Instant C++ Programming

Ian Wilks

Wrox Press Ltd. ®

Instant C++ Programming

Published by Wrox Press Ltd. 1334 Warwick Road, Birmingham, B27 6PR UK

ISBN 1-874416-29-X

Acknowledgements

My special thanks go to various family members: my wife, Sue Wilks, for her encouragement and support, my mother, Jean Wilks, for proof reading the manuscript, and my father, Eric Wilks, for advice and for the use of his printer and fax.

I also wish to thank all at Wrox Press, without whom this book would not have been written.

Trademark Acknowledgements

Credits

Author
Ian Wilks

Managing Editor
John Franklin

Style Editors
Rachel Maclean
Nina Barnsley
Wendy Entwistle
Luke Dempsey

Technical Reviewers
Julian Templeman
Julian Dobson

Production Manager
Gina Mance

Book Layout
Ewart Liburd
Eddie Fisher
Kenneth Fung

Proof Reader
Pam Brand

Cover Design
Third Wave

For more information on Third Wave, contact Ross Alderson on 44-21 456 1400

Instant

Contents Summary

Instant

C++

Contents

Instant

Introduction

Who Should Use This Book?

This book aims to teach C++ programming in the shortest possible time with the minimum of fuss. There are only two things you'll need (apart from access to a computer): a grasp of basic computing terminology (this will save us having to explain what a mouse is!), and a real desire to learn the language in double-quick time. The book will enable you to program competently and correctly in C++, and gain an understanding of the exciting world of Object Oriented Programming.

How to Use This Book

The book is a hands-on manual. It's filled with example programs, which are broken down and fully analyzed. We advise you to try out the examples as you go along so that you learn by doing and enjoying. Programming isn't merely some abstract technical exercise - it's a practical and enjoyable process, so don't be afraid to work through the examples.

Why C++?

The origins of C++ are, of course, in C. Therefore, you can always compile programs written in C on your C++ compiler (you can think of C++ as a *superset* of C). C++ has become an industry standard in a short space of time. Many of the applications you use, know and love are written, or part-written, in C or C++.

Why has this language become so dominant?

It's mainly because C and C++ are portable (given suitable access to the appropriate libraries). This feature means that programs written in the C family can theoretically be kept in their original design, and re-compiled with the appropriate compiler for other platforms. A successful C++ program written for the UNIX platform could be re-compiled to operate in a DOS environment (with, for example, some simple alteration of file handling routines) - and it would work perfectly well.

C++ is also an acceptable way for thousands of C programmers to migrate to Object Oriented Programming because they are already familiar with classes, which are the basis for objects. (In fact, the original name for C++ was 'C with Classes'.) If you are a C programmer, you'll find the transition time to C++ to be brief, as you already know the syntax and the structure.

So if you're still asking 'Why C++ ?', read on! In this book you'll see how C++ is probably the best way to enter modular programming. It's a popular language that has proved itself reliable in hundreds of applications and bespoke programming, in a relatively short period. Future development of languages may well be based on this fundamental building block.

Conventions Used

Each chapter contains example programs shaded in gray, which illustrate a new part of the language. After each program you will find 'Program Analysis' which explains the code line by line. You will see lines of code 'quoted' from the program shaded in gray, followed by an explanation bordered with further gray shading. For example:

```
This is a quote from an example program
```

And this explains the above code.

```
The output from your programs is shown like this
```

```
And you'll find syntax shown like this.
```

Each chapter ends with a summary of the topics covered and some exercises for you to try. We've provided hints for you to follow so that when you find the correct approach you'll know you did it for yourself.

Chapter

Welcome to C++

Preparing to Program

Before we go tearing in to our programming it's important to step back and consider some fundamentals which all good programmers need to be familiar with.

C++ is a high level language, so it is not necessary to know a great deal about your computer's hardware. In some cases though, an understanding of how your computer deals with the information you feed to it in your code is important. We discuss throughout the book how C++ elements will affect normal memory management in a computer. C++ is mostly platform independent but its designers have included many handy routines for file handling, etc., in the library files that come with most C++ compilers.

You should remember that computers are simple machines. They can only carry out instructions - they can't think (in fact, if they were any less intelligent you'd have to water them!) The power of the computer is the speed at which any particular instruction is carried out. Instructions are given to the computer in the form of a **program**. The program tells the machine what activity it must carry out, broken down into steps.

Unfortunately, computers can't understand plain English! The instructions in the program must be written in a language it can understand. In this way, everyday problems can be related to and solved by the computer if they are relayed to the computer in a particular computer language.

Languages

English is anything but 'plain'! Its ambiguous and metaphorical nature doesn't lend itself to exact instructions. A programming language removes a lot of the ambiguity, leaving a very concise language with strict rules governing how each word can be used, and in what context.

Low-Level Languages

Assembly languages use binary codes to create instructions for the computer. These languages are similar to the binary codes that the computer itself uses. Both assembly language and machine code are notoriously complex to use and are often designed for a particular processor and can't be easily transferred to another. In contrast, C++ can be used on most computer architectures. The advantage of low-level languages are their speed, as they need little or no translation.

High-Level Languages

C++ is a high-level language. Others include BASIC, PASCAL, COBOL, FORTRAN, and C. Their use of English-like words has made programming very much easier. High-level languages are designed to be relatively easy for people to use. They may also have evolved to solve a particular problem area.

Before a program which has been written in a high-level language can be run, it must be translated from its original form (called the **source code**) into a form that the computer can understand. Generally, a single instruction translates into many lines of machine code.

Translation Systems

Interpreters

An interpreter takes a single line of source code, translates it into machine code, and carries out the instruction immediately. It then takes the next line of source code, translates it, and carries it out. This process is repeated line by line until the whole program is translated and run. If there's a loop to earlier statements in the program, they'll be translated again, each time the loop is repeated.

An interpreter has two disadvantages. Firstly, both the source code and the interpreter are in memory *together*. This reduces the memory space available for data. Secondly, as you might expect, the program takes time to translate and run.

Compilers

A compiler translates the **whole** program before the program is run, and turns it into a self-contained program which can be run independently. The great advantage of this is its speed. Another advantage is that neither the compiler nor the source code needs to be in memory while the program is running. This ensures that the maximum amount of memory is available for program execution.

C++ is a compiled language.

Borland C++

Most C++ compilers include a full programming environment - editor, compiler, linker, and debugger, often called their **IDE** (Integrated Development Environment.) One of the most popular C++ compilers is Borland C++. Although the programs and examples in this book use the Borland C++ Integrated Development Environment, they will run on *any* C++ compiler.

Before we get started you need to install your compiler, and then we'll look at what a program is and then write one!

The following figure shows a typical Borland C++ screen. It has three parts:

```
  ≡ File  Edit  Search  Run  Compile  Debug  Project  Options  ◆  Window  Help
┌─[■]──────────────────── A:\CODE\TEST.CPP ─────────────────────1=[↑]─┐
│void main()                                                          │
│{                                                                    │
│    message1();                                                      │
│    message2();                                                      │
│    cout << "This is the end of the program.\n";                     │
│}                                                                    │
│                                                                     │
│void message1(void)                                                  │
│{                                                                    │
│    cout << "This is a test program written in C++.\n";              │
│}                                                                    │
│                                                                     │
│void message2(void)                                                  │
│{                                                                    │
│    cout << "We hope that you will find this book useful.\n";        │
│─ 27:57 ──◄▯▮▮▮▮▮▮▮▮▮▮▮▮▮▮▮▮▮▮▮▮▮▮▮▮▮▮▮▮▮▮▮▮▮▮▮▮▮▮▮▮▮▮▮▮▮▮▮▮▮▮▮▮►    │
│────────────────────────── Message ──────────────────────────2──┐    │
│•Linking C:\TEMP\TEST.EXE:                                           │
│                                                                     │
│                                                                     │
│                                                                     │
│                                                                     │
│ F1 Help  Alt-F8 Next Msg  Alt-F7 Prev Msg  Alt-F9 Compile  F9 Make  F10 Menu │
```

This is the menu bar. It lets you access all the menu commands in the Borland C++ Integrated Development Environment.

This is the status line.

This is the window area.

Windows are important in the Borland C++ IDE. You can create or open windows, and you can destroy or close windows. In the figure you can see two windows:

- The top window is the **edit** window

- The bottom window is the **message** window.

You use the edit window to type, edit, compile and run your C++ source code programs. The message window informs you of the current situation and gives details of any errors that need to be corrected before the program will compile.

Writing a Program

We've referred to 'programs' throughout this chapter but now we must find out exactly what a program is, and how to write one which is efficient and user-friendly.

What is a Program?

A program is a set of instructions arranged in sequence. It directs the computer to perform the necessary operations for the solution of a problem or the completion of a task. In whatever language the program is written the computer follows the instructions one at a time in order.

A computer program is an algorithm. An algorithm is a set of instructions which, taken in order, lead to the solution of a specific problem. Once the program structure is finalized, the programmer must then decide on how exactly the task assigned to each module will be achieved.

It's sensible to sort out the algorithm in English before you attack the problem of coding it into a computer language. Another neat way of describing an algorithm is to illustrate it. This can be done either as a flowchart or as a structure chart.

There are four main steps involved in writing a program:

- Understand the problem and plan a solution

- Produce the source code for the program

- Write the program documentation

- Test the program.

Understand and Plan

Many novice programmers make the mistake of sitting down at the keyboard straight-away and worrying about mistakes afterwards. A much better way is to design your program first. Designing code is normally left until later, once the problem is defined and a solution brokered.

At its most basic level, the analysis phase involves noting what the program should do and what problems it should solve. The most common technique is that of top-down design - the process whereby one large program is broken down into a series of related modules.

Before you can instruct someone (or some *thing*, such as a computer) how to perform a particular task, you must know how to do it yourself. This may seem obvious, but the most common reason for code being illogical and hard to follow is because of a failure to fully understand what needs to be done to perform the task in hand.

The Cupboard, The Instructions, and the Kids

Imagine you wanted to put together some self-assembly furniture (I know you probably don't but bear with me!). It would be sensible to break the task down into three initial sections: get the components of the cupboard together, get your screwdriver and the instructions, get the interfering kids to go and play in the yard.

Next you'd plan what you'd need to do to assemble each particular part of the cupboard (doors, rails, handles, tie hanger, and so on). Putting the doors on, for instance, might involve getting someone to hold them in place (but the kids are in the yard), screwing them on, and checking they are square to the cabinet.

These processes concerning the doors might in turn become smaller processes such as deciphering the instructions, checking they open and close, and paying off the kids whose basketball game you just ruined.

What began as a fairly involved task, namely 'assembling a cupboard' has been broken down into a series of minor tasks each one of which is, on its own, not so hard to do (except, in our example, deciphering the instructions!).

Back to Programming!

Preparing a well written program is similar to this. Firstly, you, the programmer, must be clear about the program **specification**, which describes exactly the required inputs, processing and output. At this point planning can begin.

Just as any complex job can be broken down into smaller constituent parts, so it's usual to break long programs down into **modules** or **procedures**. Each procedure is able to deal with a smaller, more manageable, section of the problem. It can be prepared, tested and documented on its own (by different programmers if necessary) before it's linked with the others in the main program. (It might, of course, be suitable for use in other programs - a great advantage of this modular approach).

Code to Program

The instructions in your programs are source code, and in C++ are usually stored in files with names which end in **.CPP** (most C++ compilers expect this convention). Source code should be saved to such a file before the code is compiled and run. You enter the code into the computer's memory via your program editor; many C++ compilers include a built-in editor.

Once the source code is entered and saved it is then compiled as a program into an intermediate file called the **object file**. This has **.OBJ** extension, and, once this has been combined with a start-up code and any library functions your program uses, it becomes an **executable file**. This has the **.EXE** extension. The compiler will arrange for your precious original code to be merged with any pre-defined tools that your program called for (from the library for example), before producing a finished executable program.

Documenting the Program - Making Amendments Easy

When your programming skills have matured, you'll want to write programs that are of value. You will want to keep them on disk and you will want to amend them when you develop some new ideas.

It's easy to forget how a program works. To trace it through and work out just what you did can take a lot of time, especially if the program is a substantial one - time largely wasted. Documenting a program is a bit of a chore. However, proper documentation is part of making your program easy to use and easy to amend.

Documentation must include (at the very least):

- A proper title
- The date when it was written and the author's name
- A specification of the problem and some indication as to how it has been broken down into parts
- Input and output specifications
- Language-independent charts of the algorithms used
- A program listing, suitably commented.
- Test data and sample output
- User instructions

Debugging and Testing the Program

Once your program is written you will need to debug it. There *will* be errors (bugs), and all programmers accept this. There are three types of error:

- Syntax errors
- Run-time errors
- Logic errors

Syntax errors arise when the rules of the programming language have been disobeyed, key words have been mis-typed or omitted, or punctuation has been misused. These are the easiest to find, although they're not necessarily easy to put right. The computer will warn you of their existence.

Run-time errors come to light when the program has been compiled and is running. These are due to correct commands breaching certain mathematical or logical rules. An example of this would be a program that tries to divide a number by zero.

Logic errors arise when the program has been poorly designed. It might branch off at the wrong place, or it may appear to run correctly but gives incorrect results.

You *must* test your program rigorously, deliberately feeding it perverse test data that will sort out the effectiveness (or otherwise) of your error traps. You should always work out your expected results before you test so that you can compare them with the actual results from the computer.

What Makes a Good Program?

A program that fails to do the intended task isn't very good. However, even a program that *does* solve the problem can be of poor quality. Four key questions should be asked of any program:

- Does it solve the problem reliably and efficiently?

- Would someone without much experience of computers find it reasonably easy to use - is it '**user-friendly**'?

- Will future program maintenance be easy to carry out; that is, could a moderately competent programmer follow the logic and listing to make any necessary amendments,

- Is the program well documented?

User-Friendly Programs

The people who have to work with computers are often non-technical. Because of this, the programmer must ensure that their programs are user-friendly, and guide the user through the task. Programs shouldn't crash if and when the user pushes the wrong button or tries to enter inappropriate data. Most computer users don't want to worry about the details of the computer programs they use.

A plentiful supply of prompts at the appropriate time, explaining what's happening and what action is expected of the user, will help even the most hesitant and non-technically minded people to use a program successfully. In addition, screen layout is another important factor to consider.

No matter how good your prompts, users will still push the wrong button and try to input erroneous data. A good program will contain as many error traps as necessary to ensure that all inputs are immediately checked, and that the user is asked to repeat the input if an error is made.

Program Blocks

C++ naturally segments itself into blocks, or modular form. As you build your programs, you must remain aware of the different arenas of actions. These arenas will contain statements that will be grouped within their own set of braces - { }.

It's important that your blocks are organized, as this aids readability and operation. When you have an action that depends on the results of another action (which, in turn, is altered by yet another), you'll then appreciate a clear use of braces and a standard placement of syntax.

Scope

An important concept to learn right from the start in your programming career is that of **scope.** Scope may be described as 'availability'. Let's use a simple analogy to help us understand this idea - that of an office building containing many different companies

In that office complex, the person with the greatest scope may well be the doorman. He is known to all the people entering the premises - his uniform identifies him immediately. He is known to ('available to') all the employees from all the companies who pass the gates, as his job is to scrutinise everyone. You could say that he has **global scope.**

Within an individual company in the office complex, people will pass paperwork between themselves - they may use an office messenger. That messenger will probably work in that particular office, but not in another company. He might be said to have **local scope.** We could move this metaphor in any direction - individual companies could be treated as objects; different departments could be defined as functions. The important thing is to realize that elements in C++ can be applied to a part of a module, selected modules, or all modules.

Your First Program

Now, let's develop a program called **FIRST**. There are three steps to follow:

1 Create a source code file called **FIRST.CPP**

2 Create an object file, from the source code, called **FIRST.OBJ**

3 Use the linker to create an executable file, called **FIRST.EXE**

This latter file can be loaded and run (executed). It will run either from the programming environment, or directly from DOS by typing FIRST at the DOS prompt.

Create the Source Code

You write your program source code using an Edit window. You can start working with a new file, or open an existing one, using the File menu commands. The figure below shows the complete set of commands in the File menu. Choose the New command to open a new Edit window with the name **NONAMEXX.CPP**. You can substitute any number from 00 to 99 for *xx*.

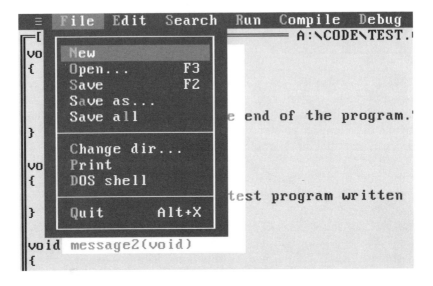

Now you can enter source code for your program. Type the following into the window:

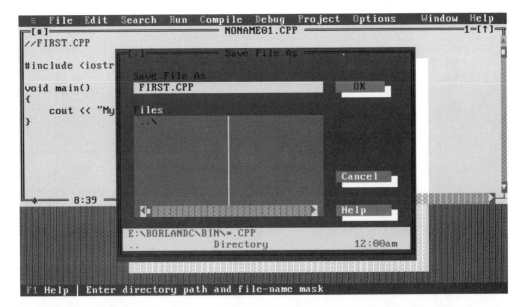

```
//FIRST.CPP

#include <iostream.h>

void main()
{
    cout << "My first C++ Program.\n";
}
```

To save the file with the name **FIRST.CPP** you'll need to pull down the File menu and select the Save as command. This will invoke a dialog box. Type in the filename **FIRST.CPP** as shown in the next figure and then press *Enter.*

Compile and Link

To compile and link your program use the Compile menu, as shown in the next figure. To compile **FIRST.CPP** to an object file choose the Compile command to create the file **FIRST.OBJ**. (When Borland C++ is compiling, a status box appears to display the progress and results). If any error has occurred in the program you'll see a flashing message saying Press any Key. Press a key to activate the Message window displaying the error message(s) or warning(s). Use the cursor keys to scroll the errors.

Each error or warning message is accompanied by the program line that is believed to have caused the error or warning. You'll have to identify any errors, and correct them.

Once the program has compiled successfully you'll need to link the object file with the appropriate library file to build an executable file. Select the Link command from the Compile menu to create **FIRST.EXE**.

Run the Program

Once the program has been linked it can be run (executed). To run the program from the programming environment, select the Run command from the Run menu.

You can see the results of running the program by opening an Output window - select the Output command from the Window menu.

To run the program outside of the programming environment, you'll need to exit from the environment. At the DOS prompt, type **FIRST** and press *Enter*. See the figure below.

```
19:45 hrs Thu   7-04-1994
[DR DOS] C:\TEMP>FIRST
My first C++ Program.

19:45 hrs Thu   7-04-1994
[DR DOS] C:\TEMP>
```

Summary

You have now seen the process of programming from start to finish, including writing good quality programs, compiling and debugging. Now you have a grasp of the fundamentals it's time to look at building more complex programs.

Chapter

Structure Of A
C++ Program

Every C++ program has basically the same structure, so the principles you'll learn in this chapter apply to even very complex C++ programs. Every C++ program consists of one or more functions, and the purpose of each function is to perform specific tasks. At the heart of your C++ compiler is a powerful library of ready-made functions for you to use in your programs. Later in this book you'll write your own functions, as part of a process of learning modular, object oriented programming.

In this chapter we'll show you the first steps in structuring a C++ program. We'll look at the basic building blocks of some simple programs before venturing further.

This chapter includes:

- A first C++ program
- Comments and headers
- Global declarations
- Naming variables
- Introducing relational operators
- Conventions
- Summary and exercises

The Very First Function

In any C++ program there must be one function which is called **main()**. This is the point from which the program starts to execute.

The minimal C++ program is shown below.

```
main()
{
}
```

This program calls the function **main()**. It's legal and it *will* compile, but on its own it does nothing.

Curly braces, **{** and **}**, are used to express grouping in C++. Expressions or statements are the things that are grouped together in C++. They might make up a simple packet of data, or represent a complete mini program or object. The grouping of related elements make the program modular in appearance. Here, they indicate the start and end of the empty body of a function called **main**.

Typically, our programs should produce output! Once you've compiled the following program it writes Welcome to Instant C++ Programming to your screen:

```
#include <iostream.h>
void main()
{
    cout << "Welcome to Instant C++ Programming\n";
}
```

Analyzing Your First Real Program

```
#include <iostream.h>
```

The first line, **#include <iostream.h>**, instructs the compiler to include one of its own special features into this program. This is a standard facility for handling input and output. You'll find the file **IOSTREAM.H** in a listing of the files that comes with your compiler.

If we don't give the compiler a **directive** that says 'IOSTREAM to be used', then anything we want to be 'streamed' won't get anywhere.

```
void main()
```

You'll have noticed that the **main()** function has been declared as **void** here. Don't worry about this for now, we'll explain it later in the chapter.

```
cout << "Welcome to Instant C++ Programming\n";
```

The standard output, **cout**, gives us a route to the screen (in the same way as **cin** helps retrieve input from the keyboard). We should make sure there is something to send. << symbolizes an **operator**, and is the insertion or 'put to' operator. It'll ensure that its second argument is written to its first argument. In this case it'll simply write our phrase **"Welcome ... "** to **cout**.

Lines ending in a semicolon (**;**) are known as **statements**. A function is a collection of one or more statements. Each statement must end with a semicolon to signal to the compiler to move on to the next statement.

"Welcome to Instant C++ Programming\n" is the phrase we want displayed on the screen. It also happens to be a **string** (a sequence of characters surrounded by double quotes). We can add things to strings, such as **\n**. This special character can automatically create a new line on the screen after our phrase.

Our output will therefore be:

```
Welcome to Instant C++ Programming
```

followed by a new line.

We can add many special characters to strings. Try entering some of the ones below to the original string:

Special Character	Effect
\a	beep
\t	tab
\\	backslash
\'	single quotation mark
\"	double quotation mark

> The C++ language is case sensitive and therefore makes a distinction between text entered in upper and lowercase letters. Be careful to type the programs *exactly* as they're written, and don't interchange upper and lower case at this stage.

We can already see that C++, like most other programming languages, needs a disciplined set of instructions in order to carry out a task. We can also see that in C++ we often need to pre-state the fact that certain parameters will be used in our program.

Comments and Headers

Comments

Let's make our simple program clear and complete. You can make your program easier to understand by adding comments. These are messages which can be put into programs at various points without affecting the results.

> Make sure you use comments in all your programs. It'll help you, and anyone else who reads your code, to understand what's going on at any point in the program. You'll find it invaluable when you write large complex programs.

We define a comment in C and C++ by adding **/*** to the front of the comment and ***/**to the end. In addition, in C++ we can start a comment with **//**. The end of the line is the end of the comment. For example:

```
//a comment
```

Let's look again at our program, which now has comments added for clarity.

```
/* ***********************************************************
 *    Welcome.Cpp                                           *
 *  Programmer: Ian M Wilks                                 *
 * *********************************************************** */

#include <iostream.h>  //A directive to include the header file
void main()            //call the essential function main
{                      //we have started the body of the function

    //display our phrase and enter a new line
    cout << "Welcome to Instant C++ Programming\n";

}                      //end the body of function main
                       //end of this program
```

Headers

In our comments we've sneaked in the term **header file**. The compiler supplies header files as pre-programmed units for your program to use. Headers are a way of including code from elsewhere. If we declare them at the start we ensure that these tools are available for basic elements in our programs. They are placed at the head of the program - hence the name.

Header files are made up of:

- Function declaration
- Variable declaration
- Macro definitions

We'll cover these terms in more detail later in the chapter. For now, let's see them as part of a bigger program.

19

Putting an Early Program Together

As you work through the next program, don't worry if some things seem unclear. Just concentrate on understanding how the various components of a C++ program fit together, and look at how the header files and **main()** function are used. We'll take the opportunity to introduce variables here, before we go on to explain their use in more depth later in the chapter.

```
/* ******************************************************
 *    HELLO.CPP                                         *
 *    Programmer: Ian Wilks                             *
 ****************************************************** */
#include <iostream.h>        //header files
#include <conio.h>

#define NO 0                 //defines NO to equal 0
#define YES 1                //defines YES to equal 1

void welcome(void);          //function declaration

void main()
{
    int answer;        //variable answer declared as type integer

    clrscr();          //clrscr() is a function defined in the
                       //header file conio.h and is called to
                       //clear the output screen

    cout << "Do you want to see a welcome message?\n";
    cout << "Enter 0 for No, 1 for Yes - and press return";
    cin >> answer;

    if (answer == YES)
         welcome();
    else
         cout << "Goodbye for now.\n";
}

void welcome (void)
{
    cout << "Welcome to Instant C++ Programming\n";
}
```

Program Analysis

The #include Directive

#include <...> The first part of the program that performs a task consists of the **pre-processor directives.** These directives instruct the compiler to do certain things before program compilation begins. The most common is the **#include** pre-processor directive. This instructs the compiler to include another source file before compilation begins. In this case, two header files are being included.

```
#include <iostream.h>
```

The first header file is **iostream.h.** We've seen this file before - it's used for input and output. If this file wasn't included then the compiler wouldn't understand our **cout** or **cin** statements.

```
#include <conio.h>
```

The second header file is **conio.h.** This is included so that we can use another function, **clrscr()**, which clears the screen.

The #define Directive

The next statements are the **#define** directives. These directives create **macro definitions** - one of the three main uses of a header file.

With the **#define** directive a definition is given to a **token** (a name). During compilation, whenever the token is encountered it will be replaced by the text held in the definition.

```
#define NO 0      //defines NO to equal 0
#define YES 1     //defines YES to equal 1
```

The above lines tell the pre-processor to replace every occurrence of the word **YES** with **1**, and every occurrence of the word **NO** with **0**. Therefore, when the compiler encounters

```
if (answer == YES)
```

the pre-processor will replace the macro **YES** with **1**. When the compiler encounters this line, the code will look like this:

```
if (answer == 1)
```

Global Declarations

The second major part of the program contains the **global** declarations. Global declarations tell the compiler about **variables** which can be used by *any* of the functions in the program. Global declarations also tell the compiler about user-defined functions that could be called *anywhere* in a program. We'll cover variables in more detail later in the chapter, but basically a variable is used to hold values that are allowed to change. The programmer gives them a name, which then becomes associated with that variable's position in memory.

Function Declaration

In this case, there are no global variables defined, but there is a function that has been defined by the programmer:

```
void welcome(void);    //function declaration
```

Here, the function type has been declared as **void**.

We've already come across the **void** function type. It's used to tell the compiler that the function is essentially self-contained. It'll achieve its task without the need for data input, and its conclusion will not be passed to any other functions for their tasks.

At this stage don't worry about functions. They'll be covered fully, later in the book.

The main() Function

The third part of the program is the **main()** function. Program execution begins in the **main()** function. In a well-structured program, execution also ends there.

Some programs may have only one function - the **main()** function. In a short program, the entire program may fit easily inside the **main()** function. A large program, however, has too much code to fit inside this function. The **main()** function in a large program may consist entirely of calls to other functions, which are either provided in the C++ library, or are defined by the programmer.

The program **HELLO.CPP** falls between these two extremes.

Some of the program's tasks are performed in **main()** function, and some are performed in the **welcome()** function.

Variable Declaration

In this program, **answer** is declared to be a variable that is a whole number.

```
int answer; //variable answer declared as type integer
```

We'll get to a full explanation of variables very soon, and that's a promise!

Next, the function **clrscr()** is called. This function is defined in the header file **conio.h**, and is called to clear the screen.

Input and Output

As we've seen, **cout** is the C++ standard output stream and outputs to the screen. In this program, **cout** is used to display two messages on the screen.

```
cout << "Do you want to see a welcome message?\n";
cout << "Enter 0 for No, 1 for Yes - and press return";
```

The C++ standard input stream is **cin**, which reads values from the keyboard. As you can see, **cin** makes use of the **>>** operator. This operator is the output operator.

```
cin >> answer;
```

In this case, the program waits until the user has entered a value and pressed return. The value the user entered at the keyboard is read by **cin** and stored in the variable we called **answer**.

The If - Else Statement

The next part of the program is the if - else statement.

You'll often want the execution of a statement to depend on a condition. In C++, the term **expression** is used rather than condition. You'll want the given statement to be executed if that expression is true; that is, if the expression evaluates to be non-zero. This is achieved by a conditional statement of the following form:

```
if (expression) statement1
```

If expression has a non-zero value (which means true), statement1 is executed. In the opposite case, with expression equal to 0, statement1 is ignored. There is also the extended form of the condition statement.

```
if (expression) statement1 else statement2
```

If expression has a non-zero value, statement1 is executed and statement2 is ignored. In the opposite case, with expression equal to 0, statement1 is ignored and statement2 is executed.

In this program the function **welcome()** is called if answer is **YES**, otherwise the program puts the message **Goodbye for now** on the screen.

The welcome() Function

The last part of the program consists of the function that has been defined by the programmer. This function consists of statements that the programmer designs to accomplish part of the programming task. These functions can be designed to do anything the programmer wants them to.

In this program the function defined by the programmer is **welcome()**. This is a short function that writes a message to the screen using **cout**. As you will see, the body of the function is enclosed in a set of braces. If you forget a brace, the compiler will catch your mistake and generate an error message. (Don't worry too much about functions at this stage - we'll look at them in greater depth later).

Variables

You'll have noticed that the last program declared an integer variable called **answer** which was used to store a number that the program user enters via the keyboard. Variables are a cornerstone of most languages. They are a fundamental link between simple words and a computer's allocated memory usage.

What's a Variable?

Computer programs handle data, which is held in the computer's memory. Data can be of two types:

- Variable data. These are values that may change during the execution of the program.

- Constant data. These are values that cannot change during program execution.

Why We Need Variables - The Organization of a Computer's Memory

The program instructions and the data are stored as a sequence of **bits** in the memory of the computer. A bit is a single cell holding a value of 0 or 1. As the computer is an electronic machine, the bit value is an electrical potential which is off (for 0) or on(for 1).

A segment of computer memory might contain bit values such as:

... 001101111110010010001110100110111100010011001000 ...

In this form, a collection of bits has no structure and you can't think of it as purposeful. You can impose organization by considering the bits in combinations. These combinations are referred to as **bytes**, which are composed of 8 bits.

The memory segment above can be organized into 6 bytes. A byte can have an address which allows us to refer to a particular collection of bits. Therefore, we can refer to the byte at addrss 2048.

However, what do the bits at an address mean? How can they be interpreted? The compiler needs to know how many bytes are going to be required to store the data, which will then be placed into memory. This is done when constants and variable values are declared within the program. Each variable must belong to a specific type. The C++ programming language supports a number of different types of variable. Initially, we'll consider three:

> int

> float

> char

Integers

The most basic data type is the integer. This is a numeric data type that represents whole numbers. Whole numbers have no fractional part.

When programmers want to use an integer in a program they declare a variable of **type int**. For example:

```
int counter;
int potatoes, cabbages;
int cars = 5;
```

Declaring an Integer

To declare an integer, type the **reserved word int**, followed by the name of the variable used to identify it. The word **int** instructs the compiler to reserve space for the integer in the computer's memory, and assigns the name following **int** - in the first example, **counter** - to represent that particular memory space.

> C++ reserves a list of words within the language as **keywords**. These reserved words can't be used as variable names.

The second example lists two variables, **potatoes** and **cabbages**. It's legal to declare multiple variables on one line, and it saves space and typing time. However, use your judgment to ensure that the program doesn't become unreadable.

The third example sets up a variable called cars *and* assigns it an initial value. You'll find if you assign an initial value to a variable it can often be very useful.

Three different modifiers can be used with the reserved word **int** to change the range of values that can be stored in this type of variable. The modifiers are **unsigned, long,** and **short**. The following table lists the various integer types, the number of bytes of memory they require, and the range of values each type can store.

IntegerType	Size	Range of Values
int	2	-32,768 to 32,767
unsigned int	2	0 to 65,535
short int	2	-32,768 to 32,767
long	4	-2,147,483,648 to 2,147,483,647
unsigned long	4	0 to 4,294,967,295

Floating-Point Numbers

The second numeric data type is the floating-point number. Unlike an integer, a floating-point number can have a fractional part. Floating-point numbers are also known as real numbers.

Declaring a floating-point variable is easy. Simply type the reserved word **float** and the variable name. When the compiler encounters the reserved word **float** it sets aside enough memory to hold a floating-point number, and assigns the variable name to represent that area of memory.

Here are some examples:

```
float radius;
float capital, interest;
float mileage = 5.25;
```

The first example declares a single variable with no initial value. The second example shows how to declare several variables on the same line, and the third example shows the assignment of an initial value. This process is known as **initialization.**

Initialization

Setting an initial value is an essential element in any mature program. You'll discover when you set your variables that you'll almost always need to set an initial value commensurate with your task.

The Range of Floating-Point Variables

Floating-point variables come in different sizes. The larger floating-point types give better precision and range, but they also use more memory. The following table summarizes the floating-point types, size (in bytes) requirements, and ranges.

Floating Point Type	Size	Range
float	4	-3.4×10^{38} to 3.4×10^{38} and -3.4×10^{-38} to 3.4×10^{-38}
double	8	-1.7×10^{308} to 1.7×10^{308} and -1.7×10^{-308} to 1.7×10^{-308}
long double	10	-3.4×10^{4932} to 3.4×10^{4932} and -3.4×10^{-4932} to 3.4×10^{-4932}

As you can see from the table, floating-point variables can represent very large numbers. The trade-off for using large numbers is the amount of memory space required to store them. For example, every floating-point variable of type long double requires 10 bytes of memory.

Besides providing a greater magnitude of values, **double** and **long double** provide more precise values as can be seen below:

Floating Point Type	Precision
float	7 digits of precision
double	15 digits of precision
long double	19 digits of precision

Characters

The basic data type for character information is denoted by the reserved word **char**. A variable of **type char** can hold a value which represents a single letter. For example:

```
char letter;
```

As the computer stores information in binary code, it's impossible to store a letter as itself. The computer uses a numeric value to represent each letter. A variable of type **char** actually stores a numeric value associated with a particular letter. We use the notation ' ' to identify a typical keyboard input to a **char** variable. Personal computers (PCs) use ASCII code to represent character data. ASCII (from the American Standards Committee for Information Interchange) developed a widely recognized code that represents 128 different character values.

A PC also uses an extended character set that contains another 128 characters. In all, the PC can use 256 characters.

Variable Declaration

The declaration of a variable can take place at a number of different points in a program. The point at which a variable is declared will affect the **scope**, or area of activity, of that variable. We'll look at this in later chapters. As we've seen, the form of a variable declaration is always the same:

```
type <identifier>;
```

Naming Variables

Identifiers

Each variable must be given a name. The name is associated with a specific memory location, and the compiler uses it to identify that location.

The name of a variable can be composed of letters, digits, and the underscore character. It must begin with either a letter or the underscore character. Upper case and lower case letters are distinct. There's no language-imposed limit on the permissible length of a name, but some compilers will limit the length.

Reserved Words

Remember the reserved words in C++ mustn't be used as variable names. The following table gives a list of these words:

A List of C++ Keywords				
asm	default	friend	private	switch
auto	delete	goto	protected	this
break	do	if	public	template
case	double	inline	register	typedef
catch	else	int	return	union
char	enum	long	short	unsigned
class	extern	new	sizeof	virtual
const	float	operator	static	void
continue	for	overload	struct	volatile

Naming Conventions

There are a number of generally accepted conventions in C++:

- A variable name is normally written in lower case letters.

- A variable is provided with a mnemonic name; that is, a name which gives some indication of its use in a program.

- A multi-word identifier either places an underscore between each word, or capitalizes the first letter of each embedded word.

An example of a multi-word identifier would be `is_empty` or `isEmpty`

Using Variables - An Example

Let's look at another example program which uses variables. You'll see that we've introduced some common **relational operators** which you'll probably be very familiar with from your math classes. We'll go on to look at them in more detail later.

```
/* *****************************************************************
 *      somefun.cpp                                               *
 *      Ian M Wilks                                               *
 *      This program is to illustrate the use of variables        *
 ***************************************************************** */
#include <iostream.h>      //header file for input and output
#include <conio.h>         //header file for clrscr();

void main()
{
    char yesOrNo;          //variable declarations
    int year = 1994;
    int birth_year;
    int ageThisYear;

    clrscr();          //clear the screen

    cout << "This program illustrates the use of variables.\n";
    cout << "Please enter your year of birth: ";
    cin >> birth_year;

    cout << "Is the year still " << year << ". (Y/N): ";
    cin >> yesOrNo;

    if ((yesOrNo == 'N') || (yesOrNo == 'n'))
    {
        cout << "Please enter current year (1994): ";
        cin >> year;
    }

    ageThisYear = year - birth_year;
```

```
        cout << "You are " << ageThisYear << " this year.\n";
        cout << "You are obviously ";

        if (ageThisYear < 13)
              cout << "a young person.";
        else
        if ((ageThisYear >= 13) && (ageThisYear < 20))
              cout << "a teenager.";
        else
        if ((ageThisYear >= 20) && (ageThisYear < 40))
             cout << "a person waiting for life to begin!!";
        else
        if (ageThisYear == 40)
              cout << "a person whose life is now beginning!!!";
        else
        if((ageThisYear > 40) && (ageThisYear < 60))
             cout << "a person who wonders if work is worth it!!";
        else
             cout << "a person in the prime of life.";
}
```

Program Analysis

```
#include <iostream.h>       //header file for input and output
#include <conio.h>          //header file for clrscr();
```

The **#include** directive is used to include the files **IOSTREAM.H** and **CONIO.H**. **IOSTREAM** is needed for input and output and **CONIO** is needed if we want to use the function **clrscr()**.

```
void main()
```

The remainder of the program is included in function **main()**.

Declaring the Variables

```
    char yesOrNo;           //variable declarations
```

The variables are declared. The first variable declaration is **char yesOrNo;** This informs the compiler to reserve space in memory for a character which will be identified as **yesOrNo**.

```
    int year = 1994;
    int birth_year;
    int ageThisYear;
```

The remaining variable declarations are for integer variables. The first of these declarations is **int year = 1994;** which assigns the value **1994** to be stored in the memory location referred to by the identifier year.

31

```
cout  <<  "This program illustrates the use of variables.\n";
cout  <<  "Please enter your year of birth:  ";
```

Two messages are sent to the screen:

```
This program illustrates the use of variables.
Please enter your year of birth:
```

```
cin >> birth_year;
```

The program then waits until the user enters their year of birth and presses *Return*. The value entered at the keyboard is stored in the memory location referred to by the identifier **birth_year.**

```
cout << "Is the year still " << year << ". (Y/N): ";
cin >> yesOrNo;
```

The program then displays the following on the screen:

```
Is the year still 1994. (Y/N):
```

and processes a simple response, entered as **Y,y** or **N,n**

```
if ((yesOrNo == 'N') || (yesOrNo == 'n'))
```

The character entered at the keyboard is stored in the memory location referred to by the identifier **yesOrNo.**

The if Statement

```
if ((yesOrNo == 'N') || (yesOrNo == 'n'))
```

What this says is 'if **yesOrNo** is equal to **'N'** *or* **yesOrNo** is equal to **'n'**. If the user has entered the character **N** or **n**, the expression in the **if** statement will evaluate to true, and the statements in the braces will be executed.

If the user has entered the character **N** or **n** then the expression in the if statement will evaluate to true, and the statements in the braces will be executed. This will result in the following output:

```
Please enter current year (1994):
```

The program will wait....

```
cin >> year;
```

The program will wait until the user has entered a value and pressed *Return*. The value entered at the keyboard will be stored in the memory location referred to by the identifier **year**.

If the user enters characters other than **N** or **n** then the expression in the if statement will evaluate to false and the statements in the braces won't be executed

```
ageThisYear = year - birth_year;
```

The program then subtracts the value stored in **birth_year** (that is, in the memory location referred to by the identifier **birth_year**) from the value stored in **year**. The answer is stored in **ageThisYear** (that is, in the memory location referred to by the identifier **ageThisYear**).

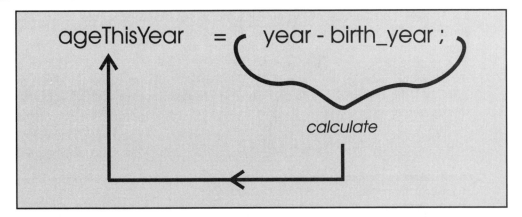

In this case we're using an **assignment operator**, **=**. The equals sign here means that the value on the right is calculated first, *before* the result is assigned to the variable on the left.

```
cout << "You are " << ageThisYear << " this year.\n";
cout << "You are obviously ";
```

The program then displays a message telling the user their age, and then displays the first part of a message on the screen:

```
You are obviously
```

The if-else Statement

The remainder of the message that will be displayed depends on the value stored in **ageThisYear**. A nested if - else statement is used to determine what the second part of the message will be. Typically, this would be:

```
else
if ((ageThisYear >= 20) && (ageThisYear < 40))
cout << "a person waiting for life to begin!!";
```

If **ageThisYear** is 20 or over, and less than 40, then output to screen will be the contents of **cout**.

Only one of the **cout** statements in the nested if - else statement will be selected.

Introducing Relational Operators

You'll have noticed that we've used some new operators in the nested if - else statement. These operators **<, >, >=**, and **==** are relational operators

The relational operators test for the relationship between values. The value on the left-hand side of the operator is compared with the value on the right-hand side, and the test will evaluate as true if the relationship is that indicated by the operator.

The following table gives a list of the relational operators.

Relational Operators	What They Mean
>	is greater than
<	is less than
>=	is greater than or equal to
<=	is less than or equal to
==	is equal to
!=	is not equal to

Constants

In a program there will often be certain values that are repeatedly used. There are a number of ways of dealing with these values.

Firstly, the value could be entered in full at each point it's used. For example:

```
    area = 3.1415926 * radius * radius;
```

You might well be happy with this approach. However, could you guarantee to get the value of PI right every time it's needed? Your program may use this value 50 times!

The second method is to use the pre-processor directive **#define**. Therefore, you could use **#define PI 3.1415926** at the start of the program, and then use

```
    area = PI * radius * radius;
```

In general, when the preprocessor encounters a **#define** directive, it replaces every occurrence of the first string of characters (PI) with the second string (3.1415926). No value can be assigned to PI because it has not been declared as a variable.

This, again, has an advantage, in that it saves all the typing and reduces the chance of a typing error. However, there are disadvantages. The short programs that we have examined so far would usually be stored in a single file. If a **#define** directive appeared at the beginning of the file, the substitution of 3.1415926 for PI would take place throughout the program. However, when you divide a program into separate files and compile all of these files into one executable file, a problem is encountered. The **#define** directive would be effective only for the single file in which it is written.

The third way is to declare PI as a variable. This saves memory, but there's always a chance that the value may be amended by mistake. This is something that shouldn't happen to a constant.

A common way around the problem is to declare the variable as a constant by modifying it using the keyword **const**. The definition of PI will now be:

```
    const float PI = 3.1415926;
```

A variable declared as a constant can't have its value changed or altered. The **const** type transforms a symbolic variable into a symbolic constant. Any attempt to change the value from within the program will result in a compile-time error.

Conventions

Case-Sensitive Language

You saw earlier that C++ is a case-sensitive language. This also applies to variable names. For example, the variable name **answer** would be regarded as different to a variable called **Answer** or **aNswer**.

Punctuation

As with any programming language, errors will result if you don't obey the syntax rules. Syntax errors are fairly easy to find, as the compiler should do most of the work.

Some of the more common mistakes you're likely to make are shown below:

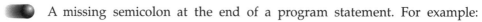 A missing semicolon at the end of a program statement. For example:

```
cout << "This is a mistake"
```

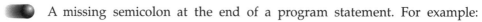 Putting a semicolon in the wrong place.

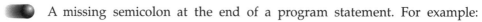 Forgetting to supply an opening or closing brace. The brace is normally used to group two or more statements together so they are treated as a single statement. If you forget to use braces when several statements are to be grouped together, only the first statement will be executed as planned.

Summary

Now you've looked at a few real C++ programs, you'll agree that they don't always reveal their purpose on first sight of the syntax. I hope, however, that you've seen how a C++ program quickly assembles itself into sections, or modules, for you to analyze task by task. By now you have a good grasp of the fundamentals of a C++ program. You've hopefully got to grips with the concept of pre-stating compiler functions which are utilized using header files, and declaring functions and variables. You know about choosing an appropriate variable, and you also know that keeping memory usage to a minimum and starting off at the right spot (initialization) is an important part of good programming technique. You'll see in future chapters how your selection of appropriate data types will help you to optimize your programs.

Programming Exercises

1 Using the source code for the program **WELCOME.CPP**, modify the program so that it initially clears the output screen and then prints your name and address on separate lines.

2 Write a program to include the following code:

```
cout << "Single Quote: \'\nDouble Quote: \"\n";
cout << "Backslash: \\\n \\n The End.\n";
```

What did it print?

Modify the code above to read as follows:

```
cout << "Single Quote: \'\nDouble Quote: \"\n"
"Backslash: \\\n \\n The End.\n";
```

What did it print?

3 Write a program to read the letter A, 21, 3.142 from the keyboard using **cin**, and output them sequentially to the standard output device, each on its own line preceded with some suitable explanatory text.

What happens if the operator inputs the wrong type, and what ought to be done about it?

4 The circumference of a circle is given by the formula $2\pi r$ and the area of a circle is given by the formula πr^2 where r is the radius of the circle. Write a program that prompts for the radius of a circle and then outputs the area and the circumference. Assume $\pi = 3.142$.

The code to use to multiply two items together is

```
answer = number1 * number2;
```

Chapter

Utilizing C++ Operators

The basic elements of C++ that we have seen so far are quite limited in terms of their ability to perform useful jobs in your programs. For example, imagine you wanted to multiply some of your program's values together before the program carries out another action or makes a decision. C++ uses standard math symbols for this task. Another important activity that you'll want to include in your programs is testing whether a given statement is true or false according to rules you have set. C++ handles this using conditional expressions which you've already encountered in Chapter 2. If you thoroughly understood that chapter, you should be able to master the additional operators covered here without any difficulty.

This chapter will include:

- Making your programs readable
- Mathematical operators
- Mathematical assignment operators
- Logical operators
- AND/OR operators
- Two other operators
- Conditional expressions
- Summary and exercises

Making Your Programs Readable

Take a quick look at the following program:

```
// operat.cpp Ian M Wilks
#include <iostream.h>
void main(){int i, j;//declare two integer variables
int answer = 0;//declare an integer variable, initialized to 0
cout << "Enter two integers ==> ";cin >> i >> j;
//multiply i by j and store the result in answer
answer = i * j;cout << "\ni * j = " << answer << endl;
//find the positive difference between the two integers
if (i > j) cout << "i - j = " << i - j << endl;
else cout << "j - i = " << j - i << endl; //find the sum of the
//two integers
answer = i + j;cout << "i + j = " << answer << endl;}
```

What does this program do? Do you understand any part of it?

As you can see, this program is difficult to read because of the way it's set out. The program will still compile and run, as there is nothing wrong with the source code.

Remember that programming statements in C++ can start in any column of any line. You can also insert blank lines and spaces to make the program readable.

The aim of any programmer should be to make programs readable and maintainable. This will helps in the future should you have to refer back to the source code to make any amendments.

Using Good Programming Style - An Example

The program has been re-written, and is shown opposite. Have a go at reading through the code and try to work out what's happening. You've covered all the elements of this program in Chapter 2; the only new statements introduced here are two mathematical operators.

```
/* ***********************************************************
 *      operat2.cpp                                          *
 *      Ian M Wilks                                          *
 * *********************************************************** */
#include <iostream.h>

void main()
{
    int i, j;           //declare two integer variables
    int answer = 0;     //declare an integer variable,
                        //initialized to 0

    cout << "Enter two integers ==> ";
    cin >> i >> j;

    //multiply i by j and store the result in answer
    answer = i * j;
    cout << "\ni * j = " << answer << endl;

    //find the positive difference between the two integers
    if (i > j)
            cout << "i - j = " << i - j << endl;
    else
            cout << "j - i = " << j - i << endl;

    //find the sum of the two integers
    answer = i + j;
    cout << "i + j = " << answer << endl;
}
```

What does this program do? Now that it's re-written, you should find the code a lot clearer. Practice reading and understanding the source code. You should be familiar with the mathematical operators from your knowledge of math, so try and understand what the program is hoping to achieve before you continue with the chapter.

Program Analysis

```
#include <iostream.h>
```

We've included our regular header file. The remainder of the program is contained in the **main()** function.

```
    int i, j;           //declare two integer variables
    int answer = 0;     //declare an integer variable,
                        //initialized to 0
```

The program initially declares three integer variables; **i,j** and **answer**, one of which is initialized to have a value of **0**.

```
cout << "Enter two integers ==> ";
```

cout is used to put a message on the user's screen which asks them to enter two integers.

```
cin >> i >> j;
```

The program waits until the user enters two values and presses *Return*. The values entered via the keyboard are stored in the variables **i** and **j**.

```
answer = i * j;
```

i is then multiplied by **j** and the result is stored in the variable **answer**. As you've seen previously, values are assigned to variables using the assignment operator **=**.

```
cout << "\ni * j = " << answer << endl;
```

This result is then displayed on the screen. Note that **endl** is the same as **"\n"**.

```
if (i > j)
        cout << "i - j = " << i - j << endl;
else
        cout << "j - i = " << j - i << endl;
```

The program then calculates the positive difference between the two integers and displays the value on the screen. An if - else statement is used.

Think about this example. If **i** had the value 5 and **j** had the value 10, then i - j = -5 and j - i = 5. However, as **i** is not greater than **j**, then the first statement is ignored and the second statement is actioned.

```
answer = i + j;
cout << "i + j = " << answer << endl;
```

The program then finds the sum of the two integers and stores the result in the variable **answer**. This is then output to the screen.

In this example, you can see we've used some *normal* adding and subtraction. C++ has rules for using these, together with the common math symbols. Some of these rules may appear awkward, but they are related to the action of a computer processing binary information. The rules are explained below.

Mathematical Operators

The program above, **OPERAT2.CPP**, demonstrated how to use some of the mathematical operators. The full set of mathematical operators are shown below:

Mathematical Operators	What They Do
+	addition
-	subtraction
*	multiplication
/	division
%	modulus

Addition, subtraction, and multiplication all work in the way familiar in math. From 2 + 3 the result is 5, from 10 - 6 the result is 4, and from 6 * 7, (six times seven), the result is 42.

Division may be a bit surprising. If you're using integers, and divide an integer by an integer, then the result will be an integer. For example, 10/2 results gives an answer of 5. However in C++, 5/2 results in an answer of 2, and **the remainder is discarded.**

If you need to know what the remainder of a division is then the modulus operator is used. The modulus operator can only be used with integer values. For example, 5 % 2 gives an answer of 1. The division is performed, but in this case the result of the division is discarded and **the remainder is kept**.

If you're working with float variables, an exact answer can be obtained. For example, 5.0/2.0 gives an answer of 2.5.

Assignment Operators

You have already come across the use of the assignment operator = to assign a value to a variable. For example, answer = 10:

You may also want to change the current value of a variable in your program, for example, if you multiply or add the result of another expression to it. To do this you would use the assignment operator as follows:

answer = 10;   answer = a + 10;

answer = answer + 10;   answer = answer * 10;

answer = answer/5;   answer = answer - 16;

Mathematical Assignment Operators

The statements above can be condensed using the **mathematical assignment operators** below:

Assignment Operators	What They Do
+=	assign sum
*=	assign product
%=	assign remainder
-=	assign difference
/=	assign quotient

They are used in the following ways:

answer += 10; is equivalent to answer = answer + 10;

Similarly:

answer *= 10; is equivalent to answer = answer * 10

The other mathematical assignment operators work in the same way.

The Logical Operators

To understand the reason why you'd need to use logical operators in your programs, first of all think about what you've already learned about conditional statements in Chapter 2.

We've seen that an if statement allows you to execute a statement, or a group of statements, if a condition is true. We have also seen that an if - else statement allows you to execute a statement (or a group of statements) if a condition is true, or execute another statement, or group of statements, if the condition is false. However, you'll frequently want to have a statement (or group of statements) executed if a set of conditions is true.

Using Nested If Statements - An Example

It's possible to execute a statement if a set of conditions is true using nested if statements. The following program illustrates this:

```
/* **********************************************************
 *    ISDIGIT.CPP                                          *
 *    Ian M Wilks                                          *
 ********************************************************** */
#include <iostream.h>        //header file for input/output
#include <conio.h>           //header file for clrscr()

void main()
{
    char digit;

    clrscr();

    cout << "\n\tProgram to test that a digit has been entered at the\n"
         << "\tkeyboard.\n";

    cout << "\n\n\tPlease enter a digit: ";
    cin >> digit;

    if (digit >= '0')
    {
        if (digit <= '9')
            cout << "\n\n\tA digit has been entered at the keyboard\n"
                 << "\tit is the number " << digit;
        else
            cout << "\n\n\tA digit was not entered.";
    }
    else
        cout << "\n\n\tNo digit was entered.";
}
```

Examine the source code. Do you understand what's happening? There are no new operators used. The only new idea is how the messages displayed on the screen by **cout** will differ according to the data entered by the user. Take a few minutes to read and understand the code. Run the program to see what happens. Does the program do what you expected it to?

In **ISDIGIT.CPP** we're trying to establish the truth of the user's mysterious keyboard entries. To do this, the program needs to follow a logical route, testing one statement after another to eliminate all possibilities. We've done this here by using nested if - else statements.

Let's examine the program, and learn why we need a logical operator to clarify things.

Program Analysis

```
#include <iostream.h>        //header file for input/output
#include <conio.h>           //header file for clrscr()
```

As you'd expect, the program starts with a comment block which provides useful information. The **#include** directive is used to tell the compiler to include the header files **IOSTREAM.H**, which, as you now know, is needed for input and output; and **CONIO.H**, which, as you also know, is needed to let us use the function **clrscr()**.

```
void main()
```

The remainder of the program is contained in the **main()** function.

```
char digit;
```

The program initially declares a character variable, **digit**.

```
cout << "\n\tProgram to test that a digit has been entered at the\n"
    << "\tkeyboard.\n";
```

cout is used to put a message on the screen which tells the user what the program does. Note how **cout** and the **<<** operators are used.

You can use as many `<<` operators as you like between `cout` and the semicolon which terminates the statement. The `<<` operators can output string constants, characters within quotation marks, or variables.

```
cout << "\n\n\tPlease enter a digit: ";
```

`cout` is then used again and **Please enter a digit:** is displayed on the screen.

```
cin >> digit;
```

The program waits until the user enters a character and presses *Return*. The value entered via the keyboard is stored in the variable `digit`.

```
if (digit >= '0')
```

An if statement is used to test whether `digit` is greater than or equal to `'0'`. As characters are stored using a numeric code (the ASCII code) it is possible to see if the ASCII code of the character stored in `digit` is greater than or equal to the ASCII code of the character `0`.

If the ASCII code of the character stored in `digit` is greater than or equal to the ASCII code of `'0'` then the next statement that will be executed is the second `if` statement. If the ASCII code of the character stored in `digit` is not greater than or equal to the ASCII code of `'0'` then the next statement that will be executed is the `else` statement following the closing brace.

```
if (digit <= '9')
```

Provided that the ASCII code of the character stored in `digit` is greater than or equal to the ASCII code of `'0'` then the second if statement will test whether the ASCII code of the character stored in `digit` is less than or equal to the ASCII code of `'9'`.

If this is true then we know a digit has been entered, and the program will display a message saying so. If a digit wasn't entered, a message will be displayed saying that a digit wasn't entered.

This program illustrates a common situation where you'll want to check that the user has entered a certain character at the keyboard., In this case you're checking to see if the user has entered a digit at the keyboard, but the program could easily be adapted to check that a lowercase letter had been entered, or whether or not a lowercase or an uppercase letter had been entered.

The AND/OR Operators

The program works, but any serious C++ or C programmer looking at this program would be shocked. As you might expect, there is a better way of doing things! C and C++ support two logical operators which allow you to combine conditions in truth tests. The operators are:

&&   The AND operator
|| The OR operator

Look at the following:

```
if ( (x > 7.5 && y < 7.5) || (x < 15 && y > 15) )
{
    .........
}
```

Actually' we've already used this operator in **SOMEFUN.CPP** in Chapter 2 without telling you much about it. Here's what it means:

if x is greater than 7.5 *and* y is less than 7.5, then execute the statement; *or* if x is less than 15 *and* y is greater than 15, execute the statement.

If we replace the multiple if statement in **ISDIGIT.CPP** with if statements using **&&** we'll have a shorter program.

Replacing Nested Ifs With AND/OR Operators

Look at how the program below is shorter and more concise than **ISDIGIT.CPP**.

```
/* ***********************************************************
 *     ISDIGIT1.CPP                                          *
 *     Ian M Wilks                                           *
 ********************************************************** */
#include <iostream.h>          //header file for input/output
#include <conio.h>             //header file for clrscr()

void main()
{
    char digit;
    clrscr();
    cout << "\n\tProgram to test that a digit has been entered at the\n"
         << "\tkeyboard.\n";
    cout << "\n\n\tPlease enter a digit: ";
    cin >> digit;
    if ((digit >= '0') && (digit <= '9'))
    {
        cout << "\n\n\tA digit has been entered at the keyboard\n"
             << "\tit is the number " << digit;
    }
    else
        cout << "\n\n\tNo digit was entered.";
}
```

Try altering the original program to see what effect it has.

It is quite common for programs to require the user to give a **Yes** or **No** input with a single key entry of the *Y* or *N* keys. The problem is that you must allow for it being given in either uppercase or lowercase.

To solve this you can use the || operator to accept as a true input either *Y* or *y*, without having to change the case of the letter.

Other Operators

Most of the operators in the C++ programming languages are simple to use and you should be able to master them without difficulty. Although a book of this size can't cover all the operators, we'll introduce the most important and frequently used ones.

We are going to discuss four more operators which you should find useful.

49

Incremental Operators

When writing programs it's common to increase or decrease the value of a variable by one unit. For example, when you move through a list of actions you may well need to step to the next action. C++ provides operators to do this. They are **++** and **--**.

If you have an integer variable **num** which has a value of 10 and use the expression:

```
num++;
```

the value of **num** will be increased by one to 11.

Similarly, if you have an integer variable **num** which has a value of 10 and use the expression:

```
num--;
```

the value of num will be decreased by one to 9.

You should note that:

```
new_num = num++;
```

is not the same as:

```
new_num = ++num;
```

The first statement says 'assign the value of **num** to **new_num** and then increase the value of **num** by 1'. Therefore, if **num** has the value 5 then 5 is assigned to **new_num**. **num** is then incremented by 1. Therefore, after the statement has been executed, **new_num** has the value 5 and **num** has the value 6.

The second statement says 'increase the value of **num** by 1 and then assign that value to **new_num**.' Therefore, if **num** has the value of 5 before the statement is executed, on execution **num** is incremented by 1 to become 6. The new value, 6, is assigned to **new_num**. Therefore, after the statement is executed both **num** and **new_num** have the value 6.

You will get similar results from

```
new_num = num--;      and      new_num = --num;
```

The NOT Operator

Before we look at the NOT operator remember that in C++ we can test for
true and **false**. We discussed **if** statements and **if-else** statements in
Chapter 2. Recall:

```
if (expression) statement1
```

If **expression** has a non-zero value (which means true), **statement1** is
executed. In the opposite case, with expression equal to 0, **statement1** is
ignored.

A non-zero value is regarded as **true**. A zero value is regarded as **false**.

So, how should the NOT operator be used? In C++, ! is the NOT operator.

A common type of programming test is to see if a variable has the value of
zero. We can write this as:

```
if (number == 0)
{
    . . . . .
}
```

If we'd written

```
if (number)
{
    . . . . .
}
```

the statements would only be executed when **number** is a value other than **0**.
This isn't what we need. The NOT operator inverts the truth of a variable or
expression. Therefore, if we write

```
if (!number)
{
    . . . . .
}
```

it's the same as writing

```
if (number == 0)
{
    . . . . .
}
```

The reason this happens is that when number is equal to 0 false is returned, but this is inverted by the NOT operator into true. Conversely, when number is equal to a value other than 0, number would return true, but the NOT operator inverts this into false.

> Although many new programmers are taught the use of the ! symbol, it's usually normal practice to use the = = system. This is a matter of choice for you as a programmer.

Conditional Expressions

Besides the conditional **if - else** statement there is also the conditional expression in which the operators **?** and **:** are used, instead of the keywords **if** and **else**. It has the following form:

```
expression1 ? expression2 : expression3
```

The test condition is **expression1** and this is evaluated first. If its value is **true** (that is, the value of the expression is non-zero) **expression2** is evaluated. If its value is **true** (that is, the value of the expression is zero) **expression3** is evaluated. The value of the chosen expression is taken as the value of the conditional expression.

FALSE

One of the most common types of selection using the **if - else** statement, is to return one of two values depending on the truth of a condition.

The following code fragment can be used to convert a lowercase letter to an uppercase letter. Look at the following:

```
if ( (letter >= 'a') && (letter <= 'z') )
    deduct = 32;
else
    deduct = 0;
```

The ASCII code for **'a'** is 97 and the ASCII code for **'A'** is 65. Similarly, the ASCII code for **'b'** is 98 and the ASCII code for **'B'** is 66. To convert a lowercase letter to an uppercase letter we must simply deduct 32 from the ASCII code. Therefore,

a - 32 = A, b - 32 = B, and so on.

However, as you can see, the test can only return one of two results depending on whether it is true or false. The previous fragment could be written as:

```
deduct = ( (letter >= 'a') && (letter <= 'z') ) ? 32 : 0;
```

Relational Operators

As well as the operators covered above, we've already discussed relational operators in Chapter 2. As you've worked through this chapter you'll have noticed that we've used them in all the example programs as well as some of the code fragments. Hopefully, you'll feel confident using them now you've seen them in a number of different situations.

Seeing Operators in Use - An Example

A common requirement in a program is to convert a lowercase letter to an uppercase, and vice versa. There are many different ways of doing this. You could use the conditional expression that we looked at earlier. Here's another way of doing it, using the logical operator **&&** as part of an if statement.

```cpp
/* ***********************************************************
 *      upper.cpp                                           *
 *      Ian M Wilks                                         *
 *********************************************************** */
#include <iostream.h>          //header file for input/output

void main()
{
    char letter;

    cout << "\n\n\tThis program converts a lowercase letter to uppercase\n";
    cout << "\n\tPlease enter a letter:  ";
    cin >> letter;

    //only convert lowercase letters, i.e. a, b, c, d, ... , z
    //ignore any other character entered
    if ( (letter >= 'a') && (letter <= 'z') )
        letter -= 32;

    cout << "\tYou entered " << letter;
}
```

Read through the program. There's nothing in the code that we haven't discussed already, and you should have no problems in understanding what's happening.

Basically, the program checks to see that the letter entered is a lowercase letter. If it is, then 32 is subtracted from the ASCII code, making the letter uppercase.

> The libraries that come with C++ compilers tend to have functions that will convert a lowercase letter to an uppercase letter, and vice versa.

Summary

As you've seen in this chapter, the style of your programs should be an important consideration. We then introduced a few more operators for you to use: logical operators, incremental operators and the NOT operator, which improved upon nested if statements. We finished by looking at how operators work in practice. You should now be gaining in confidence when you read program code.

Programming Exercises

1 Write a program which divides the value 46 by the value 11 and display the result with an appropriate message. Actually, do two divisions - the first should be an integer division, that is, 46/11, the second should be a float division, that is, 46.0/11.

2 Write a program that uses an if statement to demonstrate three of the relational operators.

3 Find the errors in the following program and correct them.

```
include <iostream.h>

void main();
{
    int i, j, k, 1, m
    i = 13;
    j = 'A';
    k = "B";
    1 = C + i;
    m = 'D' + j;
    n = i + j + k + 1;

    cout << "End of
            program"
}
```

4 Put the following code into a program and observe the results:

```
cout << "This is a long string that is \
split over more than one line.";
```

Can a string be split over more than two lines?

```
cout << "Is this legal in the C++ Programming Language?   "
        "Remember, you can always test your code.\n";
```

Can a string be split over more than two lines using this method?

5 Use the `<<` operator only once to print the following four lines:

    One double quote: "
    Two double quotes: ""
    Backslash: \
    \n

Chapter

Control Structures

Everyone would agree that computers repeat an electronic process faster than any other medium. You will often want your programs to automate repeated actions, and in C++ the process which achieves this is called looping. Loops are always constructed following standard rules, and you can use loops to repeat any number of instructions, or even a whole program. The actions performed by the loop are contained within their own braces and therefore become virtually a separate program within the parent program.

In this chapter we cover:

- **for** loops
- **while** loops
- **do-while** loops
- Which loop to use when
- The **break** and **continue** keywords
- The problem with floats
- The **goto** statement
- The **switch** statement

Looping Statements in C++

There are three looping statements available in C++. They are:

- **for**
- **while**
- **do-while**

We will discuss them each individually below.

The for Loop

If you know in advance how many times you will need your program to execute a loop, and if the loop's execution isn't dependent on any outside input or limitations, then use a **for** loop.

The general structure of a **for** loop is:

```
for (starting value; condition; changes)
     action;
```

You can include multiple actions by containing them within braces:

```
for (starting value; condition; changes)
{
     action1;
     action2;
     action3;
}
```

For Loop Parameters

The three values in the control section of a **for** loop determine how the loop will be executed. The values can be specified in many different ways.

Let's break the loop down and look at its individual components. Here is a typical **for** loop:

```
for (i = 75; i <= 125; i++)
```

The three values have been specified as follows:

```
i = 75;
```

The starting value specifies a value at which counting will begin.

```
i <=125;
```

The condition expression limits the **for** loop to a certain number of iterations.

```
i++
```

The changes expression indicates how much the starting value will be incremented or decremented by on each pass of the loop.

Here the **for** loop uses the variable **i** to count from 75 (the starting value) to 125 (the value specified in the condition expression). The changes expression increments the value of **i** by 1 on each pass through the loop.

You can see how the concept of the **for** loop applies to the program you are trying to construct here. You know you want to start the count at 75, repeat it for the number of times it takes to get to 125, and finish at 125. You don't want anything to change that outcome while the loop is executing. Therefore, the **for** loop is the right loop to use.

Infinite for Loops

You can construct a **for** loop without any arguments at all, as the example below shows.

```
for( ; ; )
    cout << "Infinite loop\n";
```

If no arguments are present, there is no condition to be met. The loop will therefore continue to run forever, or at least until the program is reset or the computer is turned off. Obviously you want to avoid this kind of situation!

The for Loop - An Example

The following program **FOR1.CPP**, is a simple, working example of the **for** loop:

```
//FOR1.CPP
#include <iostream.h>                    //header file for input/output
void main()
{
    int counter;
    for (counter=1; counter<=10; counter++)   // Loop from 1 to 10
        cout << counter << "\n";              // Body of for loop
}
```

Program Analysis

```
for (counter=1; counter<=10; counter++)
```

This program declares an integer variable, **counter**, which is used to control the **for** loop. The variable is initialized to 1 and is incremented by 1 each time the loop is executed. The loop condition, **counter <= 10;**, shows that the loop will operate while the value in the variable **counter** is less than or equal to 10.

The output from the program is:

```
1
2
3
4
5 ·
6
7
8
9
10
```

When we use a variable in our for loop, it is referred to as the index variable, and must be a numeric value.

60

Using Characters in the for Loop - An Example

Since characters are stored as numeric values, they can also be used inside your **for** loop. This is shown in the example program below, **FOR2.CPP**.

```
//FOR2.CPP
// Write the alphabet to the screen with a simple for-loop

#include <iostream.h>                //Header file for input/output

void main()
{
    char letter;

    cout << "Here is the alphabet:\n";
    for (letter = 'A'; letter <= 'Z'; letter++)      //Loops from A to Z
        cout << letter << " ";

}
```

Program Analysis

```
char letter;
```

This program declares a character variable, **letter**, which is used to control the loop. The variable is initialized to hold the character **A**.

```
letter <= 'Z';
```

The condition is that the **letter** is less than or equal to the character Z.

```
letter++
```

The variable is incremented each time the loop is executed.

As was explained in Chapter 2, the computer stores information in binary code. Therefore, it's impossible to store a letter directly. The computer uses a numeric value, the ASCII code of the letter, to represent the letter. A variable of type **char** actually stores the numeric value associated with a particular letter. These numeric values are used to control the loop.

61

In this case:

```
(letter = 'A'; letter <= 'Z'; letter++)
```

is equivalent to:

```
(letter = 65; letter <= 90; letter++).
```

The output from the program is:

```
Here is the alphabet:
A B C D E F G H I J K L M N O P Q R S T U V W X Y Z
```

Nested for Loops - An Example

A loop can be contained inside another loop when you want your program to repeat an action several times within one iteration of the first loop. When the first loop carries out its second iteration, the whole of the second loop will execute again. The program **FOR3.CPP** below is an example of a **nested for loop**.

```
//for3.cpp
// Prints a triangle of letters
#include <iostream.h>              //header file for input/output

void main()
{
    int count1;                    //Loop control variable
    char count2;                   //Loop control variable
    for (count1 = 1; count1 <= 5; count1++)        //Outer loop
    {
        for (count2 = 'A'; count2 < ('A' + count1); count2++)  //Inner loop
            cout << count2;
        cout << "\n";
    }
}
```

Program Analysis

In order to understand this program it is important to remember that the second loop finishes its actions completely before the first loop moves on to its second iteration.

```
    int count1;
    char count2;
```

First, this program declares two variables, an integer variable **count1** and a character variable **count2**.

```
for (count1 = 1; count1 <= 5; count1++)
    {
        for (count2 = 'A'; count2 < ('A' + count1); count2++)
```

The outer loop uses **count1**, which is initialized to **1** and is incremented each time the outer loop is executed. The inner loop uses **count2**, which is initialized to **A** and is incremented each time the inner loop is executed.

```
cout << count2;
        cout << "\n";
```

When the outer loop has a value of **1**, the inner loop has an initial value of **A** (ASCII code 65). The condition of the inner loop is that **count2** is less than **'A'** + **count1**, (less than B or ASCII code 66). Therefore, the inner loop can't increase and only **A** is printed.

A newline character is actioned and the inner loop then terminates.

```
for (count1 = 1; count1 <= 5; count1++)
```

When the outer loop has a value of **2**, the inner loop has an initial value of **A** (ASCII code 65). The condition of the inner loop is that **count2** is less than **'A' + count1**, (less than C or ASCII code 67). Therefore, the inner loop increases to **B** (ASCII code 66) and **AB** is printed. A newline character is printed and the inner loop then terminates. This continues until the outer loop has a value of 5 which results in **ABCDE** being printed.

The full output from **FOR3.CPP** is:

```
A
AB
ABC
ABCD
ABCDE
```

Variable Type Casts - An Example

When you look at the next program, **FOR4.CPP**, you will see that it uses integer variables instead of character variables. However, it produces the same output as **FOR3.CPP**.

This is because we are using the statement `cout << (char) count2;` which is an example of a cast. Before we examine this, read through the source code and look at the output produced by the program to see if you can work out what is actually happening.

```
//for4.cpp

#include <iostream.h>          //header file for input/output

void main()
{
     int count1, count2;              //Loop control variables

     for (count1 = 1; count1 <= 5; count1++)   //Outer loop
     {
          for (count2 = 65; count2 < (65 + count1); count2++)   //Inner loop
               cout << (char) count2;                //cast
          cout << "\n";
     }

}
```

Program Analysis

```
cout << (char) count2;
```

The above statement is the key to how this program works. We have used a cast which is a conversion of some data we specified. It allows us to convert a value from one type to another in a situation where the compiler wouldn't do it automatically. In this case, the integer value is being converted to a character. Without a cast, the program would have output integer values instead of the letters.

It is advisable in mature programs to get your syntax selected and written correctly, instead of resorting to a cast as a fix.

The while Loop

The **while** loop continues to loop **while** some condition is true. When the condition becomes false, the looping is discontinued. This is a good loop to use when you are unsure of the number of repetitions required.

The syntax is:

```
while(condition)
       action;
```

While the condition is true the action will be repeated. Multiple actions can be included, as in a **for** loop, by using braces as follows:

```
while(condition)
{
       action1;
       action2;
       action3;
}
```

The condition is tested at the very start and the actions will only be carried out if the condition is true. Therefore, if the condition is false at the start no looping will occur at all.

```
count = 0;
while (count < 6)
{
       cout << "The value of count is " << count << "\n";
       count = count + 1;
}
```

The code segment shows an integer variable, **count**, being used to control the loop. This illustrates the syntax of a **while** loop. The keyword **while** is followed by an expression in parentheses, followed by a statement. As long as the expression in parentheses is true, the statement or statements within the braces will be executed.

In this case, since the variable **count** is incremented by 1 every time the statements in the loop are executed, it will eventually reach 6 and the statement won't be executed. The loop will be terminated and program control will resume at the statement following the loop.

Using the while Loop

Two things must be pointed out before you use the **while** loop.

- It is possible to have a **while** loop that is never executed. In the example above, if the variable **count** were initially set to any number greater than **5**, the statements within the loop wouldn't be executed at all,

- If the variable wasn't incremented in the loop, the loop would never terminate, and the program would never complete.

The **while** loop is used when the programmer doesn't know how many times something will need to be done. The **while** loop looks like a **for** loop without an initialization or increment expression. As long as the condition is true the loop continues to be executed.

The while Loop - An Example

The program **WHILE1.CPP**, shows a simple example of a **while** loop.

```
//WHILE1.CPP

#include <iostream.h>                //header file for input/output

void main()
{
    char letter = 'A';               //letter initialized to A
                                     //so while-loop is entered

    while (letter != 'q')            // Loop until q is entered
    {
        cout << "Enter a character ";
        cin >> letter;
        cout << "You entered: " << letter << endl;
    }
}
```

Program Analysis

```
char letter = 'A';
```

A character variable, **letter**, is declared and initialized to hold the value **A**.

```
while (letter != 'q')
```

The loop will execute as long as the letter **q** (a lower-case q) is not entered. When the letter **q** is entered the loop will terminate and program control returns to the statement following the loop. In this case there aren't any statements following the loop, so the program will terminate.

Sample output from this program is shown below:

```
Enter a character You entered: a
Enter a character You entered: d
Enter a character You entered: A
Enter a character You entered: S
Enter a character You entered: q
```

As you can see letter **q** is shown to have been entered. The test condition is now false and the loop terminates.

The program could be altered so that the **while** loop continues until either 'q' or 'Q' is entered.

The do-while Loop

With **do-while**, you don't have to know how many repetitions will be executed, but you do know that the loop will execute at least once.

The general syntax of the **do-while** loop is:

```
do
{
     action;
}
while(condition);
```

Most compilers insist that braces are used even when there is only one statement. As this makes the code more readable we would suggest that you always use them.

The **do-while** loop is illustrated in the code segment below. This code is almost identical to that used to illustrate the **while** loop, except that the loop begins with the reserved word **do** followed by a compound statement in braces, then the reserved word **while** and finally an expression in parentheses.

The statements in the braces are executed repeatedly as long as the expression in parentheses is true. When the expression in parentheses becomes false, execution is terminated, and control passes to the program statement following the test condition.

```
count = 0;
do
{
        cout << "The value of count is now " << count << "\n";
        count = count + 1;
}
while (count < 5);
```

Using the do-while Loop

There are two things to remember when using the `do-while` loop:

- Since the test is done at the end of the loop, the statements in the braces will always be executed at least once.

- Secondly, if the variable wasn't changed within the loop, the loop would never terminate, and hence the program would never terminate.

The Do-While Loop - An Example

The program `WHILE2.CPP`, shows an example of a `do-while` loop. This example is similar to `WHILE1.CPP`.

```
//WHILE2.CPP

#include <iostream.h>

void main()
{
    char answer;

    cout << "Enter a character: ";
    cin >> answer;

    do
    {
        cout << "You entered " << answer << endl;
        cout << "Enter a character: ";
        cin >> answer;
    } while (answer != 'Q');

    cout << "\nThe program is now finishing.\n";
}
```

Program Analysis

```
char answer;
```

A character variable, **answer**, is declared.

```
    do
    {
        cout << "You entered " << answer << endl;
        cout << "Enter a character: ";
        cin >> answer;
    } while (answer != 'Q');
```

The loop will execute once without the condition being tested. The loop will continue to execute as long as the condition is true. In this case, as long as the letter ǫ (an upper-case Q) is not entered. When the letter ǫ is entered the loop will terminate and program control returns to the statement following the loop. In this case, program control returns to the **cout** statement following the loop.

Sample output from this program is shown below:

```
Enter a character: a
You entered a
Enter a character: b
You entered b
Enter a character: A
You entered A
Enter a character: Z
You entered Z
Enter a character: Q

The program is now finishing.
```

In this case the loop terminated when ǫ was entered. This meant that the loop won't be re-entered and, therefore, the program doesn't inform the user that ǫ was entered.

Nesting Loops

All three loops can be **nested**. This means that one loop can be included within the compound statement of another loop, and the nesting level has no limit. Try to keep the nesting easy and logical - there is often more than one way to nest loops for the right result.

Which Loop to Use

You have now seen how each of the three loops are used. When will you use which loop?

- The **for** loop can be used when you know in advance how many times the loop will be executed.

- The **while** loop can be used when you don't know in advance how many times the loop will be executed. Use it when you don't want the loop to execute at all - not even once - unless a condition is met.

- The **do-while** loops can be used when you don't know in advance how many times the loop will be executed. Use it when you're certain it's OK for the loop to execute at least once.

break and continue

Normally a loop will execute until the terminating condition is met but occasionally you will want to get out of a loop early.

This can be achieved by using either the **break** or the **continue** keywords.

break - An Example

If the **break** keyword is used the program will jump out of the loop and the loop will terminate.

This is illustrated in the example below:

```
int counter;

for (counter = 5; counter < 12; counter++)
{
  if (counter == 9)
    break;                    //break out of loop and terminate it
  cout << "In the break loop, counter is now " << counter << endl;
}
```

The output from this code fragment would be

```
In the break loop, counter is now 5
In the break loop, counter is now 6
In the break loop, counter is now 7
In the break loop, counter is now 8
```

Program Analysis

```
if (counter == 9)
    break;
```

Here, there is an **if** statement inside the **for** loop that calls **break** if counter equals 9. The break will cause the program to jump out of the loop and begin executing statements following the loop, effectively terminating the loop. This is a valuable statement when you need to jump out of a loop depending on the value of some results calculated within the loop. In this case, when counter reaches **9**, the loop is terminated and the last value printed will be the previous value, namely **8**.

continue - An Example

If the **continue** keyword is used the program will stop executing the remaining statements in the loop but will return to the start of the loop. The loop will continue to execute if the terminating condition hasn't been achieved.

This is illustrated below:

```
for (counter = 5; counter < 12; counter++)
  {
    if (counter == 9)
      continue;  //jump to end of loop but continue to
                 //execute loop from the next iteration

    cout << "In the loop, counter is now " << counter << endl;
  }
```

The following output is produced:

```
In the loop, counter is now 5
In the loop, counter is now 6
In the loop, counter is now 7
In the loop, counter is now 8
In the loop, counter is now 10
In the loop, counter is now 11
```

Program Analysis

```
if (counter == 9)
     continue;
```

The **for** loop contains a **continue** statement which doesn't cause the termination of the loop but which does cause the program to jump out of the present iteration. When the value of counter reaches 9 the program will jump to the end of the loop and continue executing the loop, effectively eliminating the **cout** statement during the pass through of the loop when counter is at 9.

The Problem With Floats

We said earlier that variables used in loops must have numeric values. However, we can say they must have no fractional part - floats should not be used. Let's think now about why we need to restrict our variables like this. There is a problem which arises when using floats in a relational test which is usually highlighted when you are using loops. Run the following program and see what happens:

```
/* ****************************************************************
 *    floats.cpp                                                 *
 *    Ian M Wilks                                                *
 **************************************************************** */
#include <iostream.h>

void main()
{
    float counter = 1.7;
    char letter;

    while (counter != 2.5)
    {
        cout << "Press a key: ";
        cin >> letter;
        cout << "number = " << counter << " and letter = " << letter
             << endl;

        //the next two lines provide a way of terminating the loop if
        //the loop does not terminate when counter equals 2.5
        if ((letter == 'Q') || (letter == 'q'))
            break;

        counter += 0.1;
    }
}
```

Do you understand what is happening?

This is some sample output from the program:

```
Press a key: b
number = 1.8 and letter = b
Press a key: c
number = 1.9 and letter = c
Press a key: d
number = 2 and letter = d
Press a key: e
number = 2.1 and letter = e
Press a key: f
number = 2.2 and letter = f
Press a key: g
number = 2.3 and letter = g
Press a key: h
number = 2.4 and letter = h
Press a key: i
number = 2.5 and letter = i
Press a key: j
number = 2.599999 and letter = j
Press a key: k
number = 2.699999 and letter = k
Press a key: q
number = 2.799999 and letter = q

 2:02 hrs Tue 12-04-1994
[DR DOS] C:\TEMP>
```

If you run the program you need to press a character key followed by *Return* before it prints out the current value of **number** and **letter**.

You expect the program to stop when **number** gets to 2.5. However, you will find that the program doesn't terminate. To escape from the loop and terminate the program you will have to press Q or q. Why is this? Let's find out.

Program Analysis

```
counter != 2.5
```

Look at the **while** loop condition. It reads: "while **counter** is not equal to 2.5 execute the statements in the braces". This means that when **counter** gets to 2.5 it should stop. Unfortunately, it didn't.

If you think about the way the computer deals with numbers you should realize that they don't have an accurate way or representing floating point numbers. Computers work in binary numbers and there is no way of exactly representing 0.1 in binary. There is also the possibility that the computer can't exactly represent 2.5 using binary.

> You should note that on some systems in some circumstances an exact match can be made.

How to Avoid the Problem

How will you get around this problem? The simplest way is not to test for equality or inequality on floats. Don't use == or != when using floats. If you need to use floats in tests, do so using the 'less than' and 'greater than' tests. For example, if you want to test whether something is equal to 2.5 to a degree of 0.01 you could use:

```
if ( (number > 2.49) && (number < 2.51) )
```

You are testing that the number is greater than 2.49 and less than 2.51. If this is true then it means that the number is equal to the value we require within our error limit.

In **FLOATS.CPP** the intention was to stop the loop when **counter** got to 2.5. We didn't want the loop to be performed when **counter** was in fact at 2.5 so we were only interested in those values of counter below 2.5. If the condition is altered to read:

```
while (counter < 2.5)
```

the program should then give the required result. Let's alter the program now to see if it works.

The output from your revised program should be something like

```
Press a key: a
number = 1.7 and letter = a
Press a key: b
number = 1.8 and letter = b
Press a key: c
number = 1.9 and letter = c
Press a key: d
number = 2 and letter = d
Press a key: e
number = 2.1 and letter = e
Press a key: f
number = 2.2 and letter = f
Press a key: g
number = 2.3 and letter = g
Press a key: h
number = 2.4 and letter = h
Press a key: i
number = 2.5 and letter = i
```

The goto Statement

If you have done any programming before you may think that achieving a repeated code section is easier using your old friend the **goto** command.

However, if you are familiar with the principles of structured programming you know that goto statements lead to code that is difficult to follow, difficult to understand, and difficult to debug.

C++ is a high-level language which offers excellent structuring facilities, and you should rarely need to use goto statements in your programs. Remember though, excessive use of breaks in your code can also make it unwieldy.

Take the situation where you may have some nested loops. If the center loop goes into an error condition, then all the loops have to be terminated - and remember the break statement only terminates the loop you are in. Maybe in this case, a goto statement would suffice, otherwise its best avoided.

If you need to use the goto statement, insert a label in your code at the desired location for the goto. The label is terminated by a colon.

The keyword **goto** followed by the label's name takes you to the label, for example:

```
count = 1;

goto_label:
    count++;
    if (count < 100)
        goto goto_label;
```

The switch Statement

When your **if-else** commands start building up, it can be difficult to maintain the code or keep on top of the writing. It would be good if you could write some sort of menu system into your programs to offer multiple choices or actions. This is exactly what can be done using a switch statement. You can use a switch statement instead of, or, in conjunction with multiple if-else statements

Switch statements consist of two parts:

- Firstly, the declaration of the switch, that is the variable whose value is used as the test.

- Secondly, a list of cases which state the action to be taken if the value matches the value in that case.

Sounds a little complicated!

The Structure of the switch Statement

To make things a little easier let's examine the general structure.

```
switch (choice)
{
    case 1 :
        statement;
        break;
    case 2 :
        statement;
        break;
    case 3 :
        statement;
        break;
    default :
        statement;
}
```

This isn't quite as complicated as it sounded. As you can see the switch statement begins with the keyword **switch** followed by a variable in brackets which is the switching variable, in this case **choice**. As many cases as desired are then enclosed within a pair of braces. The reserved word **case** is used to begin each case entered, followed by the value of the variable, then a colon, and the statements to be executed.

This switch statement begins by comparing the switching variable with the variable in **case 1**. If they match, the statements in **case 1** will execute. If the switching variable matches **case 2**, then the second statement will execute instead. Once an entry point into the program is found, statements will be executed until a break is found or until the program drops through the bottom brace.

It should be noted that the various case values can be in any order, and if a value isn't found, the default portion of the switch will be executed.

Case values must be an integer or character.

The break statement is vital for the execution of the switch statement. If you omitted it then all the statements from each case would execute one after another rather than stopping after the appropriate menu option. This can cause you to lose your sense of humor on program execution!

The switch Statement - An Example

The next example **SWITCH.CPP**, contains a simple example to show what's happening. Before running this program, read through the source code and ascertain what should happen. Then run the program and see if you're right.

```cpp
//switch.cpp

#include <iostream.h>

void main()
{
    int sw_var;

    for (sw_var = 0; sw_var < 10; sw_var++)
    {
        switch(sw_var)                  //switching variable is sw_var
        {
        case 0 : cout << "The value of the switching variable is 0\n";
                    break;
        case 1 : cout << "The value of the switching variable is 1\n";
                    break;
        case 2 : cout << "The value of the switching variable is 2\n";
                    break;
        case 3 :
        case 4 :
        case 5 : cout << "The value of the switching variable is"
                        " between 3 and 5\n";
            break;
        case 8 : cout << "The value of the switching variable is 8\n";
                    break;
            default: cout << "It is one of the undefined values\n";
        }       //end of switch statement
    }           //end of for-loop
}
```

Program Analysis

```
switch(sw_var)
```

As we have seen, the switch statement begins with the keyword **switch** followed by a variable in brackets (the switching variable), which in this case is **sw_var**.

```
for (sw_var = 0; sw_var < 10; sw_var++)
```

A **for** loop is used to set the value of the variable **sw_var** at the beginning of the program. During the loop's first pass it will set **sw_var** equal to 0 and so the **cout** statement will cause The value of the switching variable is   0 to be displayed, and then the **break** statement will cause the program to jump out of the switch.

```
case 3 :
case 4 :
case 5 :
```

Once an entry point is found, statements will be executed until a break is found or until the program passes through the brace at the end of the switch statement. If the variable has the value 3, the statements will begin executing where **case 3** : is found, but since there are no statements here the program will move on to the first statements which can be executed. These are found at **case 5,** and once they are executed, the **break** statement here will direct the execution out of the switch.

This method can be used when you want one of several possible selections to trigger the same action. As you have seen above, this is possible in the **switch** statement by stacking the cases.

Remember, the various case values can be in any order and if a value isn't found, the default portion of the switch will be executed.

The output from the program is shown below:

```
The  value  of  the  switching  variable  is  0
The  value  of  the  switching  variable  is  1
Teh  value  of  the  switching  variable  is  2
The  value  of  the  switching  variable  is  between  3  and  5
The  value  of  the  switching  variable  is  between  3  and  5
The  value  of  the  switching  variable  is  between  3  and  5
It  is  one  of  the  undefined  values
It  is  one  of  the  undefined  values
The  value  of  the  switching  variable  is  8
It  is  one  of  the  undefined  values
```

A Simple Menu System - An Example

Now look at the following example which demonstrates a simple menu system. Read through the source code and work out how the program works. There isn't any code in the program that you haven't seen before.

Once you realize how the program works, run the program and see if it behaves as you expect. If it doesn't, look at the source code again.

```cpp
//menu.cpp

#include <iostream.h>          //header file for input/output

void main()
{
    char letter;

    cout << "\t\t\t---- EXAMPLE MENU ----\n\n";
    cout << "\t\tA: Menu Entry 1\n";
    cout << "\t\tB: Menu Entry 2\n";
    cout << "\t\tC: Menu Entry 3\n";
    cout << "\t\tD: Menu Entry 4\n";
    cout << "\t\tE: Menu Entry 5\n\n";
    cout << "\tPlease enter capital letters to select menu\n";
    cout << "\t";

    cin >> letter;

    cout << "\n\n\n";

    switch(letter)
    {
        case 'A' : cout << "\tYou chose Menu Entry 1\n";
            break;
        case 'B' : cout << "\tYou chose Menu Entry 2\n";
            break;
        case 'C' : cout << "\tYou chose Menu Entry 3\n";
            break;
        case 'D' : cout << "\tYou chose Menu Entry 4\n";
            break;
        case 'E' : cout << "\tYou chose Menu Entry 5\n";
            break;
        default : cout << "\tYou did not chose a Menu Entry\n";
    }
}
```

As you can see this is a fairly simple program and various improvements can be made. You will have noticed that the **switch** statement only works if an upper-case letter is entered at the keyboard. Amend the program to test whether a lower-case letter is input and, if it has, to change it to an upper-case letter.

You will also notice that the program doesn't clear the screen before writing. This would be necessary in a menu program. Amend the program so that the screen is cleared.

Summary

In this chapter you have learnt how to use your computer's capacity for repetition to build some useful programming statements. The three types of loops we have looked at (**for, while** and **do-while**) can be used in a wide variety of programs. You should also now be familiar with how to use the **switch** statement to carry out a task, based on the value of a variable.

This chapter has given you a basic understanding of loops. In the next chapter we will go on to handling larger amounts of data, where loops become invaluable.

Programming Exercises

1 What does the following program do?

```
//prog41.cpp
#include <iostream.h>

void main()
{
    int input, int_var = 0;

    cout << "Enter several positive integers followed by -1\n\n";

    for (;;)
    {
    cin >> input;
    if (input == -1)
    break;
    int_var += input;
    }

cout << "The value of the variable int_var is : "
    << int_var << endl;
}
```

2 Alter the program so that only a maximum of 20 integers can be entered.

3 Re-write the revised program to do the same thing using a **while** loop.

4 Re-write the revised program in Question 1 to do the same thing using a **do - while** loop.

5 Write a program to read a sequence of positive integers and then print out the largest of the numbers entered. Use a negative integer to signal the end of the input.

6 Now alter the program so that the smallest of the numbers is printed out.

7 Write a program that reads a sequence of positive real numbers and calculates the average. Use a negative number to signal the end of the input data.

8   Write a program that displays the following message on the screen:

```
---- C++ PROGRAMMING - CONTROL STRUCTURE HELP MENU ----

A: for loops
B: while loops
C: do - while loops
D: break and continue
E: switch statements

Please enter letters in the range A - E to select help text to display
```

The user should be able to select the appropriate letter to display the following information:

A   The general structure of the **for** loop is:

> for (starting value; condition; changes)
>   action;

B   The **while** loop continues to loop while some condition is true. When the condition becomes false, the looping is discontinued.

The syntax is:

> while(condition)
>   action;

While the condition is true the action will be repeated.

C   The general syntax of the **do-while** loop is:

> do{
>   action;
>   }while(condition);

Most compilers insist that braces are used even when there is only one statement.

D   Normally a loop will execute until the terminating condition is met but occasionally you will want to get out of a loop before that condition is met.

This can be achieved by using either the **break** or the `continue` keywords.

If the **break** keyword is used the program will jump out of the loop and the loop will terminate.

If the `continue` keyword is used the program will stop executing the remaining statements in the loop but will return to the start of the loop. The loop will continue to execute if the terminating condition has not been achieved.

```
E.      switch (choice)
        {
                case 1 :
                        statement;
                        break;
                case 2 :
                        statement;
                        break;
                case 3 :
                        statement;
                        break;
                default :
                        statement;
        }
```

The screen should be cleared before the help message is displayed on the screen.

9   Once you have got the program running you should amend the program so that the user is asked if they want to see another help message. The user should indicate their decision by typing Y or N. If the user types Y, the screen should be cleared and the menu should be re-displayed.

Chapter

5

Arrays

In the programs we've examined so far, each variable was associated with a *single* data value. This type of variable is called a simple variable. We can store one value in a variable easily, but what if we wanted to store and manipulate a hundred values in that variable? We could carry out an expression on each value, then replace it and run the expression again. Each time though, we'd lose the previous value from memory. There's always the option of writing a hundred variables of course!

It is much easier to consider using an **array,** which is a grouping of related data items.

In this chapter we'll discuss:

- Why we need arrays
- One dimensional arrays
- Declaring and referencing arrays
- Bounds checking
- Multi-dimensional arrays
- Strings
- Common string controls

What is an Array?

When we are programming, we often need to process a set of data of which all the items have the same data type. Why? Think about the types of problems that this refers to.

One problem may involve the programmer in computing statistics from a set of examination marks. Another may involve computing some statistics from a set of sales figures.

The two examples are obviously of the same basic type. The programmer could allocate a variable for each data item, say each student's examination marks. However, this approach soon becomes unwieldy.

By using an array, a single variable name can be associated with a whole collection of data. The array is a data structure which is used to store a collection of data items that are all of the same type, that is: **int**, **float**, or **char**. We use arrays when we want to work with blocks of data. It's easier to work with arrays than with a collection of simple variables for certain types of problems.

As a programmer, if you want to process an individual item you need to specify the array name and indicate which array element is being referenced. Specific elements are indicated by an index or subscript. This way you can have endless variables defined quickly and actioned either individually or as a group.

Why We Need Arrays - Illustrating the Problem

The following program is a good illustration of a situation where we need an array. Suppose, for example, that you need to write a program which reads ten integer values, manipulates these values and prints the values on the screen together with the results of the manipulation. The program then displays the values in reverse order.

To do a simple averaging task of these 10 integers you might write the following program.

```
/* ***********************************************************
 *     reverse.cpp                                          *
 *     Ian M Wilks                                          *
 * ********************************************************* */
#include <iostream.h>           //header file for input/output
#include <iomanip.h>            //for input/output manipulators

void main()
{
    int first, second, third, fourth, fifth, sixth, seventh,
        eighth, ninth, tenth, sum = 0;

    float product = 1.0;
    float average;

    cout << "This Program reads ten integer numbers entered by the\n"
         << "user at the keyboard, manipulates these numbers, and then\n"
         << "displays these numbers on the screen in reverse order\n"
         << "together with the results of the manipulations.\n\n"
         << "Enter ten digits and press return.\n";

    cin >> first >> second >> third >> fourth >> fifth >> sixth >> seventh
        >> eighth >> ninth >> tenth;

/* ******************** MANIPULATE THE DATA ******************** */

    sum = first + second + third + fourth + fifth + sixth + seventh + eighth
            + ninth + tenth;

    product *= first;       product *= second;
    product *= third;       product *= fourth;
    product *= fifth;       product *= sixth;
    product *= seventh;     product *= eighth;
    product *= ninth;       product *= tenth;

    average = sum / 10.00;

/* ********************* DISPLAY THE DATA ********************* */

    cout << "\n\nThe integers that were input were: "
         << first << "  " << second << "  " << third << " " << fourth << " "
         << fifth << "  " << sixth << "  " << seventh << " " << eighth << " "
         << ninth << "  " << tenth
         << "\n\nThe sum of the integers is " << sum
         << "\n\nThe product of the integers is "
         << setiosflags(ios::fixed) << product
         << "\n\nThe average of the numbers is " << average
         << "\n\nThe integers in reverse order are: "
         << tenth << "  " << ninth << "  " << eighth << " " << seventh << " "
         << sixth << "  " << fifth << "  " << fourth << "  " << third << "  "
         << second << "  " << first;
}
```

Program Analysis

Look at the source code and ascertain what the program is doing.

```
#include <iostream.h>        //header file for input/output
#include <iomanip.h>         //for input/output manipulators
```

After the comment block the program uses the **#include** directive to include **iostream.h**, which is needed for the input/output routines, and **iomanip.h**, which is needed for input/output manipulators.

```
void main()
```

The program then enters **main()**:

```
int first, second, third, fourth, fifth, sixth, seventh,
        eighth, ninth, tenth, sum = 0;

    float product = 1.0;
    float average;
```

11 integers and 2 float variables are declared.

```
cout << "This Program reads ten integer numbers entered by the\n"
        << "user at the keyboard, manipulates these numbers, and then\n"
        << "displays these numbers on the screen in reverse order\n"
        << "together with the results of the manipulations.\n\n"
        << "Enter ten digits and press return.\n";
```

The **cout** statement is used to output a message to the screen which terminates by asking the user to enter ten integer variables.

```
cin >> first >> second >> third >> fourth >> fifth >> sixth >> seventh
        >> eighth >> ninth >> tenth;
```

cin is used to assign the integers to the appropriate variables. The program waits until ten integers are input.

```
sum = first + second + third + fourth + fifth + sixth + seventh + eighth
            + ninth  + tenth;
```

The variables input are summed.

```
product *= first;       product *= second;
product *= third;       product *= fourth;
product *= fifth;       product *= sixth;
product *= seventh;     product *= eighth;
product *= ninth;       product *= tenth;
```

The product of the input variables is calculated. The variable **product** was initialized to 1, and each of the input variables are multiplied by the value of **product** and the new answer is stored in **product**. The mathematical assignment operator ***=** is used.

```
average = sum / 10.00;
```

The arithmetic mean (average) of the input variables is calculated by dividing the sum by the number of variables.

```
cout << "\n\nThe integers that were input were: "
        << first << "  " << second << "  " << third << " " << fourth << "  "
        << fifth << "  " << sixth << "  " << seventh << " " << eighth << " "
        << ninth << "  " << tenth
        << "\n\nThe sum of the integers is " << sum
        << "\n\nThe product of the integers is "
        << setiosflags(ios::fixed) << product
        << "\n\nThe average of the numbers is " << average
        << "\n\nThe integers in reverse order are: "
        << tenth << "  " << ninth << "  " << eighth << " " << seventh << " "
        << sixth << "  " << fifth << "  " << fourth << "  " << third << "  "
        << second << "  " << first;
```

The integers that were input are then displayed, followed by the results of the manipulations. The integers are then displayed in reverse order.

```
setiosflags(ios::fixed)
```

You'll probably have noticed some unfamiliar code in the **cout** statement.

Displaying Results

There are a group of flags that are used to decide how screen output will be formatted. You don't need to understand how this works to use it. We want to ensure that output is displayed in a format that we understand.

For example, if you enter the numbers 1, 2, 3, 4, 5, 6, 7, 8, 9, and 10, then the product of the number is 3,628,800. We'd want this to be shown on the screen as   3628800. However, this number can be output as 3.6288e6. This is known as exponential format and means 3.6288×10^6

To ensure that this type of output is not generated, we can use the **ios** flag fixed**.** This prevents the output being given in exponential format.

To set the flag we use the manipulator **setiosflags** with the name of the flag, fixed, as an argument. The flag name must be prefixed with the class name, **ios**, and the **scope resolution operator (::).**

Why We Need Arrays - Solving the Problem

Now suppose our original problem changes. What happens if we now have to write the program so it reads two hundred integers, manipulates them and displays the original variables together with the results of manipulations?.

Using unique identifiers for each item of the data is an extraordinarily cumbersome approach.

The simplest way to tackle a problem like this is to use an array.

Declaring and Referencing Arrays

With the exception of declaring the size, an array is declared just like any other variable. The syntax is:

```
type  array_name[number_of_elements]
```

- The type is any of the fundamental data types, that is: **int**, **float**, or **char**.

- The array size is specified as a constant expression representing the maximum number of elements.

- The array name is introduced as an identifier.

For example, an array called **scores** with eight elements of type **integer** would be declared as

```
int scores[8];
```

An array occupies a block of consecutive memory positions. The storage space reserved for the array **scores** might appear as shown in the following figure.

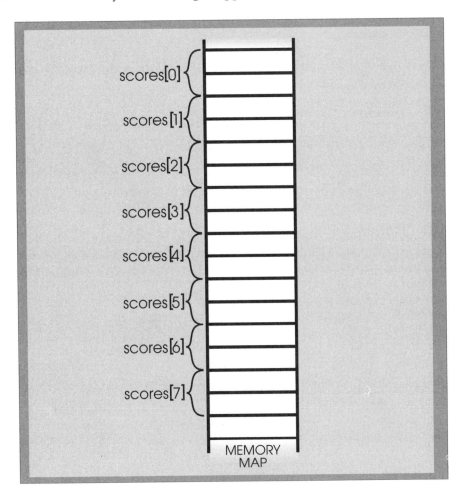

MEMORY
MAP

Subscripts

To work with the data stored in an array you need to reference each element.

The array subscript, or index, is used to distinguish different elements of the same array. A subscripted variable consists of an array name followed by an integer expression enclosed in square brackets.

For example, **scores [0]** refers to the first element in the array **scores**, **scores[1]** refers to the second element, and **scores[7]** refers to the last element. This is illustrated in the above figure.

Notice how the array declaration specifies the number of elements (eight), while the elements themselves are referenced by the subscripts 0, 1, 2, 3, 4, 5, 6, and 7.

Array Initialization

Like simple variables, arrays can be initialized when declared. To initialize an array the general form would be:

```
int  number[8]  =  {1,  2,  3,  4,  5,  6,  7,  8};
```

As you can see, the values to be allocated to the array are set in a set of braces.

This is equivalent to

```
int   number[8];

number[0]  =  1;
number[1]  =  2;
number[2]  =  3;
number[3]  =  4;
number[4]  =  5;
number[5]  =  6;
number[6]  =  7;
number[7]  =  8;
```

If the size of the array is not specified, then the compiler will construct an array of sufficient size to take the values specified. For example:

```
int  new_number[]  =  {1, 3, 5, 7, 9, 11, 13, 15, 17, 19};
```

will set up an array of 10 elements.

Using Array Elements

An array element may be used in any expression in which a simple variable of the same type could have been used.

Examples of expressions involving subscripted elements include:

```
int sum;
sum = number[0] + number[1] + number[2];
```

```
int product = 1;
product *= number[5];
```

```
number[7] = 100;
```

```
if(number[0] < number[1])
    cout << "The first element is smaller than the second\n";
```

Using Integer Values in Subscripts

You can use any expression that results in an integer value in a subscript. For example:

```
int x, y;
x = 1;
y = 2

number[x + y] = 0;
```

Here the fourth element of the array **number** = 0

```
for( int z = 0; z < 7; z++ )
    cout << number[z] << endl;
```

A **for** loop is used to output the values of the first eight elements of the array **number**.

Bounds Checking

C++ does not provide support for checking that you're working inside the array. You must be careful and ensure that the code does not attempt to access an array element that is outside the bounds of the array declaration.

For example:

```
int number[8]
number[25] = 10;
```

Since the array **number** only contains eight elements then the subscript **number[25]** cannot exist.

However, the compiler will accept the above statement and the program will run. Let's hope that the statement is not what you actually intended. What will happen? The data will probably be written on top of other data or the actual program code. This will lead to run-time errors and may even cause the computer to crash.

Shortening Code With an Array - An Example

Now, let's return to the original problem.

Ten integer values are read as input, and these values are manipulated before the program displays the values on the screen together with the results of the manipulations. The program then displays the values in reverse order.

An array is now used in the solution:

```
/* ************************************************************
 *    reverse1.cpp                                           *
 *    Ian M Wilks                                            *
 ********************************************************** */
#include <iostream.h>          //header file for input/output
#include <iomanip.h>           //for input/output manipulators

void main()
{
    const int SIZE = 10;                    //constant
    int counter, sum = 0;
    float average, product = 1.0;
    int number[SIZE];                       //array variable

    cout << "This Program reads ten integer numbers entered by the\n"
         << "user at the keyboard, manipulates these numbers, and then\n"
         << "displays these numbers on the screen in reverse order\n"
         << "together with the results of the manipulations.\n\n"
         << "Enter ten digits and press return.\n";

    for (counter = 0; counter < SIZE; counter++)
        cin >> number[counter];

/* ********************** MANIPULATE THE DATA ********************** */

    for (counter = 0; counter < SIZE; counter++)
        sum += number[counter];

    for (counter = 0; counter < SIZE; counter++)
        product *= number[counter];

    average = sum / 10.00;
```

```
/* ************************** DISPLAY THE DATA ****************************/

    cout << "\n\nThe integers that were input were: ";

    for (counter = 0; counter < SIZE; counter++)
        cout << number[counter] << "  ";

    cout << "\n\nThe sum of the integers is " << sum
        << "\n\nThe product of the integers is "
        << setiosflags(ios::fixed) << product
        << "\n\nThe average of the numbers is " << average
        << "\n\nThe integers in reverse order are: ";

    for (counter = SIZE - 1; counter >= 0; counter—)
        cout << number[counter] << "  ";
}
```

Program Analysis

The program does exactly the same as the original program, **REVERSE.CPP**. The only difference is that we're now using an array instead of ten simple variables.

```
for (counter = 0; counter < SIZE; counter++)
        cin >> number[counter];
```

A **for** loop is used to step through the array.

When **counter** is equal to 0, **number[counter]** is equivalent to **number[0]**.
When **counter** is equal to 1, **number[counter]** is equivalent to **number[1]**.

```
const int SIZE = 10;                //constant
int counter, sum = 0;
float average, product = 1.0;
int number[SIZE];                   //array variable
```

We've used a constant to declare the size of the array.

You can see from this program that using an array has shortened the code and made it easier to write.

Arrays of Other Types

It was stated earlier that array elements may be of any of the fundamental types. You can use the fundamental data types to enhance your program's security. For instance, it's good programming practice to use a constant to declare an array size as we've done above. Here are some more examples of arrays using other data types.

95

```
const int SIZE = 5;
const int NAME_SIZE = 20;
const int ADDRESS_SIZE = 30;

float real[SIZE + 1];
```

The array **real** has 6 elements of type **float**.

```
char name[NAME_SIZE], Address[ADDRESS_SIZE];
```

Both **name** and **address** are **character** arrays.

Practical Use of an Array

Let's now look at another program that uses an array. This program also calculates the average of the numbers input. The difference with this program is that we don't know how many data elements will be entered.

Therefore, in the program, we'll declare an array which is large enough to hold the anticipated number of data elements.

To calculate the average we need to know the number of data elements. We'll therefore have to count the number of elements input.

This program, although relatively simple, should help you appreciate that it's easier to use an array rather than a collection of simple variables.

Using an Array - An Example

```
/* ************************************************************
 *     average.cpp                                           *
 *     Ian M Wilks                                           *
 ************************************************************ */
#include <iostream.h>            //header file for input/output

void main()
{
    const int SIZE = 100;   //maximum number of array elements
    int counter = 0;        //variable to be used to count number of data
                            //items input
    int i = 0;              //loop variable
    float number[SIZE];     //array of floats for data
    float sum = 0.0;        //variable to sum array elements
    float average;          //variable to store answer
    char ch = `Y';          //input check
```

```
        cout << "This program prompts the user to enter a number of float\n"
             << "variables and then calculates the average of these "
             << "numbers.\n\n";

//input data to array
    while ((ch == 'Y') || (ch == 'y'))
    {
         cout << "Please enter number: ";
         cin >> number[i++];
         counter++;
         cout << "Do you wish to enter another number? (Y/N)  ";
         cin >> ch;
    }

//sum the elements in the array
    for(i = 0; i < counter; i++)
         sum += number[i];

//calculate average
    average = sum / counter;

//output average
    cout << "\n\nThe average of the numbers input is " << average;
}
```

Program Analysis

I hope you'll agree that this program is fairly easy to understand.

A **while** loop is used to enter the data and a **for** loop is used to sum the array elements as we saw in the previous program, **REVERSE1.CPP**.

- The data is entered via the keyboard by the user.

- The **while** loop is used so that the user can be asked if another number is to be entered.

- If the user enters **Y** or **y** then the loop is re-entered.

- If the user enters any other character the loop terminates.

```
        cin >> number[i++];
        counter++;
```

Each time the user enters a number, **counter** will increase by one, thus adding up the number of entries the user has made.

```
for(i = 0; i < counter; i++)
    sum += number[i];
```

The array elements are added together in the **for** loop using the **+=** operator, which is one of the mathematical assignment operators - assign sum.

```
average = sum / counter;
```

The average is then calculated and the answer is displayed on the screen.

Multi-Dimensional Arrays

C++ provides for multi-dimensional arrays.

Imagine a table containing the salary figures for several sales-areas over a number of months.

The salary figures for one area could be stored in a one-dimensional array:

```
const int MONTHS = 6;
float first_sales_area[MONTHS];
```

The salary figures for all the areas could be stored in an array of these arrays, that is, a two-dimensional array:

```
const int MONTHS = 6;
const int SALES_AREAS = 12;

float salary_figures[SALES_AREAS][MONTHS];
```

You can imagine a two-dimensional array as having rows and columns, like a sheet of graph paper or a spreadsheet. A row in this example would represent the salary figures for a single sales area. A column represents the salary figures for all the areas in a single month. The intersection of a given row and column is the salary figure for a particular sales area in a given month. See the next figure.

	JAN	FEB	MAR	APR	MAY	JUN
Sales_Areas_1						
Sales_Areas_2						
Sales_Areas_3						
Sales_Areas_4						
Sales_Areas_5						
Sales_Areas_6						
Sales_Areas_7						
Sales_Areas_8						
Sales_Areas_9						
Sales_Areas_10						
Sales_Areas_11						
Sales_Areas_12						

C++ actually treats a two-dimensional array as a one-dimensional array, each of whose elements is itself an array. Hence, a subscripted element to reference the sales of a particular district in a given month is written:

```
salary_figures[rows][column];
```

For example, `salary_figures[0][0];` references the value stored in the first row of the first column of the array `salary_figures`.

Two Dimensional Arrays - An Example

The following program shows one possible use of a two dimensional array. The user is required to enter numbers to be displayed in a table on the screen. The program prompts for the user's input by giving the coordinates of the position in the table where the input will be stored. The input values are stored in a two dimensional array.

```
/* *************************************************************
 *    array2d.cpp                                             *
 *    Ian M Wilks                                             *
 ************************************************************ */
#include <iostream.h>          //header file for input/output

void main()
{
    const int SIZE1 = 5;            //constant
    const int SIZE2 = 5;            //constant
    int count1, count2;            //variables to be used in for loops
    int array2d[SIZE1][SIZE2];     //array variable - to contain data
```

99

```
        cout << "This Program stores a table of numbers entered by the\n"
             << "user and then prints the table to the screen.\n\n"
             << "Table size is " << SIZE1 << " by " << SIZE2 << endl;


//obtain data and store in array
    for (count1 = 0; count1 < SIZE1; count1++)
        for (count2 = 0; count2 < SIZE2; count2++)
        {
            cout << "array2d[" << count1 << "] [" << count2 << "] = ";
            cin >> array2d[count1][count2];
        }

    cout << "\n\nThe integers have been stored in the array\n\n";

//display table on screen
    for (count1 = 0; count1 < SIZE1; count1++)
    {
        for (count2 = 0; count2 < SIZE2; count2++)
        {
            cout << array2d[count1][count2] << "   ";
        }
        cout << endl;
    }
}
```

Program Analysis

The program displays a message on the screen telling the user the size of the array (table) that is being used.

The program prompts the user to enter the value for each element of the array in the form of **array2d[0][0] =**. So, for example, the number that the user enters when they see the prompt **array2d[0][0]** is the number that will appear in the first row and the first column of the table.

```
for (count1 = 0; count1 < SIZE1; count1++)
    for (count2 = 0; count2 < SIZE2; count2++)
    {
        cout << "array2d[" << count1 << "] [" << count2 << "] = ";
        cin >> array2d[count1][count2];
    }
```

A nested **for** loop is used to access each element in the array and the values entered via the keyboard are stored.

```
        cout << "\n\nThe integers have been stored in the array\n\n";

//display table on screen
    for (count1 = 0; count1 < SIZE1; count1++)
    {
        for (count2 = 0; count2 < SIZE2; count2++)
        {
            cout << array2d[count1][count2] << "   ";
        }
        cout << endl;
    }
```

A message is displayed informing the user that the integers have been stored in the array and then the program displays the table on the screen:

```
1    2    3    4    5
6    7    8    9    10
11   12   13   14   15
16   17   18   19   20
21   22   23   24   25
```

Formatting the Output - An Example

In the first example program in this chapter we saw how we can control the format of the output. The following program demonstrates further methods of controlling the format of the output.

```
/* ************************************************************
 *    ioman.cpp                                             *
 *    Ian M Wilks                                           *
 ************************************************************ */
#include <iostream.h>        //header file for input/output
#include <iomanip.h>         //for input/output manipulators

void main()
{
    const int ROWS = 5;
    const int COLS = 5;

    float number[ROWS][COLS];

    cout << "This Program reads twenty-five floats, entered by the user\n"
         << "at the keyboard, and then displays a table.\n\n";

    for (int i = 0; i < ROWS; i++)
        for (int j = 0; j < COLS; j++)
        {
            cout << "Enter float value for row " << i + 1
                 << ", column " << j + 1 << ": ";
```

101

```
                    cin >> number[i][j];
        }

    cout << endl << endl
        << "                              Column\n"
        << "        1         2         3         4         5";

    for (i = 0; i < 5; i++)
    {
        cout << "\nRow " << i + 1;
        for (int j = 0; j < 5; j++)                //display table
        {
            //not exponential format
            cout << setiosflags(ios::fixed)
                 << setiosflags(ios::showpoint) //show decimal point
                 << setprecision(4)             //digits to right of
                                                //decimal point
                 << setw(10)                    //field width
                 << number[i][j];               //number from array
        }
    }
}
```

Program Analysis

Look at the output you get from the program.

```
cout << "This Program reads twenty-five floats, entered by the user\n"
    << "at the keyboard, and then displays a table.\n\n";
```

The program initially displays the following message:

```
This Program reads twenty-five floats, entered by the user
at the keyboard, and then displays a table.
```

```
for (int i = 0; i < ROWS; i++)
    for (int j = 0; j < COLS; j++)
    {
        cout << "Enter float value for row " << i + 1
            << ", column " << j + 1 << ":  ";

        cin >> number[i][j];
    }
```

The user is then asked to enter the data. This takes the following form:

```
Enter float value for row 1, column 1:  1.11111111
Enter float value for row 1, column 2:  25.2525252
```

After all the values are entered the table is output in the following format:

```
                          Column
             1        2        3        4        5
Row 1     1.1111   25.2525   2.2222   24.2424   3.3333
Row 2    23.2323    4.4444  22.2222    5.5556  21.2121
Row 3     6.6667   20.2020   7.7778  190.1902  80.8081
Row 4   180.1802   90.9091 170.1702  100.1001 160.1602
Row 5   110.1101  150.1501 120.1201  140.1401 130.1301
```

setiosflags(ios::fixed)

As we saw in the earlier example, the above expression is used to prevent exponential output.

setiosflags(ios::showpoint)

The above expression is used to ensure that the decimal point is shown. This would be useful if you're formatting a table of monetary values.

setprecision(4)

The expression **setprecision(4)** is used to set the number of digits to right of the decimal point. You use the manipulator **setprecision** with the number of digits as an argument. Again, this feature would be useful if you're formatting a table of monetary values, when you'd use 2 as the argument.

setw(10)

The expression **setw(10)** is used to set the field width. Think of each value displayed by **cout** as occupying an invisible box which has a certain width.

The default width is just big enough to hold the value. For example, 345.67 will occupy a width of six characters. You can alter the width of the box using the **setw** manipulator. The width is specified as the argument.

number[i][j];

The expression **number[i][j]** then causes the number from the array to be displayed.

Experiment with this program - change the field width and the number of digits on the right of the decimal point that should be displayed.

Strings

Strings are one-dimensional character arrays.

In Chapter 2 you discovered that a string is a sequence of characters surrounded by double quotes. A string is also known as a **string constant** or a **string literal**.

For example:

```
"Please  enter  the  data:"
"a"
```

Do not confuse `"a"` with the character constant `'a'`. The value of a character constant is the integer numeric value of the character, that is the character's ASCII code.

A string, on the other hand, is an array of characters. Internally, the null constant `'\0'` (equivalent to zero) is always stored after the final character written in a string. It is needed to detect the end of the string.

Strings can vary in length, but the maximum length of any string you use will be determined by the size of the character array holding the string. As a string is terminated by the null character, `'\0'`, the size of the string must be sufficient to include this. Remember, it's your responsibility to see that the bounds of the array are not exceeded.

The following figure shows the representation of a character array in memory. The string "abc" is implemented as a character array of size 4. The final character of the array is the null character.

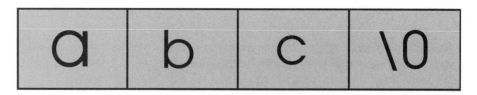

To avoid devastating results, don't forget to leave space for the null character in your strings.

Initializing Strings

A string or character array may be initialized with these same values using the construct:

```
char word[ ] = {'a', 'b', 'c', '\0'};
```

Or more easily with the more readable statement:

```
char word[ ] = "abc";
```

Your compiler will treat these two statements as identical. When you initialize the complete string as in the second example you don't need to add the null character as the compiler will do it for you automatically.

Initializing Strings - An Example

The following program demonstrates the different methods of initializing strings. Which one do you think is the easier?

```
/*  **********************************************************
 *      string.cpp                                  *
 *    Ian  M  Wilks                                     *
 *************************************************************** */
#include  <iostream.h>
#include<conio.h>
void  main()
{
    char  word1[5],  word2[8];

    char  word3[]  =  "Telephone";
    char  word4[]  =  {'N',  'u',  'm',  'b',  'e',  'r','\0'};

    clrscr();

    word1[0]  =  'N';
    word1[1]  =  'a';
    word1[2]  =  'm';
    word1[3]  =  'e';
    word1[4]  =  '\0';

    cout  <<  "\n\nEnter  the  word  ->  Address  ";
    cin  >>  word2;

    cout  <<  endl  <<  word1  <<  endl  <<  word2  <<  endl  <<  word3
          <<  "  "  <<  word4;
}
```

Program Analysis

```
char word1[5], word2[8];
```

This program initially declares two character arrays (strings) one being of length 5 and the other being of length 8.

This means that the first string can hold a word having up to 4 characters and the second string can hold a word having up to 7 characters.

Two more character arrays are then declared. They are also initialized.

```
char word3[] = "Telephone";
char word4[] = {'N', 'u', 'm', 'b', 'e', 'r','\0'};
```

The first one is initialized using the method which is easier to type and read, the final string is initialized using the other method.

```
word1[0] = 'N';
word1[1] = 'a';
word1[2] = 'm';
word1[3] = 'e';
word1[4] = '\0';
```

The program then assigns values to the first character array.

```
cout << "\n\nEnter the word -> Address ";
cin >> word2;
```

The program then asks the user to type a word at the keyboard which is stored in the remaining character array.

```
cout << endl << word1 << endl << word2 << endl << word3
     << " " << word4;
```

The program then outputs the character arrays to the string. The output is:

```
Name
Address
Telephone Number
```

Controlling Text - A Typical Problem

Now consider the following example. This program illustrates what happens when you want to enter more than one word via the keyboard using **cin**.

```
//inp_str.cpp

#include <iostream.h>

void main()
{
    const int MAX = 80;              //max characters in string
    char str[MAX];                   //string variable

    cout << "\nEnter a string: ";
    cin >> str;                      //put string in str
    cout << "You entered " << str;
}
```

Run the program and type the following string at the keyboard:

```
This is a test program
```

The final output from the program will be:

```
You entered This
```

What has happened to the rest of the string?

Solution

The problem here is that the insertion operator **>>** considers a blank space to be a terminating character. It reads a single word and discards the rest of the string.

How do we get round this? We can use the **cin.get** function to solve this problem. Alter the program so that it reads as below and then we'll discuss this new function.

```
//blankinp.cpp
#include <iostream.h>
void main()
{
    const int MAX = 80;              //max characters in string
    char str[MAX];                   //string variable

    cout << "\nEnter a string: ";
    cin.get(str, MAX);               //put string in str
    cout << "You entered " << str;
}
```

107

Run the program and type the following string at the keyboard:

```
This is a test program
```

You should now find that the full string is stored in the array.

Program Analysis

As we've just seen **cin** or **cin.get()** are used to input strings. The program above illustrates the use of **cin.get()**. The first argument to **cin.get()** is the destination of the string that is being input, and the second argument specifies the maximum size of the string. Another argument can be given to **cin.get()**.

Look at question 4 in the programming exercises to discover more about this.

String Handling

Now we've discovered that strings are nothing more than an array of characters, how do we deal with them?

Fortunately, there are a number of string handling routines available.

The basic way of printing a string is to use **cout**, as the following examples will demonstrate.

There are several powerful string handling routines to use within your C++ compiler, they are addressed in similar ways. Here we're going to explain some of the more popular and useful ones. A full listing is available in Appendix A.

Copying Strings

This is one operation you'll almost certainly want to do. In C++ you can't simply assign the value of one string to another string.

However the following program shows two ways of accomplishing the copy.

- The first method involves using a **for** loop.
- The second method involves using the string function **strcpy()**.

The function **strcpy()** needs to be passed two arguments, the first is the name of the array into which the string is to be copied and the second is the name of the array containing the string.

For example,

```
strcpy(destination, source);
```

Copying Strings - An Example

Now look at the example:

```
/* **********************************************************
 *    strcopy.cpp                                           *
 *    Ian M Wilks                                           *
 ********************************************************** */
#include <iostream.h>          //header file for input/output
#include <string.h>            //header file for string handling functions

void main()
{
    const int MAX = 80;

    char string1[] = "\t\tInstant C++ Programming; Scrape by in C++";
    char string2[MAX];
    char string3[MAX];

    cout << "\n\tstring1 contains the following text - \n\n"
        << string1 << endl;

//copy string using for-loop. Note: strlen() returns the number of characters
//in the string but does not count the terminating null character. Therefore,
//we must copy one additional character as shown below
    for(int i = 0; i <= strlen(string1); i++)
        string2[i] = string1[i];

    //Alternatively we could put the character in as follows:
    /*    for(int i = 0; i < strlen(string1); i++)
            string2[i] = string1[i];
        string2[i] = '\0';                              */

    cout << "\n\tstring2 contains the following text - \n\n"
        << string2 << endl;

    //copy string using strcpy()
    strcpy(string3, string1);

    cout << "\n\tstring3 contains the following text - \n\n"
        << string3 << endl;
}
```

Program Analysis

```
#include <iostream.h>
#include <string.h>
```

After the comment block the **#include** directive is used to include the header files **iostream.h**, which is needed for the input and output routines, and **string.h**, which is needed for the string handling functions.

```
void main()
```

The program then enters **main()**:

```
const int MAX = 80;

char string1[] = "\t\tInstant C++ Programming; Scrape by in C++";
char string2[MAX];
char string3[MAX];
```

A constant is declared and initialized. Three character arrays are declared. The first array is initialized to hold a string.

```
cout << "\n\tstring1 contains the following text - \n\n"
     << string1 << endl;
```

cout is used to display the contents of **string1** on the screen.

```
for(int i = 0; i <= strlen(string1); i++)
    string2[i] = string1[i];
```

A **for** loop is then used to copy the contents of **string1** into **string2**. To use the **for** loop we need to know how many characters to copy (that is, when is the loop to terminate?) If we don't know the size of the string we can use the function **strlen()** to determine the length of the string.

Unfortunately, the function returns the number of characters in the string *but* doesn't count the terminating null character. Therefore, we must copy one additional character, the null character, into **string2**.

```
for(int i = 0; i <= strlen(string1); i++)
     string2[i] = string1[i];
```

The null character can be copied using the **for** loop as shown.

```
for(int i = 0; i < strlen(string1); i++)
     string2[i] = string1[i];
string2[i] = '\0';
```

Alternatively, we could put the character in as above.

If you comment out the first method in the program and delete the comment operators around the second method so that the second method is used, you'll find the results are the same.

```
cout << "\n\tstring2 contains the following text - \n\n"
     << string2 << endl;
```

cout is then used to display **string2** on the screen.

```
strcpy(string3, string1);
```

string1 is again copied. This time the function **strcpy()** is used.

```
cout << "\n\tstring3 contains the following text - \n\n"
     << string3 << endl;
```

cout is then used to display **string3** on the screen.

Joining Strings

Another useful operation is joining strings. This is technically known as concatenating them.

The function that does this is called **strcat().**

Look at the following program:

```
/* ********************************************************
 *    strcat.cpp                                          *
 *    Ian M Wilks                                         *
 ******************************************************** */
#include <iostream.h>        //header file for input/output
#include <string.h>          //header file for string handling functions

void main()
{
    const int MAX = 80;

    char string1[] = "Instant C++ Programming; Scrape by in C++";
    char string2[MAX] = "Ian M Wilks";
    char string3[MAX];

    cout << "\n\tstring1 contains the following text - \n\n"
        << string1 << endl;


    cout << "\n\tstring2 contains the following text - \n\n"
        << string2 << endl;

    //copy string1 to string3 using strcpy()
    strcpy(string3, string1);

    //add text to the new string using strcat()
    strcat(string3, " written by ");

    //add string2 to string3 using strcat
    strcat(string3, string2);

    cout << "\n\tstring3 contains the following text - \n\n"
        << string3 << endl;
}
```

Program Analysis

```
#include <iostream.h>
#include <string.h>
```

After the comment block the **#include** directive is used to include the header files **iostream.h**, which is needed for the input and output routines, and **string.h**, which is needed for the string handling functions.

```
void main()
```

The program then enters **main()**.

```
const int MAX = 80;

char string1[] = "Instant C++ Programming; Scrape by in C++";
char string2[MAX] = "Ian M Wilks";
char string3[MAX];
```

A constant is declared and initialized. Three character arrays are declared. The first two arrays are initialized to hold strings.

```
cout << "\n\tstring1 contains the following text - \n\n"
     << string1 << endl;
```

cout is used to display the contents of **string1** on the screen.

```
strcpy(string3, string1);
```

string1 is then copied to **string3** using the **strcpy()** function.

```
strcat(string3, " written by ");
```

The string " **written by** " is then added to **string3** using the **strcat()** function.

```
strcat(string3, string2);
```

string2 is then added to **string3** using the **strcat()** function.

```
cout << "\n\tstring3 contains the following text - \n\n"
     << string3 << endl;
```

cout is then used to display **string3** on the screen.

Comparing Strings

The final string function we'll look at is **strcmp()**.

This function compares two strings and is the equivalent of the equality operator, **==**.

This function compares two strings character by character.

If the strings are the same it returns 0. If the strings are not the same it returns another value.

Consider the program:

```
/* ************************************************************
 *    strcmp.cpp                                             *
 *    Ian M Wilks                                            *
 ************************************************************ */
#include <iostream.h>
#include <string.h>

void main()
{
    char yes1[] = "yes";
    char yes2[] = "Yes";
    char yes3[] = "YES";

    char no1[] = "no";
    char no2[] = "No";
    char no3[] = "NO";

    char input[4];

    char question[] = "\t\tAnyone can fall in love.\n\n";

    char response1[] = "\t\tYou are an incurable romantic.\n\n";
    char response2[] = "\t\tHow sad!\n\n";

    cout << "\n\t\tDo you agree with the following statement - \n"
         << question << "\t\t\t";

    cin >> input;

    if ( (strcmp(input, yes1) == 0) || (strcmp(input, yes2) == 0)
                          || (strcmp(input, yes3) == 0) )
        cout << response1;
    else
    if ( (strcmp(input, no1) == 0) || (strcmp(input, no2) == 0)
                          || (strcmp(input, no3) == 0) )
        cout << response2;
    else
        cout << "\n\t\tIncorrect Response";
}
```

Program Analysis

```
char yes1[] = "yes";
char yes2[] = "Yes";
char yes3[] = "YES";

char no1[] = "no";
char no2[] = "No";
char no3[] = "NO";

char input[4];

char question[] = "\t\tAnyone can fall in love.\n\n";

char response1[] = "\t\tYou are an incurable romantic.\n\n";
char response2[] = "\t\tHow sad!\n\n";
```

A number of character arrays are declared.

- There are three arrays holding different versions of the word **YES**.
- Three arrays holding different versions of the word **NO**.
- A string to accept the string input by the user.
- An array that holds a string that users are asked if they agree with.
- Two arrays that the program displays on the screen depending on the answer given by the user.

```
cout << "\n\t\tDo you agree with the following statement - \n"
     << question << "\t\t\t";
```

cout is used to ask users if they agree with the statement.

```
cin >> input;
```

The program then waits for the user to enter a response.

```
        if ( (strcmp(input, yes1) == 0) || (strcmp(input, yes2) == 0)
                            || (strcmp(input, yes3) == 0) )
            cout << response1;
        else
        if ( (strcmp(input, no1) == 0) || (strcmp(input, no2) == 0)
                            || (strcmp(input, no3) == 0) )
            cout << response2;
        else
            cout << "\n\t\tIncorrect Response";
```

If the input string is the same as one of the three versions of **YES** an appropriate message is displayed on the screen. Similarly, if the input string is the same as one of the three versions of **NO** another appropriate message is display. If the input string is not the same as a **YES** or a **NO** then the following message is displayed:

```
        Incorrect Response
```

Compare the Different Compares

There is another function **strcmpi()** which compares two strings without taking the case of the letter into account. Alter the above program so that the strings **yes2**, **yes3**, **no2**, and **no3** are not needed. You'll need to use the function **strcmpi()** for the comparison.

Summary

In this chapter we've explored the world of arrays. We've looked at the different sorts of arrays and examined how they're used practically. You've learnt about bounds checking and you've worked with strings including handling, copying, joining and comparing them. Now have a go at the following programming exercises before moving on to the next chapter and the exciting world of functions.

Programming Exercises

1   Write a program to output the five times table.

2   Write a program to write out the multiplication tables from 1 to 12 using a **for** loop within a loop (nested **for** loop).

3   Write a program that uses an array to store the names of the months of the year. The user should be able to input the months via the keyboard. The program should then display the months on the screen in the order they were entered and should then re-display the months in the reverse order that they were entered.

4   Run the program **BLANKINP.CPP** from the section on controlling text and attempt to enter the following via the keyboard:

```
C++ is a very interesting
programming language that
I am going to master
```

Make sure you put newlines after interesting, that and master.

What happened?

Now change the line:

```
cin.get(str, MAX);
```

so that it reads:

```
cin.get(str, MAX, '$');
```

Now compile the program and run it. Enter the following via the keyboard:

```
C++ is a very interesting
programming language that
I am going to master
$
```

Again put the newline characters in and finish the string with the dollar sign, **$**

Now what happens?

5   Several of the example programs in this chapter use a **for** loop to access the array elements. Re-write these programs using

🔵   a **while** loop, and

🔵   a **do-while** loop

to access the array elements without using a **for** loop.

6   The following program sorts the elements of an array of integers into descending order.

```
/* *********************************************************
 *    sort.cpp                                             *
 *                                                         *
 ********************************************************* */
#include <iostream.h>
void main()
{
    const int MAX = 10;
    int table[MAX];

    cout << "\n\n\tThis program demonstrates sorting array "
         << "elements into\n\tdescending order\n\n"
         << "\tEnter ten integers: ";

    for(int i = 0; i < MAX; i++)
        cin >> table[i];

    cout << "\n\n\tThe unsorted array is: ";
    for(i = 0; i < MAX; i++)
        cout << table[i] << "  ";

    //sort
    int temp, test = 0;

    while(test == 0)
    {
        test = 1;
        for (i = 0; i < (MAX - 1); i++)
        {
            if (table[i] < table[i + 1])
            {
                temp = table[i];
                table[i] = table[ i + 1];
                table[i + 1] = temp;
                test = 0;
            }
        }
    }
    cout << "\n\n\tThe sorted array is: ";
```

```
        for(i = 0; i < MAX; i++)
            cout << table[i] << "  ";
    }
```

You should have no problems in following the sort algorithm.

Alter this program so that the elements in the array are in ascending order.

Chapter

Functions

In Chapter 1 you learnt that a procedural program is a list of instructions. Each statement tells the computer to do something. In a very small program no other model, is required. However, when programs become larger, a single list of instructions becomes difficult to manage. Functions are used to make the program modular and flexible. A function groups a number of statements into a unit which is given a function name, and callable (executed) from another part of the program.

You can give these functions values to process and you can also receive values from them to use in your program. Your compiler already comes with a host of pre-written functions.The most important reason for using functions is to assist in the organization of a program; dividing it into functions is one of the most important parts of structured programming. Use functions to reduce the size of your program. If you have to repeat a series of instructions in a program then you should consider writing a function.

In this chapter we cover:

- What a function is
- General syntax
- Local/global variables
- Prototypes
- Return values and argument types
- Recursion
- Arrays with functions
- Default arguments

Function Basics

As you've seen, each C++ program must have a function called **main()**. This is the point from which the program starts to execute. It is the function where you normally set up the top level of program flow control. Your first experience of a function was using **main()** and in large, mature programs **main()** is often used purely to call all the other functions you may have written or utilized from a library. When your function is called, the instructions in it are executed and on completion, control returns to the command that comes immediately after the original function call.

How Functions Work

The basic form of a function is:

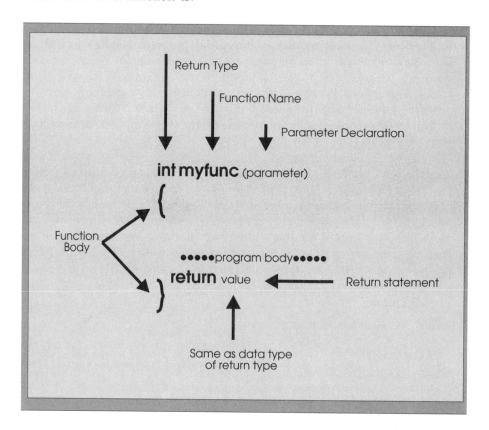

You can see that this structure is the same as the structure of the **main()** function that you are already familiar with. Let's look at each section in turn.

Function Return Type

The first part, return type, specifies the type of value that will be returned for use in the rest of the program. In this case, it is specified as an integer type. If your function will return a value on completion of the function's task, you should include the statement: `return value;`

If there's to be no resultant from your function (indicated by declaring a void type), then you can either include:

```
return;
```

as your return statement or you can omit the line altogether.

Naming Your Functions

The function name you use must be unique. It can include up to 32 letters or numbers and must begin with a letter. Try to use meaningful names that indicate what the function does.

> Don't use function names that begin with an underscore - this will create a conflict with Borland identifiers.

The Parameter Declaration

The final part of the function, enclosed in the brackets (), is the parameter or argument declaration. When your function is called, any values that need to be passed to it will be received by the variables set up here.

Function Prototypes

Before you can utilize the marvelous function you have designed you will have to inform the compiler of the framework of that function. You do this by simply declaring a function prototype. For example:

```
float   my_total (int  a,  int  b,  int  c )
```

will tell the compiler that it will require 3 integer arguments when it's called, and will produce a float resultant. We declare the prototype so that the compiler can verify that the function is used correctly.

Variables

With the use of functions, you'll soon realize the importance of variable **scope**.

Variables declared outside of any particular function (not included in that function's braces) will be available to all parts of the program that follow their declaration in the program list. They are **global** variables.

You can declare variables outside functions anywhere in the code but it is better practice to put such declarations at the start of the source code.

Variables declared in a function are known only to that function and are called **local variables**. An important point to remember is that if you have two variables of the same name declared in two different functions, they are different variables. An assignment made to one of these variables in one of the functions has no effect on the other. When you're referring to a local variable within a function, and another variable has the same name but is outside the body of the function (i.e not in scope), the local variable will *mask* the presence of the global (see scope resolution operator to overcome this).

Using Functions - An Example

Let's go straight into an example function structure. This program illustrates how functions are used, and you should concentrate on understanding how program control is passed from one function to the next.

```
/* ************************************************************
 *   sumOfSqr.cpp                                            *
 *   Ian M Wilks                                             *
 ************************************************************ */
#include <iostream.h>  //header file for input/output

int sum;              //a global variable which can be
                      //used in any function

void main()
{
    int counter;              //variable only available in main()

//function prototypes
    void begin(void);
    void sumAndSquare(int dummy);
    void end();

    begin();          //this calls the function begin() control passes
                      //to the begin() function and the statements in
                      //that function are executed sequentially.  When
                      //begin() is completed, control returns to the
```

```
                        //statement following this call

        for(counter = 1; counter <= 7; counter++)
            sumAndSquare(counter);   //this call the function
                                     //sumAndSquare() which is passed an
                                     //argument - counter.  The value of
                                     //counter is used in the function.
                                     //As before control passes to this
                                     //function and on completion control
                                     //returns to the next statement -
                                     //which will either be the loop
                                     //or end()

                                        //this calls the function end()
        end();          //control passes to the end() function and the
                        //statements in that function are executed
                        //sequentially.  When end() is completed control
                        //returns to the statement following this call

        cout << "\n\nThe program is now finished.";
    }

void begin()
{
    sum = 0;            //Initialize the variable sum
    cout << "\nThis is the begin() function.\n\n";
}

void sumAndSquare(int dummy)
{
    int number_squared;

    number_squared = dummy * dummy;    //this produces the square
    sum += number_squared;             //this sums the squares
    cout << "The square of " << dummy << " is " << number_squared << endl;
}

void end()
{
    cout << "\nThis is the end() function.\n\n";
    cout << "The sum of the squares is " << sum << endl;
}
```

Read through the source code and try to ascertain what is happening. Run the program and see if that helps. The flow of control of this program is shown in the diagram on the next page.

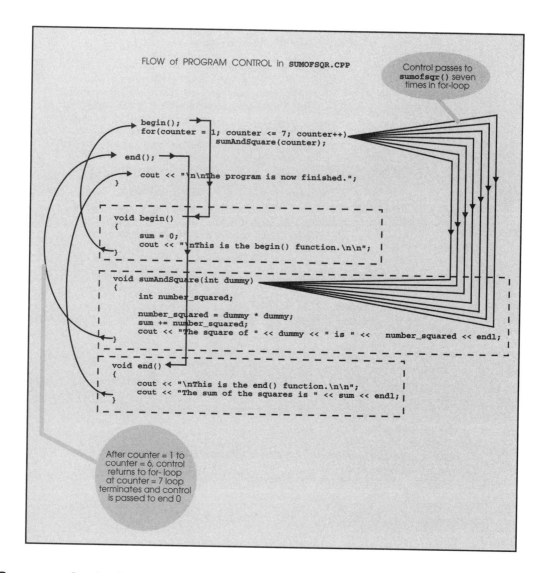

FLOW of PROGRAM CONTROL in **SUMOFSQR.CPP**

Control passes to **sumofsqr()** seven times in for-loop

```
begin();
for(counter = 1; counter <= 7; counter++)
                sumAndSquare(counter);
end();

cout << "\n\nThe program is now finished.";
}

void begin()
{
    sum = 0;
    cout << "\nThis is the begin() function.\n\n";
}

void sumAndSquare(int dummy)
{
    int number_squared;

    number_squared = dummy * dummy;
    sum += number_squared;
    cout << "The square of " << dummy << " is " <<    number_squared << endl;
}

void end()
{
    cout << "\nThis is the end() function.\n\n";
    cout << "The sum of the squares is " << sum << endl;
}
```

After counter = 1 to counter = 6, control returns to for- loop at counter = 7 loop terminates and control is passed to end 0

Program Analysis

```
#include <iostream.h>
```

As you would expect, after the comment block the **#include** directive is used to include **iostream.h**, the header file needed for the input and output routines.

```
int sum;
```

A global integer variable, **sum**, is declared. This variable can be used in any function.

```
void main()
{
    int counter;
```

An integer variable, **counter**, is declared. This is a local variable which is only available in **main()**.

The next part of the program consists of the function prototypes also known as a function declaration. These specify the names of functions, their argument types, and return values. It tells the compiler that these functions will occur, and allows the compiler to check that the data passed to the function is of the correct type.

In this case there are three prototypes:

```
void begin(void);
void sumAndSquare(int dummy);
void end();
```

The keyword **void** specifies that the function has no return value. If no type is given for the return value, compiler will assume a **type int**.

The keyword **void** in the *brackets* specifies that the function takes no arguments. This is the same as the last prototype, **void end();**, the only difference being, that the brackets were left empty rather than using the keyword void.

```
void sumAndSquare(int dummy);
```

Is different in that the function takes an integer value as an argument.

```
begin();
```

The program then calls the function **begin()**. The only thing needed to call the function is its name followed by brackets and the statement is terminated with a semi-colon.

Control passes to the function and the statements in the function definition (we will discuss this shortly) are executed sequentially. When the function has finished, control returns to the statement following the function call.

```
sum = 0;          //Initialize the variable sum
cout << "\nThis is the begin() function.\n\n";
```

In this case the function definition contains only two statements, and these are both self explanatory.

```
for(counter = 1; counter <= 7; counter++)
     sumAndSquare(counter);
```

A **for** loop is then used. The loop operates 7 times - when counter is equal to 1, 2, ... , 7. On each pass the function **sumAndSquare()** is called.

As you can see from the source code the function is called with an argument, **counter**. The function is called seven times and each time its argument has a different value.

As with the previous function call, control passes to this function and the statements in its definition are executed sequentially. When the function has finished, control returns to the statement following the function call.

This function only has four statements in its definition. The first of which is a local integer declaration:

```
int number_squared;
number_squared = dummy * dummy;
```

This is used to store the answer generated when the function argument is squared.

```
sum += number_squared;
cout << "The square of " << dummy << " is " << number_squared << endl;
```

The global variable, **sum** has the generated answer added to its existing value using one of the mathematical assignment operators - **assign sum**. The square is then output to the screen.

```
end();
```

The program then calls the function, **end()**. Control passes to the function and the statements in that function are executed sequentially. When the function has finished, control returns to the statement following this call.

```
    cout << "\nThis is the end() function.\n\n";
    cout << "The sum of the squares is " << sum << endl;
```

The function only contains two statements and you should have no trouble understanding what this function does.

```
cout << "\n\nThe program is now finished.";
```

The last statement is self-explanatory.

Following the terminating brace of **main()** you'll see the three function definitions. The function definition is the actual function which contains the source code for the function.

As you can see, the definitions start off with a line similar to the prototype but without the semi-colon.

The function body is composed of statements making up the function and is contained in a pair of braces.

When a function is called, control passes to the first statement in the function body. The other statements are executed sequentially, and when the closing brace is encountered control returns to the calling program.

Creating Functions

We'll write some programs that use functions. You will see how important it is to think about the steps you want your program to carry out before you actually sit down and start typing in the code.

Creating Functions - A Solid Rectangle

Let's consider some text-screen based graphics which produce the following types of output:

```
++++++++++++++++++++        *******************
++++++++++++++++++++        *                 *
++++++++++++++++++++        *                 *
++++++++++++++++++++        *                 *
++++++++++++++++++++        *                 *
++++++++++++++++++++        *                 *
++++++++++++++++++++        *******************
++++++++++++++++++++
```

```
*                =====                =
**               ====                ===
***              ===                =====
****             ==                ======
*****            =                ========
******
```

Let's write a function to draw a solid rectangle letting the user specify the size.

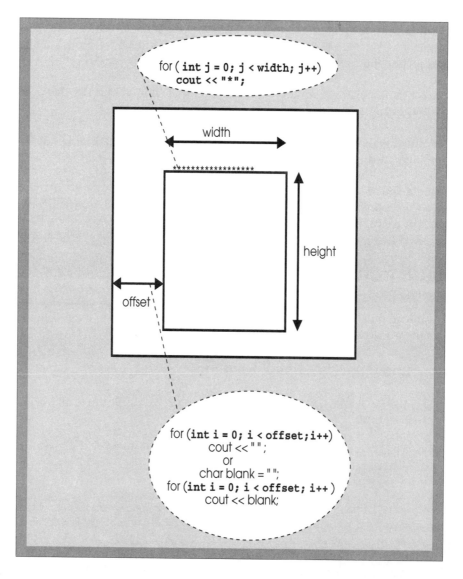

Setting the Basics

As you can see there are three distances that interest us. The offset from the left-hand side of the screen, the width of the rectangle, and the height.

How can we use the distances to put blank spaces for the offset and characters for the lines.

To write a space to the screen we would simply use the statement:

```
cout << " ";
```

So how can we write a number of spaces? Think back to the chapter on loops. Which loop would we use if we know how many times we wanted to do something?

So, use a **for** loop to write the blank spaces to the screen.

```
for(i = 0; i < offset; i++)
    cout << " ";
```

What about the characters? The same construct should work:

```
for(i = 0; i < width; i++)
    cout << character;
```

Now we have a line. How do we make that into a rectangle? Well, a number of lines will be our rectangle and we should be able to make use of the **for** loop again.

Consider:

```
for(count = 0; count < height; count++)
{
    for(i = 0; i < offset; i++)
        cout << " ";
    for(i = 0; i < width; i++)
        cout << character;
    cout << endl;
}
```

Setting Arguments

Now that we have the basis of our function we can finish it off. The function won't need to return a value to the calling program but it will have to be passed some arguments.

The arguments it will need are **offset, width, height**, which are all integers, and **character**, which is a character variable.

The prototype will look like this:

```
void solid_box(int offset, int width, int height, char character);
```

Can you put it all together now? We've done this one for you and it's shown below:

```
void solid_box(int offset, int width, int height, char character)
{
    int count, i;              //loop control variables

    for(count = 0; count < height; count++)
    {
        for(i = 0; i < offset; i++)
            cout << " ";
        for(i = 0; i < width; i++)
            cout << character;
        cout << endl;
    }
}
```

To call the function from your program you simply put the following into your program:

```
solid_box(10, 25, 10, '*');
```

Alternatively, you could pass variables to the function and call it in the following manner:

```
solid_box(offset,  width,  height,  character);
```

Write a program to test this function. Ask the user to enter the values via the keyboard and store the values in appropriate variables.

Creating Functions - A Hollow Box

Let's now write a function that will produce a hollow box.

When we visualize a hollow box we see that there are three parts to the problem:

- The top line
- The vertical sides
- The bottom line

As the first and third points are the same we can write a function to do this. Try it - write a function called:

```
line_of_char()
```

that will write a line of characters. Remember to take account of the offset. If you're having problems the solution will be shown after the programming exercises at the end of the chapter.

Now you've written that function we can continue with the function to draw a hollow box. To draw the top line and the bottom line will simply entail a call to the procedure you've written:

```
line_of_char(offset, width, character);
```

The middle part of this function requires us to:

- Write spaces to the screen in respect of the offset
- Write a character
- Write spaces to the screen in respect of the hollow
- Write a character

A single line can be written as follows:

```
for(i = 0; i < offset; i++)          //offset
    cout << blank;
cout << character;                    //write first character
for(i= 0; i < width - 2; i++)        //hollow - there is a char on each
    cout << blank;                    //side the distance is width - 2
cout << character;                    //write second character
```

Can you finish this part of the function? It is now similar to the first function we wrote. You need to enclose the above code in another **for** loop and insert a newline in the appropriate place.

Now you've done that put it all together into a function. If you're having difficulty there is a copy after the programming exercises at the end of the chapter.

You should now incorporate these functions:

```
line_of_char() and hollow_box()
```

into your test program.

To increase your confidence try writing functions to generate a solid right-angled triangle with the point uppermost. Now write a function to generate a solid right-angled triangle with the point at the bottom. When you've done these consider writing functions to generate hollow versions of the two triangles.

Creating Functions - Squaring a Number

Now look at another example program that uses a function. This function squares a value that is passed to it as an argument and then returns an answer, the computed value, to the calling program.

```
/* ***********************************************************
 *     square.cpp                                            *
 *     Ian M Wilks                                           *
 *********************************************************** */
#include <iostream.h>              //header file for input/output

void main()
{
    int counter, answer;          //variables only available in main()
//function prototype
    int square(int dummy);

    for(counter = 1; counter <= 7; counter++)
    {
        answer = square(counter);     //this calls square() which
                                      //is passed an argument - counter.  The
                                      //value is used in the function.
                                      //Control passes to square() and the
                                      //statements in this function are
                                      //executed sequentially.  On
                                      //completion control returns to the
                                      //next statement

        cout << "The square of " << counter << " is " << answer << endl;
    }

    for(counter = 1; counter <= 7; counter++)
        cout << "The square of " << counter << " is " << square(counter)
            << endl;
}

int square(int number)
{
    int square;

    square = number * number;     //this produces the square
    return(square);               //this returns square to main() so
                                  //the value can be stored in answer
}
```

Program Analysis

This program only demonstrates one new point and you should understand what it's doing.

```
void main()
```

The program enters the **main()** function:

```
int counter, answer;
```

Two local variables are defined - **counter** and **answer**.

```
    int square(int dummy);
```

A function prototype is defined - **int square(int dummy)**.

Remember that the values used in your prototypes can be local or global.

This function will return an integer value to the calling program.

The function takes one argument, an integer variable. It should be noted that the variable name given as the argument in the prototype is simply a dummy. Any name could be used. All it's doing is telling the compiler that an integer value will be passed to it.

If you look forward to the function definition you'll see that the argument is called **number**. Again it doesn't matter what the name is, except that the same name is used in the function definition when the argument is being manipulated.

```
For (counter = 1; counter<=7; counter++)
    {
```

As we've seen before, a **for** loop is used to put values into the function. However, the statement:

```
answer = square(counter);
```

is new to us.

From what you already know, you'll have no trouble in understanding that the `square(counter)` portion of the statement is a call to the function `square()` taking `counter` as an argument.

Looking ahead to the function definition you see that the argument is called into the function, squares it and stores the answer in the variable `square`.

```
    return(square);
```

The final statement in the function definition is `return(square);` The value within the brackets is assigned to the function itself and is returned as a useable value in `main()`.

Therefore, the function call `square(counter)` is assigned the value of the `square` of `counter` and this value is returned to `main()` so that the variable `answer` is then set equal to that value. If `counter` had the value of 4 prior to the function call, `answer` would be assigned the value 16 as a result of this line of code.

```
        cout << "The square of " << counter << " is " << answer << endl;
```

Within the loop `cout` is used to display the answers on the screen.

```
    for(counter = 1; counter <= 7; counter++)
        cout << "The square of " << counter << " is " << square(counter)
            << endl;
```

Another `for` loop is then used with a `cout` statement.

It's possible to *think* of `square(counter)` as another variable with a value that is the square of the variable `counter`, and that this can be used in any place that it's legal to use a variable of this type.

To illustrate this point, the function call `square(counter)` is placed in the `cout` statement rather than assigning the generated value to another variable.

After then closing brace of `main()`, the `square()` function definition appears. We've already discussed this.

Floating Point Functions - An Example

For completeness the next example program looks at a function with a floating point return.

```
/* ************************************************************
 *     fltsqu.cpp                                            *
 *     Ian M Wilks                                           *
 ************************************************************ */
#include <iostream.h>          //header file for input/output
void main()
{
     float argument = 2.5;
//function prototype
     float square(float input);
     cout << "The square of " << argument << " is " << square(argument) <<
endl;
}

float square(float input)
{
     return(input * input);  //return calculated value to main()
}
```

Program Analysis

```
void main()
```

The program enters the **main()** function:

```
float argument = 2.5;
```

A local variable is declared and initialized.

```
float square(float input);
```

A function prototype is declared. As you can see, the function returns a float value to the calling program and take a float as an argument.

```
        cout << "The square of " << argument << " is " << square(argument)
           << endl;
```

A **cout** statement is the last statement in **main()**. This statement outputs the message

```
   'The square of 2.5 is 6.25'.
```

As you can see the number 2.5 is output as the value of the variable argument and the value 6.25 is the value generated by the function call, **square(argument)**.

```
float square(float input)
{
    return(input * input);  //return calculated value to main()
}
```

After the closing brace of **main()** the function definition is found. You'll see that this is different from the other versions of function **square()** in the other examples.

The only calculation needed to generate a square is to multiply the number to be squared by itself. Remember that you can use an expression which evaluates to a simple variable anywhere that you can use a variable. So, there's no reason that the calculation cannot be done in the actual return statement. This saves the compiler from having to allocate memory space for a variable to hold the answer in. You should also note that the value to be returned can be put in brackets to make it clearer.

Scope of Variables

As we've already said, variables that are declared outside of functions are known to all functions following their declaration. It's good practice to put these declarations at the start of the source code. As these variables are known to all functions they are said to be global variables. You should remember that until a variable is initialized it may contain garbage values left over from a previous use of that memory location. No variable should be used until it has been initialized to hold a value.

Variables declared in a function are known only to that function and are called local variables. In general, local variables are allocated storage in the computer's memory at the time the function is called. They are said to come into scope. The memory storage is allocated from the program's stack which is a reserved sequence of memory locations used for the temporary storage of

138

data, functions and interrupt instructions. As with global variables, until a local variable is initialized it may contain garbage values left over from a previous use of that memory location. This is more likely if the function has been called previously in the program. No variable should be used until it has been initialized to hold a value.

When the function is completed the memory locations allocated for the local variables are de-allocated. The variables are said to go out of scope upon the termination of the function. Any values they contained will be lost.

As variables declared in a function are local to that function there's no reason why you can't declare and use another variable of the same name in a different function.

Recursion

A recursive function is nothing more than a function that calls itself. The following example program is probably one of the simplest recursive programs that it's possible to write.

```
/* *************************************************************
 *      count.cpp                                             *
 *      Ian M Wilks                                           *
 ************************************************************* */
#include <iostream.h>

void main()
{
    int argument = 10;

//function prototype
    void count_down(int value);

    count_down(argument);
}

void count_down(int value)
{
    value--;
    cout << "value is now: " << value << endl;
    if (value > 0)
        count_down(value);
    cout << "Now value is: " << value << endl;
}
```

Program Analysis

```
void main()
```

The program enters the **main()** function:

```
int argument = 10;
```

A local variable is declared and initialized.

```
void count_down(int value);
```

A function prototype is declared.

As you can see the function returns no value to the calling program and has an integer argument.

The only other statement in **main()** is a call to the function.

After **main()** you'll see the function definition.

Recursion - How Does it Work?

As we said earlier, recursion occurs when a function calls itself. It is, therefore, a loop which must have a way of terminating. In the program the variable argument is set to 10, and is used as the argument to the function. The function simply decrements the variable, prints the value to the screen, and if the variable is not 0, it calls itself using the reduced value as the argument where it starts the process again. Finally the variable will reach 0, and the function will not call itself again. Instead it returns to the prior time it called itself and outputs another message to the screen, then it returns again, until it returns to **main()**.

To assist you in understanding what's happening, you can think of it as having 10 copies of the function available and it simply calls them one at a time, keeping track of which copy it was in, at a given time.

What actually happens is that when the function calls itself it stores all of the variables and the internal flags that it needs to complete the function on the stack. The next time it calls itself it does the same thing, creating and storing another block of the things needed to complete that function call. It continues making the blocks and storing them until it reaches the last function when it starts to retrieve the blocks and use them to complete each function call.

Recursion - An Example Using an Array

Consider the following program which is another example of recursion:

```
/* ***********************************************************
 *     RECUR.CPP                                            *
 *     Ian M Wilks                                          *
 *     This program prints the elements of an array in      *
 *     reverse order recursively.                           *
 *********************************************************** */
#include <iostream.h>
//function prototype
void reverseIt ( int arr[], int number );
//constants
const int MAXIMUM = 10;
void main()
{
    int count;
    int array[MAXIMUM];
    cout << "This prints the elements of an array in reverse order.\n";
//give values to the array elements using a for-loop
    for ( count = 0; count < MAXIMUM; count++ )
    {
        //assign values to the array
        array[count] = count;
    }
//write the array values to the screen in reverse order
    reverseIt (array, MAXIMUM - 1);
}

void reverseIt ( int arr[], int number)
{ // Prints the elements of arr in reverse order
    if ( number == 0 )                 //terminating condition
    {                                  // the stopping case
        cout << arr[number] << "\n";
    }
    else
    {                                  // recursion
        cout << arr[number] << "\n";
        reverseIt ( arr, number - 1);
    }
} // end of Reverse
```

```
void reverseIt ( int arr[], int number );
```

A function prototype is declared.

As you can see the function returns no value to the calling program and has two arguments, an integer array and an integer variable.

```
void main()
```

The program then enters the **main()** function:

```
int count;
int array[MAXIMUM];
```

Two local variables are declared. An integer variable and an integer array.

```
cout << "This prints the elements of an array in reverse order.\n";
```

A **cout** statement is used to display a message on the screen.

```
for ( count = 0; count < MAXIMUM; count++ )
{
    array[count] = count;
}
```

A **for** loop is used to initialize the array with the numbers 0, 1, 2, ... , 9.

```
reverseIt (array, MAXIMUM - 1);
```

The only other statement in **main()** is a call to the function.

```
void reverseIt ( int arr[], int number)
```

After **main()** you will see the function definition.

The function displays the element of the array that corresponds to the number passed to the function as an argument. For example, the first time the function is called the second argument to the function is **MAXIMUM - 1**, which is 9. The array element displayed is **arr[9]**. If the value of the integer variable is not 0 the function calls itself again.

You need to remember that if you use recursion there must be a point when something will reach a pre-defined value that will stop the function calls. Otherwise you will have an infinite loop and the stack will fill up and overflow which would result in the program stopping abruptly.

If you use recursion you can use indirect recursion as opposed to direct recursion which we have seen demonstrated in the last two examples. Indirect recursion is when function "A" calls function "B" which in turn calls function "A", etc. There's no reason why you couldn't do this with three, or even more, functions calling each other in a circle.

Try altering this program to see what happens if you comment out the terminating code and only execute the code found in the else clause.

You can also write a program that does the same as this but using iteration. Which is the easiest to understand?

Arrays and Functions

As the last example program showed, arrays, just like any other variable, can be passed from one function to another.

In the example program the array was declared as:

```
int   array[MAXIMUM];
```

The array was initialized in the **for** loop.

```
for ( count = 0; count < MAXIMUM; count++ )
{
    array[count] = count;
}
```

and the array was passed to the function:

```
reverseIt (array, MAXIMUM - 1);
```

As you can see only the array name has to be given. There's no need for the [] operator or a subscript.

143

However, this would be correct:

```
reverseIt (array, array[9]);
```

as in this case, the array is passed as before, using only the name, and the integer value stored at **array[9]** is passed as the integer variable. The second case is only passing a single integer variable.

Default Arguments

It's possible to write a function that can be called without having to specify all of its arguments. For this to occur the function prototype must provide default arguments for the values not specified.

The following example program should illustrate the position.

```
//defarg.cpp
//demonstrates missing and default arguments
#include <iostream.h>
//function prototype with default arguments
void lineOfChar(int length = 30, char ch = '*');

void main()
{
     lineOfChar();              //prints a line of 30 *'s
     lineOfChar(10);            //prints a line of 10 *'s
     lineOfChar(15, '#');       //prints a line of 15 #'s
}

void lineOfChar(int n, char ch)    //defaults supplied
{
     for(int i = 0; i < n; i++)
          cout << ch;
     cout << endl;
}
```

Program Analysis

This program should present you with no problems.

```
void lineOfChar(int length = 30, char ch = '*');
```

The function **lineOfChar()** takes two arguments.

```
void  main()
{
    lineOfChar();              //prints a line of 30 *'s
    lineOfChar(10);            //prints a line of 10 *'s
    lineOfChar(15, '#');       //prints a line of 15 #'s
}
```

It's called three times from **main()**.

The first time it's called with no arguments and the function uses the default arguments supplied.

In the second case one argument is passed and the function uses the default argument for the one not supplied.

In the third case the function arguments are used.

If one argument is missing when the function is called, it's assumed to be the last argument. You can leave out the last four arguments but you can't leave out an argument in the middle and put the remaining ones in. Arguments that are going to be omitted must be at the end of the list.

Summary

In this chapter you've learnt what a function is and how it is used. Now you've had some experience in writing your own functions you should feel confident in using them in your programs. You should also understand the issue of scope when declaring your variables to be used in your functions.

Programming Exercises

1   To convert a temperature in degrees Fahrenheit to degrees Celsius take 32 away from the temperature to be converted and multiply the result by 5/9. Write a function to do this conversion and put the function in a program to test that it works.

2   Now write a function that converts a temperature in degrees Celsius to degrees Fahrenheit. Put this function in the program you used in question 1. Amend the program so that the user is asked whether they want to convert from Fahrenheit to Celsius or Celsius to Fahrenheit and do the appropriate calculation.

3   The following code will generate a solid right-angled triangle with its point uppermost:

```
void solid_triangle(int offset, int height, char character)
{
    int i, j, k;                             //loop counter

    for(i = 0; i < height; i++)
    {
        for(j = 0; j < offset; j++)
            cout << blank;
        for(k = 0; k < i + 1; k++)
            cout << character;
        cout << endl;
    }
}
```

Put the above function into a program and test that it works.

Write a function that produces hollow right-angled triangle point uppermost.

Earlier in the chapter it was suggested that you wrote functions to generate: (i) a solid right-angled triangle, point down, (ii) a hollow right-angled triangle, point up, and (iii) a hollow right-angled triangle, point down.

You should now finalize these functions, put them in your program and test that they work.

Now consider an isosceles triangle.

4   Write a function to inform you whether the character entered via the keyboard is a number, an uppercase letter, a lowercase letter, or a punctuation mark.

146

5 Raising a number N to the power p is the same as multiplying the N by itself p times.

For example, 2^2 means raise the number 2 to the power of 2 (2 x 2 = 4). Another example is 2^3 which means raise the number 2 to the power 3 (2 x 2 x 2 = 8).

Write a function called double power (double N, int p). Now alter the function and use a default argument of 2 for p, so that if this argument is omitted, the number will be squared.

These functions should be put in a program that obtains values from the user and displays the results on the screen.

Solutions

A solution to the **line_of_char()** function:

```
void line_of_char(int offset, int width, char character)
{
    int count;                  //loop counters

    for(count = 0; count < offset; count++)
        cout << blank;
    for(count = 0; count < width; count++)
        cout << character;
}
```

A solution to the **hollow_box()** function is:

```
void hollow_block(int offset, int height, int width, char character)
{
    int count, i;                        //loop counters

line_of_char(offset, width, character); //top line

    for(count = 0; count < height - 2; count++)
    {                                    //vertical sides
        cout << endl;
        for(i = 0; i < offset; i++)
            cout << " ";
        cout << character;
        for(i = 0; i < width - 2; i++)
            cout << " ";
        cout << character;
    }
    cout << endl;

    line_of_char(offset, width, character);      //bottom line
}
```

Instant

Where Are We Now ?

Don't be surprised if the pace of the book seems a little fast. If you are very new to programming, you've done as well as any juggler - keeping all those concepts in the air at the same time! If you are coming to the book with some experience of another language, then you will have recognized all the normal terms and conditions, and will have digested the basic style of building a program in the C++ world.

So, where exactly do we stand now in terms of the complete language?

You have seen several examples of C++ programs. You know that all C++ programs must include a function called **main()** where execution of the program begins. You have met the standard C++ types.

You have seen that variables can be initialized using an assignment statement and have been told that uninitialized variables contain garbage values. The value of a variable can be kept fixed if it is declared to be a constant.

You have used the input and output routines.

You have also met and used statements that allow iteration and branching in your programs. All of these statements are controlled by the evaluation of one or more expressions.

You have met functions which are a predominant tool in building modular programs. Functions can return values of specified types and can accept arguments.

As you have seen, C++ allows elements of the same type to be combined into larger structures, called arrays. Arrays in C++ can be comprised of any data type. Array elements are accessed by using the name of the array and the index of the element. In C++, array indices start from 0.

So what can you do?

At this stage you can write quite long programs in C++. You can pass arguments to functions, use the built-in C++ libraries (similar to the ones you have already seen in operation), use the standard input and output facilities, control the flow of execution in a program by using several loops, and branching with **if**, **if-else**, and `switch` statements.

You know enough of the language to write useful programs.

You should have enough experience and knowledge of the language to study additional new library functions and C++ constructions on your own.

Let's consider another example. There is an algorithm, called Zeller's algorithm, which can calculate the weekday (i.e Monday, Tuesday) given the date. The algorithm works as follows:

- The date should be given in the form 19 11 1954, i.e. DD MM YYYY
- If the month is January it is taken as month 11 of the previous year
- If the month is February it is taken as month 12 of the previous year
- Once the months are numbered, with March as month 1 of the year, use the following formula:

$$day = (DD + (13 \times MM - 1)/5 + 5 \times (\ YYYY \bmod 100)/4 - (7 \times \ YYYY)/400) \bmod 7,$$

where mod means modulus.

- The algorithm returns numbers between 0 and 6. 0 represents Sunday, 1 represents Monday and so on.

Now we know the algorithm, we can write a function to perform the calculation. Have a go and see if you can do this.

My version of the function is shown below:

```
int calc_day(int d, int m, int y)
{
    int day, month, year;

    year = y;
    month = m - 2;

    if (month <= 0)
    {
        month += 12;
        year--;
    }

    day = ( d + (13 * month - 1)/5 +
            5 * (year % 100)/4 - 7 * year/400) % 7;
    return(day);
}
```

As you can see the function presents no problems. You should now write a program that asks the user to enter a date in the form DD MM YYYY. The program should use the above function to calculate the day and this should be output to the screen.

It's great isn't it! And it uses all the things you have learnt so far. We can now continue learning C++, moving on to the next chapter.

Chapter

Mixed Data Types

As we've seen, an array can hold a collection of data under one name. The only problem is that the data all has to be of the same type. You'll often want to group data of a different type together. C++ allows you to do this and asks you simply to tell the compiler what form the mixed data structure will take by setting up a template that the compiler will understand.

This chapter covers:

- What a structure is
- The structure specifier
- The structure member operator
- Declaring structure variables
- Initializing structure variables
- Arrays of structures
- Nested structures
- Structures and functions
- Unions

Structures

An example of a typically grouped collection might include employee records, like these:

```
Name              char name[80];
Address           char address[80];
Age               int age;
Position          char position[20];
Salary            float salary;
```

There are obviously other examples. What about customer records, supplier information, invoice details, and so on.

The items described above can be held together in a structure. A structure is a grouping of related data which is grouped in a way convenient to the programmer or user. It's a user-defined data type which is a combination of several different previously defined data types.

If we wanted to make the employee records into a structure we'd have to give the compiler a *template* of what the structure will hold. The template is a description of the individual components or **members** of the structure. So in this case we'd declare a template as follows:

```
struct employees
{
    char name[80];
    char address[80];
    int age;
    char position[20];
    float salary;
};
```

With this template we're telling the compiler to recognize a type of structure called employees. The structure will consist of five variables.

Structures in a Program - An Example

It will probably be easier if we look at an example of a structure being used in a program:

```
/* ************************************************************
 *     struct1.cpp                                            *
 *     Ian M Wilks                                            *
 * ********************************************************** */
#include <iostream.h>          //header file for input/output
void main()
{
     const int MAX = 80;

     struct
     {
          char name[MAX];
          int age;
     } person;

     cout << "This program introduces structures.\n\n"
          << "Please enter your name: ";
     cin.get(person.name, MAX);
     cout << "Please enter your age: ";
     cin >> person.age;
     cout << "\n\nThis person is " << person.name
          << " and they are aged " << person.age << endl;
}
```

Program Analysis

```
#include <iostream.h>
void main()
```

After the comment block, the **#include** directive is used to include
IOSTREAM.H. Then the **main()** function is entered.

```
     const int MAX = 80;
```

A constant integer is defined.

```
     struct
     {
          char name[MAX];
          int age;
     } person;
```

A simple structure is defined.

Structure Declaration

This construction is often called a structure declaration. However, the word declaration is also used in another sense - so for clarity let's call it a structure specifier.

Defining an Aggregate Variable

The keyword **struct** is followed by some simple variables between the braces. These variables are the components of the structure. After the closing brace a variable is declared, **person**. According to the definition of a structure, **person** is now an aggregate variable composed of two elements - **name** and **age**.

If you're familiar with database terminology you'll understand what a field is: a regular, named component of a complete record of any data. Your telephone number (field) would be a component of your complete name and address (record).

So, each of the two fields in our **struct** are associated with (the record of) **person**, and each can store a variable of its respective type. We can now say that two variables have been declared.

At this stage we should point out that each of the elements of **person** are simple variables. You can use these anywhere in a C++ program where a variable of their type could be used.

For example, the age element is an integer variable and can therefore be used anywhere in a program where it is legal to use an integer variable; in calculations, as a counter, in input/output operations, and so on.

To access the variable **age** which is part of the compound variable **person**, you need to use both names with a full stop between them, with the name of the struct variable first.

Thus **person.age** is the complete variable name for the **age** field of **person**.

You can use this construct anywhere in a C++ program where you want to refer to this field. In fact, it is not advisable to use the name **person** or **age** alone because they are only partial definitions of the complete field. (You may of course pass a structure of this name to a function). On its own, the name refers to nothing.

The cout Statement

```
cout << "This program introduces structures.\n\n"
     << "Please enter your name: ";
```

The **cout** statement is used to put a message on the screen and asks the user to enter a name.

```
cin.get(person.name, MAX);
```

As the user can input a full name with spaces between words, the **cin.get()** function is used to put the text into **person.name**.

```
cout << "Please enter your age: ";
cin >> person.age;
```

cout is used to ask the user to enter an age, while **cin** is used to put the data in **person.age**.

As you can see, it's possible to assign a value to each of the fields of **person**. **person.name** is actually a character string. Since it was set up that way in the structure, it must be assigned a string. You'll see that **person.name** is assigned the string input via the keyboard. The remaining field is assigned a value in accordance with its type.

Notice that the order of assignment is not critical.

```
cout << "\n\nThis person is " << person.name
     << " and they are aged " << person.age << endl;
```

cout is then used to output the information stored in the structure to the screen.

Look at the **cout** statement. There's nothing special about it. The compound name of each variable is specified because that's the only valid name by which these variables can be referred.

Structures are a useful method of grouping data together in order to make a program easier to write and understand.

Compile and run **STRUCT1.CPP** and observe the output.

Structures and Arrays Compared

To recap - a structure is a collection of simple variables. The variables in a structure can be of different types: some can be int, some can be float, and so on. Structures differ from arrays, where all the variables must be of the same type.

Structures and Class

In books on C programming, structures are often considered to be an advanced feature of the language and are introduced towards the end. For C++ programmers however, structures are one of the two important building blocks in the understanding of objects and classes. In fact the syntax of a structure is almost identical to that of a class. We'll cover this in the chapters on object-oriented programming.

A structure (as typically used) is a collection of data, while a class is a collection of both data and functions.

Structures in C++ serve a similar purpose to records in BASIC and PASCAL.

Structures in C++ - An Example

Let's look now at how structure variables can be declared in your program.

```
/* **************************************************************
 *     struct2.cpp                                             *
 *     Ian M Wilks                                             *
 ************************************************************** */
#include <iostream.h>          //header file for input/output
void main()
{
    const int MAX = 80;

    struct person
    {
        char name[MAX];
        int age;
    };

    person person1;

    cout << "This program introduces structures.\n\n"
        << "Please enter your name: ";

    cin.get(person1.name, MAX);
    cout << "Please enter your age: ";
    cin >> person1.age;
    cout << "\n\nThis person is " << person1.name
        << " and they are aged " << person1.age << endl;
}
```

Program Analysis

Look at the program and you'll see that it's almost the same as the first program. The only difference is the syntax of the structure specifier.

```
struct person
{
    char name[MAX];
    int age;
};
```

and the following line:

```
person person1;
```

As you've seen, the keyword struct introduces the specifier and is followed by the structure name, which in this case is **person**. The declarations of the structure members - **name[MAX]** and **age** - are enclosed in braces. A semicolon, following the closing brace, terminates the structure. Note that this use of the semicolon is unlike the usage for a block of code.

As you saw earlier, the specifier serves as a blueprint for the creation of variables of type **person**. The specifier doesn't itself define any variables; that is, it doesn't set aside any space in memory. It's merely a specification for how such structure variables will look when they're defined.

The next statement defines a variable, called **person1**.

```
person person1;
```

This definition reserves space in memory for person1. Enough space is reserved in memory to hold all the members of person1.

In some ways it's possible to think of a structure as the specification for a new data type. You can see that the format for defining a structure variable is the same as that for defining a built-in data type such as int.

Once the structure has been defined, its members can be accessed using the dot operator - as shown earlier. The structure member is written in three parts:

- The name of the structure variable
- The dot operator
- The member name. i.e. **person1.age** (This means the age member of person1).

Compile and run this program - it does exactly the same as the first program.

An Array of Structures

Look at the following example program which demonstrates an array of structures. You'll recall that an array is a data structure used to store a collection of data items that are all of the same type. A structure variable is regarded as a data type so an array can be used.

Using an Array of Structures - An Example

```
/* **************************************************************
 *     struct3.cpp                                              *
 *     Ian M Wilks                                              *
 ************************************************************** */
#include <iostream.h>            //header file for input/output

void main()
{
    struct Example
    {
        char initial;
        int number;
    };

    Example test1, test2[10];

    cout << "This program continues the introduction to structures.\n\n"
        << "Please enter a letter: ";
    cin >> test1.initial;
    cout << "Please enter a number: ";
    cin >> test1.number;

    cout << "\n\nThe initial is " << test1.initial
        << " and the number is " << test1.number << endl;

    for(int count = 0; count < 10; count++)
    {
        test2[count].initial = 'a' + count;
        test2[count].number = count + 25;
    }

    for(count = 0; count < 10; count++)
    {
        cout << "test2[" << count << "].initial = "
            << test2[count].initial << " and test2["
            << count << "].number = " << test2[count].number << endl;
    }

    int answer = test2[1].number + test2[3].number;

    cout << "\n\nanswer = " << answer;
}
```

Program Analysis

```
void main()
```

The program enters **main()**.

```
struct Example
{
    char initial;
    int number;
};
```

A structure specifier for structure **Example** which has two simple variables - **char   initial** and **int   number**.

```
Example test1, test2[10];
```

Type **Example** variables are defined - **test1** and an array **test2[10]**.

This program contains a single structure variable and an array of 10 variables named **test2**. This program therefore contains 10 x 2 = 20 + 2 = 22 simple variables, each of which can store one item of data provided that it's of the correct type.

```
cout << "This program continues the introduction to structures.\n\n"
     << "Please enter a letter: ";
cin >> test1.initial;
cout << "Please enter a number: ";
cin >> test1.number;
```

cout is used to display a message on the screen and asks the user to enter some data. **cin** is used to store the data in the **test1** structure variable.

```
cout << "\n\nThe initial is " << test1.initial
     << " and the number is " << test1.number << endl;
```

The data stored in **test1** is displayed on the screen.

```
for(int count = 0; count < 10; count++)
{
     test2[count].initial = 'a' + count;
     test2[count].number = count + 25;
}
```

The next part of the program operates on the array of structures. A **for** loop
is used to assign values to the array elements and each pass through the loop
results in assigning a value to the two fields. One pass through the loop
assigns all of the values for one of the **test2** elements. This would not be a
very useful way to assign data in a real situation, but a loop could read the
data in from a file and store it in the correct fields.

```
for(count = 0; count < 10; count++)
{
     cout << "test2[" << count << "].initial = "
          << test2[count].initial << " and test2["
          << count << "].number = " << test2[count].number << endl;
}
```

A **for** loop is then used to output the information stored in **test2** to the
screen.

```
int answer = test2[1].number + test2[3].number;
```

To confirm that simple variables in a structure can be used in the same way as
stand alone variables, an addition of two elements from the array is carried
out.

```
cout << "\n\nanswer = " << answer;
```

The answer is then displayed on the screen.

Initializing a Structure

The next example shows how structure members can be initialized when the
structure variable is defined. The example is working with imperial
measurement - yards, feet and inches.

For those people who can't remember, 12 inches make 1 foot, and 3 feet make
a yard !

Initializing a Structure - An Example

```cpp
/* ***********************************************************
 *      struct4.cpp                                        *
 *      Ian M Wilks                                        *
 ************************************************************ */
#include <iostream.h>          //header file for input/output

void main()
{
     struct yardsFeetInches
     {
          int yards;
          int feet;
          float inches;
     };

     yardsFeetInches m1, m3, m2 = {2, 2, 9.75};

     cout << "This program continues the introduction to structures.\n\n"
          << "Please enter yard, feet and inches: ";
     cin >> m1.yards >> m1.feet >> m1.inches;
     m3.yards = m1.yards + m2.yards;
     m3.feet = m1.feet + m2.feet;
     m3.inches = m1.inches + m2.inches;
     while (m3.inches >= 12 )
     {
          m3.inches -= 12;
          m3.feet++;
     }
     while (m3.feet >= 3 )
     {
          m3.feet -= 3;
          m3.yards++;
     }
     cout << m1.yards << "yd " << m1.feet << "ft " << m1.inches << "in + "
          << m2.yards << "yd " << m2.feet << "ft " << m2.inches << "in = "
          << m3.yards << "yd " << m3.feet << "ft " << m3.inches << "in.";
}
```

Program Analysis

```cpp
void main()
```

The program enters `main()`.

```
struct yardsFeetInches
    {
            int yards;
            int feet;
            float inches;
    };
```

A structure specifier for structure **yardsFeetInches** which has three simple variables:

```
yardsFeetInches m1, m3, m2 = {2, 2, 9.75};
```

The yardsFeetInches variables are defined – **m1, m3** and **m2**. You'll also see that m2 is initialized to hold the values **2 yards 2 feet 9.75** inches using the expression **m2 = {2, 2, 9.75}**

This program contains three structure variables and therefore contains 3 x 3 = 9 simple variables, each of which can store one item of data provided that it's of the correct type.

```
        cout << "This program continues the introduction to
structures.\n\n"
            << "Please enter yard, feet and inches: ";
        cin >> m1.yards >> m1.feet >> m1.inches;
```

cout is used to display a message on the screen and asks the user to enter some data. **cin** is used to store the data in **m1**.

```
        m3.yards = m1.yards + m2.yards;
        m3.feet = m1.feet + m2.feet;
        m3.inches = m1.inches + m2.inches;
        while (m3.inches >= 12 )
        {
                m3.inches -= 12;
                m3.feet++;
        }
        while (m3.feet >= 3 )
        {
                m3.feet -= 3;
                m3.yards++;
        }
```

m1 and **m2** are added together and the answer is stored in **m3**. Note how the while statement is used to check if **m3.inches** is greater than 12. If it's greater than 12 **m3.inches** is reduced by 12 and **m3.feet** is incremented. A similar procedure is used to check if **m3.feet** is greater than 3.

Why did we use a **while** loop? In this example an if statement would have sufficed. Try altering all the example programs and experiment.

You may have a value like 13 yards 17 feet 39 inches before the **while** loop. If we used an if statement this would alter the values to 14 yards, 15 feet, 27 inches when, in fact, the values should be 19 yards, 2 feet, 3 inches. Therefore, the **while** loop is used in case you have several **yardsFeetInches** variables being added together and these types of values are generated.

```
cout << m1.yards << "yd " << m1.feet << "ft " << m1.inches << "in + "
     << m2.yards << "yd " << m2.feet << "ft " << m2.inches << "in = "
     << m3.yards << "yd " << m3.feet << "ft " << m3.inches << "in.";
```

The values and the answer are then displayed on the screen.

You'll have noticed that it wasn't possible to add two distances with a program statement like:

```
m3 = m1 + m2;
```

This is because there's no routine built into C++ that knows how to add variables of type **yardsFeetInches**. See Chapter 10 on overloading.

Nested Structures

The next example builds on the previous one and shows that structures can use the usual nested approach and create structures within structures.

```
/* ***********************************************************
 *    struct5.cpp                                           *
 *    Ian M Wilks                                           *
 *********************************************************** */
#include <iostream.h>          //header file for input/output

void main()
{
    struct yardsFeetInches
    {
        int yards;
        int feet;
        float inches;
    };


    struct area
    {
        yardsFeetInches Length;
        yardsFeetInches Width;
    };
```

```
        area garden;

        garden.Length.yards = 5;
        garden.Length.feet = 2;
        garden.Length.inches = 6;
        garden.Width.yards = 3;
        garden.Width.feet = 1;
        garden.Width.inches = 9;

        float len = garden.Length.yards
                + (garden.Length.feet + garden.Length.inches/12)/3;
        float wid = garden.Width.yards
                + (garden.Width.feet + garden.Width.inches/12)/3;

        cout << "\nThe garden area is " << len * wid << " sq yards\n\n";

        len = garden.Length.yards * 3 + garden.Length.feet +
                                garden.Length.inches/12;
        wid = garden.Width.yards * 3 + garden.Width.feet
                                + garden.Width.inches/12;

        cout << "\nThe garden area is " << len * wid << " sq feet";
    }
```

Program Analysis

```
void main()
```

The program enters **main()**.

```
struct yardsFeetInches
    {
        int   yards;
        int   feet;
        float  inches;
    };
```

```
    struct  area
    {
        yardsFeetInches  Length;
        yardsFeetInches  Width;
    };
```

Two structure specifiers are present. The first specifier is for the structure **YardsFeetInches** which was used in the last example. The second is for structure **area** which has two structure variables - **YardsFeetInches Length** and **YardsFeetInches Width**.

```
area garden;
```

An area variable is defined.

```
garden.Length.yards = 5;
garden.Length.feet = 2;
garden.Length.inches = 6;
garden.Width.yards = 3;
garden.Width.feet = 1;
garden.Width.inches = 9.
```

Values are then assigned to the structures.

```
garden.Length.feet = 2;
```

As one structure is nested inside another, the dot operator must be applied twice to access structure members.

In the statement, garden is the name of the structure variable. As before:

Length is the name of a member in the outer structure **(area)**.

feet is the name of a member of the inner structure **(YardsFeetInches)**.

The statement means "take the feet member of the Length member of the variable garden and assign it the value 2".

```
float len = garden.Length.yards
          + (garden.Length.feet + garden.Length.inches/12)/3;
float wid = garden.Width.yards
          + (garden.Width.feet + garden.Width.inches/12)/3;
```

Two float variables are created and assigned the values that are in **area**. In order that the program can calculate the area in square yards, the inches are divided by 12 (to make them fractions of feet), and added to the feet value.

This value is then divided by 3 (to make it a fraction of yards) and added to the yards value.

```
cout << "\nThe garden area is "<< len * wid << "sq yards\n\n";
```

The area is calculated and displayed on the screen.

```
len = garden.Length.yards * 3 + garden.Length.feet + garden.Length.inches/12;
wid = garden.Width.yards * 3 + garden.Width.feet + garden.Width.inches/12;
```

The program then calculates the area in square feet. To enable this to be done, the yards are multiplied by 3 and added to feet. The inches are divided by 12 (to make them fractions of a foot) and added to the value.

```
cout << "\nThe garden area is " << len * wid << " sq feet";
```

The area is calculated and the answer is displayed on the screen.

Assigning Strings to Structure Elements - An Example

The following example program, **STRUCT6.CPP**, shows how to assign strings to structure elements using a string function defined in the header file, **STRING.H**.

```
/* ***********************************************************
 *     struct6.cpp                                          *
 *     Ian M Wilks                                          *
 ********************************************************** */
#include <iostream.h>         //header file for input/output
#include <string.h>           //header file for string operations

void main()
{
    const int MAX = 80;

    struct person
    {
        char name[MAX];
        int age;
    };

    person person1;

    strcpy(person1.name, "Ian M Wilks");
    person1.age = 39;

    cout << "\n\nThis person is " << person1.name
        << " and they are aged " << person1.age << endl;

}
```

Program Analysis

Run the program. You should have no trouble in understanding the code. As we saw in Chapter 5 we're utilizing the **strcpy()** function to copy the string into the character array (copying one string into another). To use this function you must include the header file, **STRING.H**.

Structures and Functions

Structures can be passed as arguments into functions, and functions can return structures to the calling program.

The following example shows a function that will accept a structure argument. Consider the earlier examples that looked at the structure **yardsFeetInches** and remember the task of **STRUCT4.CPP** and **STRUCT5.CPP**.

We used the following code to output the values to the screen:

```
cout << m1.yards<< "yd " << m1.feet<< "ft " << m1.inches<< "in + "
     << m2.yards<< "yd " << m2.feet<< "ft " << m2.inches<< "in = "
     << m3.yards<< "yd " << m3.feet<< "ft " << m3.inches<< "in.";
```

We could have written a function to output the data as follows:

```
void out_measure(yardsFeetInches m)
{
    cout << m.yards<< "yd " << m.feet<< "ft " << m.inches<< "in";
}
```

Put this function into the program **STRUCT4.CPP** and alter the program to output the measurements using this function. Remember, the function prototype will be as follows:

```
void out_measure(yardsFeetInches m);
```

To call the function you'll use the function call:

```
out_measure(m1);
```

When you try to run the program you'll probably encounter an error.

The structure specifier should be global and you'll have to put it outside of **main()**.

169

Value Flow in Structures and Functions - An Example

The following example shows how to pass arguments to a function and how to return structure variables. Again, we'll use the example of the structure `yardsFeetInches`. When we added the structure variables together we used the following code:

```
m3.yards = m1.yards + m2.yards;
m3.feet = m1.feet + m2.feet;
m3.inches = m1.inches + m2.inches;
while (m3.inches >= 12 )
{
     m3.inches -= 12;
     m3.feet++;
}
while (m3.feet >= 3 )
{
     m3.feet -= 3;
     m3.yards++;
}
```

We could have written a function to do the addition and return the answer to **main()** as we've done below.

```
yardsFeetInches add_measure(yardsFeetInches mm1,yardsFeetInches mm2)
{
     yardsFeetInches ans;    //new variable for answer
     ans.yards = mm1.yards + mm2.yards;
     ans.feet = mm1.feet + mm2.feet;
     ans.inches = mm1.inches + mm2.inches;

   while (ans.inches > 12 )
      {
           ans.inches -= 12;
           ans.feet++;
      }
   while (ans.feet > 3 )
      {
           ans.feet -= 3;
           ans.yards++;
      }
     return(ans);
}
```

Put this function into the program **struct4.cpp** and alter the program to add the measurements using this function.

Remember, the function prototype will be as follows:

```
yardsFeetInches add_measure(yardsFeetInches mm1,
                            yardsFeetInches mm2);
```

And to call the function you'll use the function call:

```
add_measure(m1, m2);
```

Unions

To round things off, we'll briefly consider unions. However, don't worry if you don't understand all of this section immediately. Unions aren't used very frequently and almost never by novice programmers.

At first sight unions look very much like a structure. They're set up in a similar way to a structure:

```
union  name
{
    members
}  identifier;
```

The only difference is the union keyword.

The difference between a union and a structure is that a union only allows you to hold one value at a time.

As you can see, unions exhibit many of the characteristics of structures, but use memory differently. Like a structure, a union can declare a group of different data objects, but in a union only one member is active at a time.

A union type is allocated enough memory to hold only the largest member found in the union declaration. If a smaller member is active, the remaining space is padding and a waste of space.

Enough memory is allocated to hold only the word[MAX] member. As word[MAX] is declared as a char, four bytes of memory are allocated. These four bytes are the total memory allocated for the union.

Basically, a union is a structure with members that 'overlay' each other.

For example:

```
union  example
{
        int  i;
        char  one;
        char  two;
};
```

You should note that the variables are not distinct. They are different names for the same memory location. They could be used to view information in two different ways. A more practical use for unions is to extract bytes (8 bits) from words (16 bits). As the following example shows, the union can hold three letter word like "Jan", "Feb", "Mar" or, a number like 1,2,3 or 12. It doesn't matter which is selected, as they are both held in the same area of memory.

Unions - An Example

Look at the following program:

```
/* ****************************************************************
 *     union1.cpp                                                 *
 *     Ian M Wilks                                                *
 ***************************************************************** */
#include <iostream.h>         //header file for input/output
#include <string.h>           //header file for string operations
void main()
{
    const int MAX = 4;
    struct date
    {
            int day;
            union
            {
                    char word[MAX];
                    int num;
            } month;
            int year;
    };

    date date1;
    date1.day = 19;
    date1.month.num = 11;
    date1.year = 54;
    date date2 = {15, "May", 55};
    char ch, buffer[MAX];
    date date3;
    cout << "Date1 is: " << date1.day << "/" << date1.month.num << "/"
         << date1.year << endl;
```

```
    cout << "Date2 is: " << date2.day << " " << date2.month.word << " "
        << date2.year << endl;
    cout << "\nIf you enter the month using letters press L and return.";
    cout << "\nIf you enter the month using numbers press N and return.";
    cin >> ch;
    if ((ch == 'L') || (ch == 'l'))
    {
        cout << "Enter day: ";
        cin >> date3.day;
        cout << "Enter month: ";
        cin >> buffer;
        strcpy(date3.month.word, buffer);
        cout << "Enter year: ";
        cin >> date3.year;
        cout << "\nThe date you entered was " << date3.day << " "
            << date3.month.word << " " << date3.year << endl;
    }
    if ((ch == 'N') || (ch == 'n'))
    {
        cout << "Enter day: ";
        cin >> date3.day;
        cout << "Enter month: ";
        cin >> date3.month.num;
        cout << "Enter year: ";
        cin >> date3.year;
        cout << "\nThe date you entered was " << date3.day << "/"
            << date3.month.num << "/" << date3.year << endl;
    }
}
```

Program Analysis

```
#include <iostream.h>
#include <string.h>
```

Following the comment block the **#include** directive is used to include **IOSTREAM.H** for the input/output routines and **STRING.H** for the string operation routines.

```
void main()
```

The program then enters **main().**

```
const int MAX = 4;
```

A constant is declared and initialized.

```
struct date
{
      int day;
      union
      {
            char word[MAX];
            int num;
      } month;
      int year;
};
```

A structure specifier is declared - **date**. The structure has three elements:

> **int   day**
>
> **int   year**
>
> **union   month.**

The pattern allows for a date to be entered as all numbers or for the month to be entered as a three letter word.

```
date date1;
date1.day = 19;
date1.month.num = 11;
date1.year = 54;
```

date1, a date variable is declared. It is initialized to hold the date as numbers.

```
date date2 = {15, "May", 55};
```

date2, a date variable is declared and initialized to hold the date which has the month shown using a three letter word.

```
cout << "Date1 is: " << date1.day << "/" << date1.month.num << "/"
      << date1.year << endl;
cout << "Date2 is: " << date2.day << " " << date2.month.word << " "
      << date2.year << endl;
```

Both dates are displayed on the screen.

```
        cout << "\nIf you enter the month using letters press L and return.";
        cout << "\nIf you enter the month using numbers press N and return.";
        cin >> ch;
        if ((ch == 'L') || (ch == 'l'))
        {
            cout << "Enter day: ";
            cin >> date3.day;
            cout << "Enter month: ";
            cin >> buffer;
            strcpy(date3.month.word, buffer);
            cout << "Enter year: ";
            cin >> date3.year;
            cout << "\nThe date you entered was " << date3.day << " "
                << date3.month.word << " " << date3.year << endl;
        }
        if ((ch == 'N') || (ch == 'n'))
        {
            cout << "Enter day: ";
            cin >> date3.day;
            cout << "Enter month: ";
            cin >> date3.month.num;
            cout << "Enter year: ";
            cin >> date3.year;
            cout << "\nThe date you entered was " << date3.day << "/"
                << date3.month.num << "/" << date3.year << endl;
        }
```

The user is asked if they'll enter the month using letters or numbers. Depending on the selection, the program then enters the appropriate **if** statement to accept the date entered via the keyboard, and then to display it on the screen.

Experiment With the Program.

As you can see, union members can be accessed with the structure member operator in the same way as structures. The programmer must be aware of which member is active - the compiler does not keep track of an active member.

In this example there are two elements to the union, the first part being the character string, which is stored as a four byte variable in the computer's memory. The second element is an integer variable. This variable is stored in the same storage locations that the string is stored in. A union allows the programmer to store different types of data in the same physical storage locations.

Summary

In this chapter you've learnt about using structures and arrays in C++ programs. We've looked at different types of structures, as well as how to initialize them and use loops with them. We went on to see how structures can be passed as arguments into functions, and rounded off by dipping into unions. The following exercises will help to consolidate your learning.

Programming Exercises

1   A point in the three-dimensional space can be represented by three numbers - X coordinate, Y coordinate, and Z coordinate.

For example (1, 2, 3) represents a point 1 unit to the right of the origin along the X-axis, 2 units up the Y-axis, and 3 units along the Z-axis.

Write a program that uses a structure to model a point.

Define three structure variables and initialize one of them. Ask the user to enter details via the keyboard for the second point. Set the third point equal to the sum of the other two. For example Point A = (1, 2, 3), Point B = (7, 8, 9), Point A + Point B = (8, 10, 12).

2   The example program **STRUCT4.CPP** uses the **yardsFeetInches** structure and adds two measurements together. Earlier you were asked to insert and test the **out_measure()** and **add_measure()** functions.

Write a function that subtracts two structure variables.

3   The example program **STRUCT5.CPP** uses the **yardsFeetInches** structure and the **area** structure. The program computed the area in square feet and in square yards.

Write a function to calculate the area in square yards. The function should accept a structure as its argument and return a structure to the calling program.

Now write a second function to calculate the area in square feet. As previously, the function should accept a structure as its argument and return a structure to the calling program.

4   Write a program that uses a structure variable to store the name, address and telephone number of several people. The user should be able to add the information via the keyboard.

5   Write a program using a structure variable to store a list of dates and the anniversary/occasion. The user should be able to add the information via the keyboard.

Chapter

8

Pointers

A pointer is a variable that points to the location of other variables in memory. Essentially pointers give you the advantage of being able to pass back multiple values, instead of being restricted to one parameter in the return command.

Use pointers as an alternative way of accessing array elements allowing arguments to be passed to functions, when the function needs to modify the original argument. It also allows arrays to be passed as arguments to functions. It enables you to obtain memory from the system dynamically and lets you create certain data structures.

This chapter covers:

- Some of the uses of pointers
- Addresses and pointer variables
- Incremental operators
- Void pointers
- Pointers and arrays/strings/functions
- Passing by reference
- Passing arrays to functions
- Arrays of pointers
- Pointers and structures
- Casting

Pointers and Addresses

As we have said, pointers aren't complicated; they are based on a simple idea.

Every byte in the computer's memory has an address, an integer number. The numbers start at 0. If you have 640k of memory, the highest address is 655,359; if you have 1mb of memory it is 1,048,575.

A program occupies a particular range of these addresses when loaded into the computer's memory. This means that each variable and each function starts at a particular address.

If you have the following line of code in your program:

```
int number = 10;
```

there will be two bytes of memory that are allocated for this variable and will hold the value 10. You can refer to this address by using the address operator & in front of the variable name. For example: `&number;`.

Pointers and Addresses - An Example

Consider the following program:

```
/* ***********************************************************
 *    pointer1.cpp                                          *
 *    Ian M Wilks                                           *
 *********************************************************** */
#include <iostream.h>              //header file for I/O

void main()
{
    int first_num = 258;          //define and initialize variable
    int second_num = 582;         //define and initialize variable

    cout << "\nThe value of first_num is " << first_num << endl;
    cout << "\nThe address of first_num is " << &first_num << endl;
    cout << "\nThe value of second_num is " << second_num << endl;
    cout << "\nThe address of second_num is " << &second_num << endl;

}
```

The actual addresses occupied by the variables in a program will vary for different computers depending on factors like the size of the operating system and whether any other programs are currently in memory.

The output of the program will look like this.

```
The value of first_num is 258

The address of first_num is 0x89e90ffe

The value of second_num is 582

The address of second_num is 0x89e90ffc
```

Program Analysis

Run the program and look at the output. You will immediately see that the address of a variable is not the same as its contents.

```
void main()
```

The program enters **main()**.

```
int first_num = 258;        //define and initialize variable
int second_num = 582;       //define and initialize variable
```

Two integer variables are declared and initialized.

```
cout << "\nThe value of first_num is " << first_num << endl;
cout << "\nThe address of first_num is " << &first_num << endl;
cout << "\nThe value of second_num is " << second_num << endl;
cout << "\nThe address of second_num is " << &second_num << endl;
```

cout statements are then used to output messages containing the values stored in memory and to output the address of the variables.

As you can see from the sample output, the **<<** (insertion operator) outputs the addresses in hexadecimal notation. **0x** at the start of each number indicates this. This is the customary way to show memory addresses.

You can see that each variable has a unique address which differs by exactly two bytes. This is because integers occupy two bytes of memory. As the variables are stored on the stack, the addresses appear in descending order.

Pointer Variables

Now that we can discover the address of a variable, what can we do with it? You will probably be thinking that displaying the address of a variable on the screen isn't all that useful.

We need a further concept to boost programming ability and that is variables that hold address values. A variable that holds an address is called a pointer variable, or simply a pointer.

Pointer Variables - An Example

Consider the following example:

```
/* ***********************************************************
 *    pointer2.cpp                                          *
 *    Ian M Wilks                                           *
 ************************************************************ */
#include <iostream.h>              //header file for I/O

void main()
{
    int first_num = 258;          //define and initialize variable
    int second_num = 582;         //define and initialize variable

    int * ptr;                    //define pointer to integer

    ptr = &first_num;             //pointer points to first_num

    cout << "\nThe value of first_num is " << first_num << endl;
    cout << "\nThe address of first_num is " << &first_num << endl;
    cout << "\nThe value stored in the pointer is " << ptr << endl;
    cout << "\nThe contents of the pointer is " << *ptr << endl;

    ptr = &second_num;            //pointer now points to second_num

    cout << "\nThe value of second_num is " << second_num << endl;
    cout << "\nThe address of second_num is " << &second_num << endl;
    cout << "\nThe value stored in the pointer is " << ptr << endl;
    cout << "\nThe contents of the pointer is " << *ptr << endl;
}
```

Program Analysis

Before we analyze the program, look at the output generated by the program:

```
The value of first_num is 258

The address of first_num is 0x89de0ffe
```

```
The value stored in the pointer is 0x89de0ffe

The contents of the pointer is 258

The value of second_num is 582

The address of second_num is 0x89de0ffc

The value stored in the pointer is 0x89de0ffc

The contents of the pointer is 582
```

```
void main()
```

The program enters **main()**.

```
int first_num = 258;
int second_num = 582;
```

Two integer variables are declared and initialized.

```
int * ptr;
```

A pointer to an integer variable is defined using the statement **int * ptr;**.

Unlike variable declarations, the statement doesn't mean that the pointer is of type **int**. It means it can point to integer variables and only integer variables.

In some reference material, you will see that the asterisk is placed closer to the variable name than to the type. It doesn't matter to the compiler. However, some people consider that placing the asterisk next to the type helps to emphasis that the asterisk is part of the variable type (pointer to char), not part of the name itself.

To define more than one pointer of the same type on one line use the following:

```
int* point1, * point2, * point3;
```

or

```
int *point1, *point2, *point3;
```

```
ptr = &first_num;        //pointer points to first_num
```

The next statement `ptr = &first_num;` sets the pointer pointing to the variable `first_num`. This means that the address of `first_num` is stored in the pointer variable `ptr`.

```
cout << "\nThe value of first_num is " << first_num << endl;
cout << "\nThe address of first_num is " << &first_num << endl;
cout << "\nThe value stored in the pointer is " << ptr << endl;
cout << "\nThe contents of the pointer is " << *ptr << endl;
```

`cout` statements are used to display the following on the screen:

1 The value stored in the variable `first_num`

2 The address of the variable `first_num` using the address of operator as follows: `&first_num`

3 The value stored in the pointer (the address of the variable) using the pointer variable name in the same way you would use a variable name - `ptr`

4 The value stored at the memory location pointed to by the pointer - `*ptr`

`ptr` = where the pointer points to. For example, to an address.
`*ptr` = what the pointer points at. For example, what is at the address.

Note, the * placed in front of the pointer name is the indirection operator or the de-referencing operator . Whereas the * used in the declaration (**int * ptr;**) means pointer to.

```
ptr = &second_num;          //pointer now points to second_num
```

The pointer then points to **second_num** and the appropriate values are then displayed using the **cout** statement.

You need to remember that when a variable is first declared it doesn't contain an address unless it's initialized at the same time. Like a variable, before it's initialized a pointer may hold a garbage value which has no meaning in your program.

When dealing with pointers you must bear in mind that the value may not represent a valid address. Your computer, under direction of the program, will try to use whatever is contained in the pointer variable as a valid address. If this is a garbage value, it may turn out to be anywhere in memory: in your program, your data or in the operating system! For this reason, using an uninitialized pointer may result in your computer crashing, and your program will be difficult to debug.

Pinpointing Variables

The example above has shown that you can access a variable either by using the variable name or by using a pointer to the variable's address. Look at the following examples which we'll explain as we go along.

Assume the following declarations have been made in your program:

```
int first_num, second_num;
int * ptr;
```

You have defined two integer variables, and a pointer to an integer.

```
ptr = &first_num;
```

You next initialize the pointer to the address of the variable `first_num`.

```
*ptr = 258;
```

This statement is equivalent to the statement `first_num = 258;`.

```
second_num = *ptr;
```

This statement is equivalent to the statement `second_num = first_num;`.

You can assign values to variables and access the variables without using their names providing you know their addresses.

Try writing a program that incorporates these statements to see that they work. Use `cout` statements to output the values to the screen.

The figure below illustrates these points.

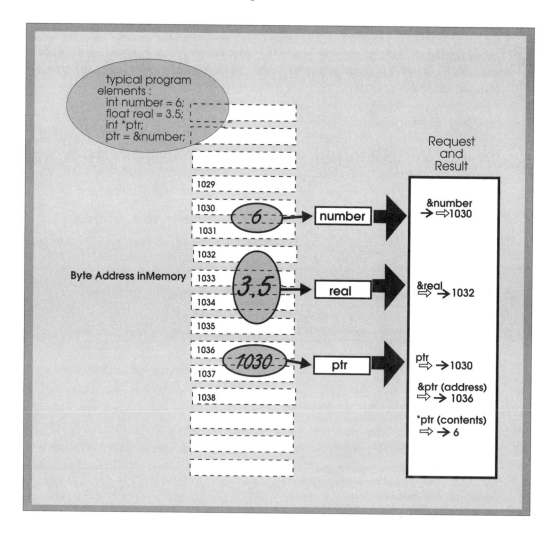

Incremental Operators

As we have seen, C++ provides us with the incremental operators **++** and **--** that allow us to increment or decrement variables by one unit. For example, **number++;** will increase the value stored in **number** by one unit.

The difference comes when the variable is a pointer. In the case of a pointer the numeric change will be equal to the size of the object in bytes to which the pointer is pointing.

For example, if you have a pointer to integers, it is pointing to a two-byte variable. To increase the pointer to point to the next variable in memory will require an increment of two. If you use the incremental operator on a pointer to an integer, the increase will be two.

Incremental Operators - An Example

For example:

```
int numbers[ ] = { 582,583,584,585,586 };
int *pointer = numbers;

for ( i= 0; i <  5,i ++ )
{
        cout << "\n\tThe data stored at memory address " << pointer
             << " is " << *pointer;
        pointer++ ;
}
```

Produces the following output :

```
The data stored at memory address 0x60660ff4 is 582
The data stored at memory address 0x60660ff6 is 583
The data stored at memory address 0x60660ff8 is 584
The data stored at memory address 0x60660ffa is 585
The data stored at memory address 0x60660ffc is 586
```

As you can see, incrementing the pointer, using the command pointer **++**, increases the address value by 2. The memory addresses are shown in hexadecimal notation. 0x60660ff4 translates to 1,617,301,492 in decimal notation. Similarly, 0x060660ff6 translates to 1,617,301,494, and so on. The address value is the address of the byte in memory where the data is situated. As an integer occupies two bytes of memory, the address is increased by two as we move through the data.

However,

```
int numbers[ ] = { 582,583,584,585,586 };
int *pointer = numbers;

for (i= 0; i < 5; i++)
{
        cout << "\n\tThe data stored at memory address " << pointer
               << " is " << *pointer++;
}
```

and

```
int numbers[ ] = { 582,583,584,585,586 };
int *pointer = numbers;

for (i= 0; i < 5; i++)
{
        cout << "\n\tThe data stored at memory address " << pointer
               << " is " << *(pointer++);
}
```

produce the same output. Therefore, you can see that **pointer++**, ***pointer++**, and ***(pointer++)** all increment the pointer address and allow us to step through the data.

Now look at the following code:

```
int numbers[ ] = { 582,583,584,585,586 };
pointer = numbers;

for ( i= 0; i  < 5; i++ )
{
        cout << "\n\tThe data stored at memory address " << pointer
               << " is " <<   (*pointer )++;
        pointer++ ;
}
```

The resulting output is shown below :

```
The data stored at memory address 0x60660ff4 is 582
The data stored at memory address 0x60660ff4 is 583
The data stored at memory address 0x60660ff4 is 584
The data stored at memory address 0x60660ff4 is 585
The data stored at memory address 0x60660ff4 is 586
```

The results are different! The memory address isn't changing but we are now increasing the data value by one. Therefore, **(*pointer)++** works on the data stored at the address.

This should have been expected. The expression in the brackets, *pointer, refers to the data stored at the address to which the pointer is pointing. The incremental operator is working on the data and not on the address.

Try incorporating this code into a small program to confirm these results. You could also write similar code for an array of floats and an array of characters (a string). The resulting output will confirm your earlier observations.

Pointers to Void

Normally, the address assigned to a pointer must be for a variable of a type that the pointer can point to. For example, the address of a float variable can't be assigned to a pointer of integers, if you attempt it, it will lead to the compiler trapping the violation.

There is a pointer that can point to any data type. This is called a pointer to void, and is defined like this:

```
void*  ptr;
```

Such pointers have certain specialized uses, such as obtaining memory from the system dynamically. They are seldom used for their own sake, but as an intermediate in some other operation.

The Void Pointer - An Example

The following program illustrates the use of the **void** pointer. Read through the source code to ascertain what's happening.

```
/* **************************************************************
 *                                                            *
 *    pointer5.cpp                                            *
 *    Ian M Wilks                                             *
 ************************************************** */
#include <iostream.h>            //header file for I/O

void main()
{
    int int_num = 582;          //define int variable
    float flo_num = 258.05;     //define float variable
    char char_let = 'I';        //define char variable
    int * int_ptr;              //define pointer to integer
    float * flo_ptr;            //define pointer to float
    char * char_ptr;            //define pointer to char
    void * void_ptr;            //define pointer to void

    int_ptr = &int_num;         //pointer set to address of int_num
```

```
//    int_ptr = &flo_num;          //illegal - cannot point integer pointer
                                   //              at a float
//    int_ptr = &char_let;         //illegal - cannot point integer pointer
                                   //              at a char
      flo_ptr = &flo_num;          //pointer set to address of flo_num
//    flo_ptr = &int_num;          //illegal - cannot point float pointer
                                   //              at an integer
//    flo_ptr = &char_let;         //illegal - cannot point float pointer
                                   //              at a character
      char_ptr = &char_let;        //pointer set to address of char_let
//    char_ptr = &int_num;         //illegal - cannot point char pointer
                                   //              at an integer
//    char_ptr = &flo_num;         //illegal - cannot point char pointer
                                   //              at a float
      cout << "\nThe value stored in int_ptr is " << int_ptr << endl;
      cout << "\nThe contents of int_ptr is " << *int_ptr << endl;
      cout << "\nThe value stored in flo_ptr is " << flo_ptr << endl;
      cout << "\nThe contents of flo_ptr is " << *flo_ptr << endl;
      cout << "\nThe value stored in char_ptr is " << char_ptr << endl;
      cout << "\nThe contents of char_ptr is " << *char_ptr << endl;

      void_ptr = &int_num;              //correct - void pointer set to point to
                                        //              int_num
      cout << "\nThe value stored in void_ptr is " << void_ptr << endl;

//    cout << "\nThe contents of void_ptr is " << *void_ptr << endl;
//    The attempt to "dereference" the void_ptr (access the contents) is
//    illegal.
//    There is no type information to guide the compiler in interpreting
//    the underlying data.

      void_ptr = &flo_num;              //correct - void pointer set to point to
                                        //              flo_num
      cout << "\nThe value stored in void_ptr is " << void_ptr << endl;

//    cout << "\nThe contents of void_ptr is " << *void_ptr << endl;
//    The attempt to "dereference" the void_ptr (access the contents) is
illegal.

      void_ptr = &char_let;             //correct - void pointer set to point to
                                        //              char_let
      cout << "\nThe value stored in void_ptr is " << void_ptr << endl;

//    cout << "\nThe contents of void_ptr is " << *void_ptr << endl;
//    The attempt to "dereference" the void_ptr (access the contents) is
illegal.
}
```

Program Analysis

Hopefully, the comments should explain what the program is doing. Run the program and look at the output.

```
void main()
```

The program enters **main()**.

```
int int_num = 582;
float flo_num = 258.05;
char char_let = 'I';
```

Three variables are declared and initialized: an integer, a float and a character.

```
int * int_ptr;
float * flo_ptr;
char * char_ptr;
void * void_ptr;
```

Four pointer variables are defined.

```
int_ptr = &int_num;          //pointer set to address of int_num
```

Several pointer assignments are then made (or were attempted to be made). The pointer is set to the address of **int_num**.

```
//   int_ptr = &flo_num;
```

This pointer assignment caused a compiler error. It is illegal. You can't assign the address of a float variable to an integer pointer.

```
//   int_ptr = &char_let;
```

This pointer assignment also caused a compiler error. It's illegal. You can't assign the address of a character variable to an integer pointer.

```
flo_ptr = &flo_num;
```

The pointer is set to the address of **flo_num**.

```
//   flo_ptr = &int_num;
```

This pointer assignment caused another compiler error. It's illegal. You can't assign the address of an integer variable to a float pointer.

191

```
//    flo_ptr = &char_let;
```

This pointer assignment also caused a compiler error. It's illegal. You can't assign the address of a character variable to a float pointer.

```
char_ptr = &char_let;
```

The pointer is set to the address of **char_let**.

```
//    char_ptr = &int_num;
```

This pointer assignment also caused a compiler error. It's illegal. You can't assign the address of an integer variable to a character pointer.

```
//    char_ptr = &flo_num;
```

This pointer assignment caused a compiler error. It's illegal. You can't assign the address of a float variable to a character pointer.

```
cout << "\nThe value stored in int_ptr is " << int_ptr << endl;
cout << "\nThe contents of int_ptr is " << *int_ptr << endl;
cout << "\nThe value stored in flo_ptr is " << flo_ptr << endl;
cout << "\nThe contents of flo_ptr is " << *flo_ptr << endl;
cout << "\nThe value stored in char_ptr is " << char_ptr << endl;
cout << "\nThe contents of char_ptr is " << *char_ptr << endl;
```

cout statements are used to output the variables' values and the variables' addresses, using either the name of the appropriate pointer with the indirection operator, or simply the name of the pointer.

```
void_ptr = &int_num;
```

The address of the integer variable is assigned to the **void** pointer. This is a correct assignment to the pointer.

```
cout << "\nThe value stored in void_ptr is " << void_ptr << endl;
```

The address, stored in the **void** pointer, is displayed on the screen using a **cout** statement.

```
//    cout << "\nThe contents of void_ptr is " << *void_ptr << endl;
```

However, the attempt to de-reference the **void_ptr** (access the contents) is illegal and causes a compiler error. This is because there is no type information to guide the compiler in interpreting the underlying data.

```
void_ptr = &flo_num;
cout << "\nThe value stored in void_ptr is " << void_ptr << endl;

//    cout << "\nThe contents of void_ptr is " << *void_ptr << endl;
```

The same operations are carried out in respect of the float variable and the character variable. In other words they assign the addresses to the **void** pointer, display the address of the variables on the screen, and attempt to de-reference the pointer. On both attempts to de-reference the pointer the compiler generated an error.

Pointers and Arrays

Pointers and arrays can be used in a similar way to access memory. There are some differences. A pointer is a variable that takes an address in memory as its value. An array name is the initial location in memory where the array elements are stored.

Since an array name is an address, it is also a pointer to its first element. However, the array can't be relocated in memory whilst the program is running so the address associated with the array name can't be changed.

We have already seen that array elements can be accessed using pointers (see the section on incremental operators earlier in the chapter). You will also recall that we can assign the address of an array to a pointer using the syntax below:

```
float table  [SIZE];
float * pointer;

pointer = table;
```

and we can then step through the array using syntax, such as:

```
pointer++;  or  *pointer++;  or  *(pointer++);
```

In fact, if **ptr** is a pointer to a specific element in an array then **ptr + 1** points to the next element. Generally, if **num** is an integer then **ptr + num** points **num** elements after **ptr**. Similarly, **ptr - num** points **num** elements before **ptr**.

Therefore, if **ptr** points to **table[0]** using the expression **ptr = table;** then ***(ptr + num)** refers to the contents of **table[num]**.

As an array name is a pointer to the first element in the array, then expressions involving **table[num]** can, for all practical purposes, be regarded as having been changed to ***(table + num)** and these two statements are equivalent and interchangeable.

Accessing Arrays Using Pointers - An Example

In Chapter 5 we looked at an example program which demonstrated how to access an array using a **for** loop. Statements from the program are shown below:

```
float table[SIZE];              //array of floats for data
float sum = 0.0;                //variable to sum array elements

cout << "Please enter five numbers: ";

//input data to array
for(counter = 0; counter < SIZE; counter++)
    cin >> table[counter];

//sum the elements in the array
for(counter = 0; counter < SIZE; counter++)
    sum += table[counter];
```

Array elements can also be accessed using pointer notation and the program **AVERAGE.CPP** has been re-written to demonstrate this:

```
/* **********************************************************
 *      average.cpp                                        *
 *      Ian M Wilks                                        *
 ********************************************************** */
#include <iostream.h>           //header file for input/output
#include <conio.h>              //header file for clrscr()

void main()
{
    const int SIZE = 5;                 //number of array elements
    int counter;                        //variable to be used in for-loop
    float table[SIZE];                  //array of floats for data
    float sum = 0.0;                    //variable to sum array elements
    float average;                      //variable to store answer
    float * flo_ptr;                    //pointer to float
```

```
        clrscr();                          //clears the screen

        cout << "This program prompts the user to enter five numbers\n"
             << "and then calculates the average of these numbers.\n\n"
             << "Please enter five numbers.";

        //input data to array
        for(counter = 0; counter < SIZE; counter++)
             cin >> *(table + counter);            //NOT *(table++)

        flo_ptr = table;

        //sum the elements in the array
        for(counter = 0; counter < SIZE; counter++)
             sum += *(flo_ptr++);

        //calculate average
        average = sum / SIZE;
        //output average
        cout << "\n\nThe average of the numbers input is " << average;
}
```

Program Analysis

Does this program do the same as the original version?

```
    float * flo_ptr;
```

The initial difference is that a pointer to a float variable is declared.

```
        cin >> *(table + counter);
```

The next is that when the data is input in the **for** loop the above statement is used. As we have discussed, the expression ***(table + counter)** has exactly the same effect as **table[counter]** in the original program.

For example, suppose that **counter = 2**, so the expression is equivalent to ***(table + 2)**. This represents the third element of the array (remember the first element of an array is numbered 0) because the name of an array is its address.

The expression **table + counter** is an address with something added to it.

As we saw in the section on incremental operators, in the case of a pointer the numeric change will be equal to the size of the object (in bytes) to which the pointer is pointing. So, as the compiler takes the size of data into account when arithmetic is performed on addresses, the third element of the array is accessed.

As we wish to take the value the indirection operator is used.

You will see from the comment in the program that you shouldn't use ***(table++)**. The name of an array is an address constant and a constant can't have its value changed. A pointer is a variable holding an address and can be incremented.

```
flo_ptr = table;
```

Study the statement. As you know, this assigns the address of the array table to the pointer. This now means that the contents of the array can be accessed using ***(flo_ptr++);**. The pointer expression in the brackets steps through the array elements and the indirection operator, *****, is used to access the data at these addresses.

```
for(counter = 0; counter < SIZE; counter++)
      sum += *(flo_ptr++);
```

This allows the array contents to be summed, using a **for** loop.

The pointer variable **flo_ptr** starts with the same address as **table**. This allows the first array element, **table[0]**, to be accessed as before. Now, as **flo_ptr** is a variable, it can be incremented to point to the next element in the array.

Pointers and Functions

The ampersand, &, is also used as the reference operation to pass arguments to functions. We will demonstrate this idea by first looking at a simple program which uses functions, and then modifying it showing how to pass arguments by reference using this operator.

Pointers and Functions - An Example

Look at the example first and then we'll discuss passing by reference.

```cpp
/* **********************************************************
 *    pointer7.cpp                                          *
 *    Ian M Wilks                                           *
 ********************************************************** */
#include <iostream.h>

void main()
{
    void swap(int x, int y);

    int first_num = 10;
    int second_num = 50;

    cout << "\nThe value of first_num is " << first_num << endl
         << "The value of second_num is " << second_num << endl;

    swap(first_num, second_num);

    cout << "\nThe value of first_num is now " << first_num << endl
         << "The value of second_num is now " << second_num << endl;
}

void swap(int x, int y)
{
    int local_int;

    local_int = x;
    x = y;
    y = local_int;

    cout << "\nIn the function first_num is " << x << endl
         << "In the function second_num is " << y << endl;
}
```

Program Analysis

The output generated by the program is shown below

```
The value of first_num is 10
The value of second_num is 50

In the function first_num is 50
In the function second_num is 10

The value of first_num is now 10
The value of second_num is now 50
```

Well, what's happening?

197

```
void main()
```

The program enters **main()**.

```
void swap(int x, int y);
```

A function prototype is declared. The function takes two integer arguments and doesn't return a value to the calling program.

```
int first_num = 10;
int second_num = 50;
```

Two variables are declared and initialized.

```
cout << "\nThe value of first_num is " << first_num << endl
     << "The value of second_num is " << second_num << endl;
```

cout is used to output the values assigned to the variables.

```
swap(first_num, second_num);
```

The function **swap()** is called with the two variables passed as the arguments.

If you look ahead to the function definition you will see that a local integer variable is declared. The value of the first argument to the function is assigned to the local variable. The value of the second argument is assigned to the first argument. Then the value of the local variable is assigned to the second argument.

In effect the values of the variables are swapped. The values of the variables are then displayed on the screen.

```
cout << "\nThe value of first_num is now " << first_num << endl
     << "The value of second_num is now " << second_num << endl;
```

Control then returns to **main()**. **cout** statements are used to display the value of the variables on the screen. The values assigned to the variables are the original values - no swap has occurred.

Passing by Value

In the example, our values didn't swap. Why not? When a variable is passed to a function as an argument, the original variable isn't actually passed. What happens is a copy of the variable is passed to the function. This is to prevent variables having their values altered unintentionally. This property is known as passing by value.

In this case, copies of the variables were passed into the function and these copies had their values altered. The original variables weren't altered.

Passing By Reference

Sometimes a programmer will want a function to alter the values stored in a variable, and C++ provides a mechanism for doing this. This is known as passing by reference.

A reference provides an alias, a different name, for a variable. By far the most important use for references is passing arguments to a function.

When arguments are passed by value (without the reference operator), the function called creates a new variable of the same type as the argument and copies the argument's value into it. The function doesn't have access to the original variable in the calling program. Passing arguments by value is useful when the function doesn't need to modify the original variable in the calling program. It offers insurance that the function can't harm the original variable.

Passing arguments by reference uses a different mechanism. Instead of a value being passed to the function, a reference to the original variable in the calling program is passed. The primary advantage of passing by reference is that the function can access the actual variables in the calling program.

Passing by Reference - An Example

Look at the following program which is almost identical to the last one.

```
/* ************************************************************
 *     pointer8.cpp                                          *
 *     Ian M Wilks                                           *
 ************************************************************ */
#include <iostream.h>
void main()
{
    void swap(int& x, int& y);
    int first_num = 10;
    int second_num = 50;

    cout << "\nThe value of first_num is " << first_num << endl
         << "The value of second_num is " << second_num << endl;

    swap(first_num, second_num);

    cout << "\nThe value of first_num is now " << first_num << endl
         << "The value of second_num is now " << second_num << endl;
}

void swap(int& x, int& y)
{
    int local_int;

    local_int = x;
    x = y;
    y = local_int;

    cout << "\nIn the function first_num is " << x << endl
         << "In the function second_num is " << y << endl;
}
```

Program Analysis

When you read through the source code you will see that there are only two changes to the program

1 In the function prototype

2 In the first line of the function definition

The difference is that **&**, the reference operator, has been added as a suffix to the argument types:

```
int&.
```

When you run the program you will see that the output is as follows:

```
The value of first_num is 10
The value of second_num is 50

In the function first_num is 50
In the function second_num is 10

The value of first_num is now 50
The value of second_num is now 10
```

Passing Arguments Using Pointers

However, it is possible to use pointers to pass the address of the argument to a function. This also allows the function to alter the original values.

Passing Arguments Using Pointers - An Example

Look at the following example which is similar to the last two programs:

```
/* **********************************************************
 *    pointer9.cpp                                          *
 *    Ian M Wilks                                           *
 ********************************************************** */
#include <iostream.h>

void main()
{
    void swap(int* x, int* y);

    int first_num = 10;
    int second_num = 50;

    cout << "\nThe value of first_num is " << first_num << endl
         << "The value of second_num is " << second_num << endl;

    swap(&first_num, &second_num);

    cout << "\nThe value of first_num is now " << first_num << endl
         << "The value of second_num is now " << second_num << endl;
}

void swap(int* x, int* y)
{
    int local_int;

    local_int = *x;
    *x = *y;
    *y = local_int;

    cout << "\nIn the function first_num is " << *x << endl
         << "In the function second_num is " << *y << endl;
}
```

Program Analysis

Run the program and you will see that the output is the same as in the last program.

The changes in the code are as follows:

```
void swap(int* x, int* y);
```

The function prototype shows that the function's arguments are pointers to integers.

```
void swap(int* x, int* y)
```

The first line of the function definition shows that the function's arguments are pointers to integers. In the function definition the indirection operator has to be used.

```
swap(&first_num, &second_num);
```

When **main()** calls the function it supplies the addresses of the variables as the arguments. Remember, the variables aren't being passed to the function. It is the addresses of the variables that are being passed.

```
local_int = *x;
*x = *y;
*y = local_int;
```

As **swap()** has been passed two addresses, indirection operators (***x** and ***y**) are used to access the values stored at these addresses.

This approach is similar to passing by reference. They both permit the variable in the calling program to be modified. However, the mechanism is different. A reference is an alias for the original variable, while a pointer is the address of the variable.

Passing Arrays to Functions - An Example

The following example passes integer arguments into a simple function using pointers. The code is simple and shouldn't present you with any difficulties. We will alter this program to show how arrays can be passed to functions.

```cpp
/* ***********************************************************
 *      point10.cpp                                         *
 *      Ian M Wilks                                         *
 *********************************************************** */
#include <iostream.h>

void main()
{
    void square(int* x);

    int first_num = 10;
    int second_num = 50;

    cout << "\nThe value of first_num is " << first_num << endl
         << "The value of second_num is " << second_num << endl;

    square(&first_num);
    square(&second_num);

    cout << "\nThe value of first_num is now " << first_num << endl
         << "The value of second_num is now " << second_num << endl;
}

void square(int* x)
{
    *x *= *x;

    cout << "\nIn the function the value is " << *x << endl;
}
```

Program Analysis

This program doesn't need much explanation and you should be able to see what's happening.

```cpp
    void square(int* x);
    .
    .
    .
    square(&first_num);
```

As you can see, the argument that is passed to the function is a pointer to integers. When **main()** calls the function it supplies the address of the variable as the argument.

```
void square(int* x)
{
    *x *= *x;

    cout << "\nIn the function the value is " << *x << endl;
}
```

As **square()** has been passed an address, the indirection operator (***x**) is used to access the value stored at the address.

It is fairly common to use pointer notation instead of array notation when arrays are passed to functions.

Functions With Arrays as Arguments - An Example

Look at the next example, which is a copy of the above program, but modified so that the function takes an array as its argument.

```
/* ********************************************************
 *    point11.cpp                                         *
 *    Ian M Wilks                                         *
 ******************************************************** */
#include <iostream.h>
void main()
{
    void square(int* x);
    const int MAXIMUM = 5;
    int new_array[MAXIMUM];

    //initialize array
    for (int i = 5; i < 10; i++)
        new_array[i - 5] = i;

    //put values on screen
    for (i = 0; i < 5; i++)
        cout << new_array[i] << "   ";

    square(new_array);

    cout << "\nThe value in the array are now " << endl;

    for (i = 0; i < 5; i++)
        cout << new_array[i] << "   ";
}

void square(int* x)
{
    for (int j = 0; j < 5; j++)
        *x++ *= *x;
}
```

Program Analysis

The function prototype for the function is the same as in the previous example. The function's argument is a pointer to integers. In array notation this would be written as:

```
void square(int[]);
```

In this case, **int*** is equivalent to **int[].**

As the name of an array is the address of the array, there is no need to use the address operator, **&**, when calling the function. Read through the source code and run the program. You shouldn't have any difficulty in understanding what the program is doing.

Pointers and Strings

Before we leave the subject of arrays we should consider strings. As you know, strings are one-dimensional arrays of characters. Therefore, pointers can be applied to characters in the strings, just as they can to elements in arrays.

The following example has two strings defined:

- One is defined as an array of characters

- One is defined as a pointer to characters

As you will see these two definitions are similar in several ways. Both strings can be displayed on the screen and both can be passed to functions as arguments.

Pointers and Strings - An Example

Run the following program to help you clarify the distinction.

```
/* **********************************************************
 *    point12.cpp                                          *
 *    Ian M Wilks                                          *
 ********************************************************** */
#include <iostream.h>

void main()
{
    char first_string[] = "C++ Programming is Fun";
    char * second_string = "Instant C++ Programming";

    cout << endl << first_string << endl;
    cout << second_string << endl;
```

```
//    first_string += 11;        //illegal - this is a constant
      second_string += 11;       //this is a pointer and can be incremented

      cout << " This book is part of the \"The Instant" << second_string << "\"
series.\n";
}
```

Program Analysis

Well, as you can see I have given you some help!

```
char first_string[] = "C++ Programming is Fun";
char * second_string = "Instant C++ Programming";
```

The difference is that **first_string** is an address (pointer) constant and
second_string is a pointer variable. Therefore, **second_string** can have its
value (address) changed but **first_string** can't.

Strings as Function Arguments - An Example

The following simple program, which shouldn't require any explanation,
demonstrates how to use strings as function arguments. This program has a
function which takes a character pointer as its argument. The function displays
the string on the screen using a **cout** statement.

```
/* ********************************************************
 *    point13.cpp                                         *
 *    Ian M Wilks                                         *
 ******************************************************** */
#include <iostream.h>

void main()
{
    void display(char * str_ptr);

    char str[] = "Instant C++ Programming.";

    display(str);
}

void display(char * str_ptr)
{
    cout << endl;
    while (*str_ptr)                 //equivalent to *str_ptr != 0
        cout << *str_ptr++;
    cout << endl;
}
```

As you can see the function displays the string by accessing each character.

Arrays of Pointers - An Example

As we have seen there are arrays of integers, floats, characters, and structures. You can also have arrays of pointers.

The following program demonstrates the use of an array of pointers. It is a useful program in that it demonstrates that memory can be saved using strings which aren't part of an array of characters. The program in itself is fairly simple and you should understand what's happening without any further explanation.

```
/* ***********************************************************
 *    point14.cpp                                           *
 *    Ian M Wilks                                           *
 ********************************************************* */
#include <iostream.h>

void main()
{
    int number;

    char * days[] = {"Sunday", "Monday", "Tuesday", "Wednesday",
                        "Thursday", "Friday", "Saturday"};

    cout << "\nEnter a number: ";
    cin >> number;
    while((number < 1) || (number > 7))
    {
        cout << "Please enter a number between 1 and 7: ";
        cin >> number;
    }
    number--;
    cout <<"\nThe day is " << days[number] << endl;
}
```

Program Analysis

Hopefully you understand what the program is doing. The program stores the days of the week (strings) in an array of pointers to characters.

The user is asked to enter a number, between 1 and 7, and the program then displays the appropriate day.

The following figure shows how strings, as part of a normal array, would be stored in memory.

	= Wasted space									
S	u	n	d	a	y	'\0'			
M	o	n	d	a	y	'\0'			
T	u	e	s	d	a	y	'\0'		
W	e	d	n	e	s	d	a	y	'\0'
T	h	u	r	s	d	a	y	'\0'	
F	r	i	d	a	y	'\0'			
S	a	t	u	r	d	a	y	'\0'	

Strings stored in memory in a conventional array

When strings aren't part of an array, C++ places them contiguously in memory, so there is no wasted space. See the next figure.

S	u	n	d	a	y	M	o	n	d
a	y	T	u	e	s	d	a	y	W
e	d	n	e	s	d	a	y	T	h
u	r	s	d	a	y	F	r	i	d
a	y	S	a	t	u	r	d	a	y

String stored in memory as an array of character pointers

Pointers and Structures - An Example

This example shows how you can use pointers to access the members of a structure. We also look at a new operator, `->`, which a pointer uses to refer to members of a structure.

```cpp
/* *********************************************************
 *    point16.cpp                                         *
 *    Ian M Wilks                                         *
 ********************************************************* */
#include <iostream.h>
#include <string.h>

void main()
{
    struct newType
    {
        char letter;
        int number;
    };

    newType struct_arr[10], one_more, * point;

    for(int i = 0; i < 10; i++)
    {
        point = struct_arr + i;

        (*point).letter = 'a' + i;
        (*point).number = 121 + i;
    }

    cout << endl;


    for(i = 0; i < 10; i++)
    {
        point = struct_arr + i;
        cout << i << " " << point->letter << " " << point->number << endl;
    }

    cout << endl;

    one_more = struct_arr[5];

    cout << "one_more: " << one_more.letter << " " << one_more.number
        << endl;

    *point = one_more;

    cout << "point: " << (*point).letter << " " << point->number << endl;
}
```

Program Analysis

```
void main()
```

The program enters **main()**.

```
struct newType
    {
        char letter;
        int number;
    };
```

A simple structure, **newType**, is defined.

```
newType struct_arr[10], one_more, * point;
```

newType variables are defined: a ten element array, a single structure variable, and a pointer to a structure.

```
for(int i = 0; i < 10; i++)
{
    point = struct_arr + i;

    (*point).letter = 'a' + i;
    (*point).number = 121 + i;
}
```

A **for** loop is used to assign values to the array. You will see that **point** is assigned the address of an element of the array and then uses the indirection operator to assign values into the structure members.

You will recall that **struct_arr** is an address constant and can't be changed in value but **point** is a pointer variable and can be assigned any value consistent with its being required to point to the structure.

Adding one to **point** will cause it to point to the next array element. The system knows that the structure contains two variables and it knows how many bytes are required to store the structure.

```
for(i = 0; i < 10; i++)
{
    point = struct_arr + i;

    cout << i << " " << point->letter << " " << point->number
        << endl;
}
```

A **for** loop is used to output the values contained in each structure in the array.

```
cout << i << " " << point->letter << " " << point->number << endl;
```

As before **point** is assigned the address of an element of the array and then uses a new operator, **->**, to access the structure members.

Referring to the members of a structure with a pointer occurs so often in C++ that a special operator was devised. Using **point->letter** is the same as using **(*point).letter**.

```
one_more = struct_arr[5];

cout << "one_more: " << one_more.letter << " " << one_more.number
    << endl;
```

An element of the array is assigned to the variable **one_more**. A **cout** statement is then used to output the values stored in this variable.

```
*point = one_more;
```

The values stored in **one_more** are then assigned to the pointer. ***point = one_more;**.

```
cout << "point: " << (*point).letter << " " << point->number << endl;
```

A **cout** statement is then used to output the values pointed to by the pointer.

Casting

Sometimes you will discover that the variable you are dealing with isn't in the form you require for a specific use. An example would be in programming graphical routines where it is sometimes necessary to assign a specific value to a pointer.

It is possible to cast one variable onto another. This allows a copy of a variable to be assigned to a variable of a different type. The syntax is:

```
variable1  =  (type)  variable2
```

where *type* is the type of the first variable.

For example, if you wish to assign an integer variable to a pointer to characters, you would use the expression:

```
char_ptr = (char *) int_var;
```

To assign the value of a float variable to a character variable, you would use the expression:

```
char_var = (char) float_var;
```

Summary

In this chapter you have seen how pointers are very useful in a number of different situations. You've learnt that pointers are variables that point to the address of another variable in memory. You've covered the basic uses of pointers and the mechanism of passing arguments to functions by value and by reference. You've also seen how to pass arrays to functions as arguments, and have looked at using pointers to access structure members.

Programming Exercises

1 Write a function called **copy_string()** that takes two arguments both being pointers to characters and copies one string to the other.

For example: **copy_string(char * source, char * dest);**

Write a program to test that the function works.

2 Write a function that takes two pointers to integers as its arguments and swaps the values if the first argument is greater than the second argument,

For example, **order(int * var1, int * var2);**

If **var1** holds the value 20 and **var2** holds the value 5 then after the function call **var1** will hold the value 5 and **var2** will hold the value 20.

Put the function in a program and test that it works correctly.

3 If you have an array of integers holding N numbers then it is possible to order them so that the smallest element would be at **array[0]** and the largest at **array[N-1]**. The elements in between will be such that **array[n + 1] > array[n]**.

The following function, taken together with the function you wrote for question 2, will accomplish this.

```
void bsort(int * ptr, int N)
{
    int i, j;

    for(i = 0; i < N - 1; i++)
        for(j = i + 1; j < N; j++)
            order(ptr+i, ptr+j);
}
```

Use this code to write a program that orders an array containing 25 integers.

Chapter

File Handling

As you start to write more complex programs you will start to use disk files and other ancillary equipment. This chapter examines some ways to perform these activities using C++ streams.

Input/output can be a difficult area in many languages because it depends on both the operating system and the hardware. C++ allows a programmer to use the input/output devices (disks, tapes, terminals, or printers) as if they were files.

In this chapter we cover:

- DOS predefined filenames for hardware devices
- Streams
- ofstream, ifstream, and fstream file objects
- Reading from and writing to files
- Checking for errors and the end-of-file marker
- File pointers
- Text files and binary files
- Output to the printer
- Command line arguments

DOS Filenames

The compiler has to be told what device the program will use. DOS predefines a number of special filenames for hardware devices:

Name	Device
CON	Console (keyboard and screen)
AUX or COM1	First serial port
COM2	Second serial port
PRN or LPT1	First parallel printer
LPT2	Second parallel printer
LPT3	Third parallel printer
NUL	Dummy (non-existent) device

Streams

A stream is a general name given to a flow of data. They are usually associated with input and output operations but really refer to the transfer of data from one object to another. For example, you can think of a function used to move data from one memory location to another as a stream operation.

Streams are your first real introduction to object-oriented programming. The stream library has many classes and they are arranged in a complex hierarchy. However, you don't need to know this to program input/output routines.

Streams bring many of the features of operator overloading and object-orientation to input and output routines. The goal was to allow uniform notation across the different types, allowing the compiler to work out the details. As you have already seen with output to the screen and input from the keyboard, stream statements use the following notation:

```
output_stream << typed_variable;
```

```
input_stream >> typed_variable;
```

The object is always put on the left-hand side of the operator. The operators indicate the flow of data from one object to another. Any C++ type can be used with input/output operations.

File Input/Output - An Example

The simplicity of stream operations are available for file operations.

Look at the example program below:

```
/* ************************************************************
 *    file1.cpp                                              *
 *    Ian M Wilks                                            *
 ************************************************************ */
#include <fstream.h>          //header file needed for file handling
                             //this header file includes iostream.h
                             //so there is no need to include it in
                             //this source code
void main()
{
    ofstream file_out("a:\\file1.txt");      //create file for output

    cout << "This program demonstrates file handling.\n\n";

    file_out << "Instant C++ Programming.\n";
    file_out << "by Ian M Wilks\n\n"
             << "Published by Wrox Press.\n";
}
```

Program Analysis

This program outputs some text into a file.

The program produces a text file which is a sequence of ASCII characters divided into lines. Each line is terminated with a newline character.

Read through the source code to see what the program is doing. Run the program to assist you (unless you alter the program, you will have to have a disc in the **a:** drive). If you perform a directory listing of the **a:** drive you will see that a file, **FILE1.TXT**, has been produced. Open the file, with any standard editor, and you will see what has been written to the file. This is shown below:

```
Instant C++ Programming.
by Ian M Wilks

Published by Wrox Press.
*****START*****
#include <fstream.h>          //header file needed for file handling
```

After the comment block, the **#include** directive is used to include the header file, **fstream.h**. This supports the file streams. The header file includes **iostream.h** if it has not already been included, so there's no need to put this statement in yourself.

```
void main()
```

The program enters **main()**

```
ofstream file_out("a:\\file1.txt");        //create file for output
```

This statement will be new to you. Let's examine it in more detail

ofstream file objects

ofstream is a class. A class is a user-defined type, and the class name can be used to declare variables, in the same way that types built into the language are used (like **int** and **char**).

In this case, an object called **file_out** has been defined to be a member of the **ofstream** class. In the same statement, **file_out** is initialized to the file name **A:\FILE1.TXT**. A full path name can be used but this isn't necessary if the file is in the current directory.

Two backslash characters are required to separate directories in the path name, because this is one of the special characters that are used in strings.

This initialization opens the disk file, and sets aside various resources for the file.

Basically, with this statement, you are defining an output file object that is associated with the filename. As no value is returned, you don't know whether this operation has been successful or not.

```
cout << "This program demonstrates file handling.\n\n";
```

A message is displayed on the screen using the **cout** statement.

```
file_out << "Instant C++ Programming.\n";
file_out << "by Ian M Wilks\n\n"
         << "Published by Wrox Press.\n";
```

The strings are then output to the file using the output file object you have defined, **file_out**, together with the **<<** operator.

Closing the File

When the program terminates, the object **file_out** goes out of scope. This calls the object destructor which closes the file. Therefore, there's no need for the file to be closed in the program. However, good programming practice means it would be prudent to close the file to ensure all the reading/writing has been completed. To close the file you would use the statement **file_out.close();**.

As you will have seen, when the program is run the strings are written to the file without being echoed to the screen.

Modify the program to output your own message to a file. Change the file name so that a new file is created. You can put a full path name in and then alter the code so that the file is created in the current directory.

Reading the File

To read the same file we need to create an object of class **ifstream**.

Reading the File - An Example

This is done in the following example, which opens the file, reads the text, and displays it on the screen. This program also demonstrates how to check that the file has been opened successfully before you attempt to read or write it.

```
/* *************************************************************
 *    file2.cpp                                               *
 *    Ian M Wilks                                             *
 ************************************************** */
#include <fstream.h>                //header file needed for file
handling

void main()
{
    const int MAXIMUM = 80;        //size of character store
    char store[MAXIMUM];                  //character store

    ifstream file_in("a:\\file1.txt"); //open file for output

    cout << "This program demonstrates file handling.\n\n";

    while(file_in)
    {
        file_in.getline(store, MAXIMUM);    //read a line of text
        cout << store << endl;          //output text to the screen
    }
}
```

Program Analysis

```
#include <fstream.h>
```

After the comment block, the **#include** directive is used to include the header file, **FSTREAM.H**.

```
void main()
```

The program enters **main()**.

```
const int MAXIMUM = 80;        //size of character store
char store[MAXIMUM];                //character store
```

A constant integer and a character array are declared.

```
ifstream file_in("a:\\file1.txt"); //open file for output
```

This statement is similar to the one in the previous program. However, the class being used now is **ifstream**. As you will recall, a class is a user defined type and is used to declare variables of that type.

The ifstream file object

In this case, an object called **file_in** has been defined to be a member of the **ifstream** class. In the same statement, **file_in** is initialized to the file name **A:\FILE1.TXT**. As before, the initialization opens the disk file and sets aside various resources for the file.

Basically, with this statement you are defining an input file object that's associated with the file name. As no value is returned, you don't know whether this operation has been successful.

Checking for Errors

Errors can occur during the course of stream operations. The program may try to open a file that isn't in the directory or read past the end-of-file. These and other conditions cause errors and it is your job, as the programmer, to detect any errors so they can be dealt with.

```
while(file_in)
```

There are several ways to test for errors and this program uses the **while** loop.

An **ifstream** object and an **ofstream** object have values that can be tested for error conditions. If an error occurs, the object returns a zero value. If an error doesn't occur, the object returns a non-zero value.

Therefore, **while(file_in)** is testing that no errors have occurred, in other words a non-zero value has been returned.

```
while(file_in)
{
    file_in.getline(store, MAXIMUM);
    cout << store << endl;
}
```

If no errors have occurred the statements in the loop are executed. The loop continues to be entered until either an error occurs or the end-of-file marker is encountered.

```
file_in.getline(store, MAXIMUM);
```

In this case, **file_in.getline()** reads the text from the file one line at a time. This function reads characters until it encounters the **\n** character, placing the characters in the string supplied as an argument to the function. The maximum size of the string is given as the second argument. The **getline()** function (see Chapter 5) is used because the insertion operator **<<** considers a blank space to be a terminating character.

```
cout << store << endl;
```

The **cout** statement displays the string after each line.

Another test that could have been done would have been to use an **if** statement as follows:

```
if(!file_in)
{
    ...
}
```

The **if** statement would have been entered if errors had occurred and could, therefore, contain statements to prevent the error continuing. This will be demonstrated later.

There are other tests you can do:

```
if (file_in.bad())
{
    ...
}
```

This tests to see whether errors have occurred.

```
if (file_in.eof())
{
    ...
}
```

This tests to see if the end-of-file marker has been encountered.

```
if (file_in.good())
{
    ...
}
```

This tests to see that no errors were encountered.

Checking for Errors in ofstream Objects

These tests can be used with **ofstream** objects as well.

Consider the following example:

```
/* ***********************************************************
 *     file2a.cpp                              *
 *     Ian M Wilks                             *
 *********************************************************** */
#include <fstream.h>          //header file for file I/O

void main()
{
     //open existing file
     ifstream infile("a:\\file1.txt");
     //open a file and truncate it
     ofstream copy_file("a:\\copy1.txt");

     //check for errors when opening file
     if(!infile)
          cout << "\nCould not open a:\\file1.txt\n";

     if(!copy_file)
          cout << "\nCould not open a:\\copy1.txt\n";

     //copy file
     while(infile && copy_file)
     {
          char store[80];
          infile.getline(store, sizeof(store) );
          copy_file << store << endl;
     }
}
```

Program Analysis

Read through the source code to see what the program is doing. You shouldn't have any problems with this as the example simply incorporates the first two programs.

```
#include <fstream.h>          //header file for file I/O
```

After the comment block, the **#include** directive is used to include the header file, **FSTREAM.H**.

```
void main()
```

The program then enters **main()**.

```
ifstream infile("a:\\file1.txt");
```

An **ifstream** object, **infile**, is declared and initialized with the file
A:\FILE1.TXT. As with the earlier examples, the initialization opens the disk
file and sets aside various resources for the file.

```
ofstream copy_file("a:\\copy1.txt");
```

An **ofstream** object, **copy_file**, is declared and initialized with the file
A:\COPY1.TXT. the initialization opens the disk file and sets aside various
resources for the file.

```
if(!infile)
        cout << "\nCould not open a:\\file1.txt\n";

if(!copy_file)
        cout << "\nCould not open a:\\copy1.txt\n";
```

if statements are then used to check that the files have been opened without
error.

```
while(infile && copy_file)
{
        char store[80];
        infile.getline(store, sizeof(store) );
        copy_file << store << endl;
}
```

A **while** loop is then used which tests that the end-of-file marker hasn't been
reached in either file. While this condition is true the **getline()** function is
used to read the characters on a line until the **\n** character is encountered,
placing the characters in the string supplied as an argument to the function.
The maximum size of the string is given as the second argument.

```
copy_file << store << endl;
```

The program then writes the string to the **copy_file**.

The put() and get() Functions

The **put()** function outputs a single character at a time and the **get()** function inputs a single character at a time.

The following code fragment shows how the **put()** function can be used with a **for** loop to output the contents of a string.

```
for(int i = 0; i < MAX; i++)
    file_out.put(lineOfText[i]);
}
```

Similarly, the following code fragment shows how the **get()** function can be used in a **while** loop to read a character.

```
while(file_in)
{
    file_in.get(ch);
    cout << ch;
}
```

Binary Files

Binary files can also be used as output or input files. Binary files deal with binary values, not characters. The data is stored in the file as a sequence of bytes and makes no assumption as to how these bytes should be handled.

Binary files do not contain *white space* characters (spaces or tabs) and is not organized into lines with newline characters. However, there is no problem with using binary files.

Binary Files - An Example

The following program uses binary files to store a series of employee records. A structure has been used to define a type called **Data** which contains four elements:

- A character string to hold **first_name**
- A character string to hold **surname**
- An integer variable to hold **age**
- A float variable to hold **salary**

The program is used to enter the employee's details into a binary file.

Read through the code and you should be able to understand what's happening. There is only one new expression in the code and this relates to the opening of the file. As you will see, opening the file is the same as for text files except that the **ios::binary** flag is passed to the open function.

```cpp
/* ***********************************************************
 *    file5.cpp                                             *
 *    Ian M Wilks                                           *
 *********************************************************** */
#include <fstream.h>

struct Data
{
    char first_name[15];
    char surname[25];
    int age;
    float salary;
};

void enter_data(Data&);

void main()
{
    Data employee;

    ofstream employ_record("a:\\file5.dat", ios::binary);

    //check for errors
    if(!employ_record)
        cout << "\nCould not open file\n";

    char ch;

    do{
        if(employ_record)
        {
            enter_data(employee);
            employ_record.write((char *) &employee, sizeof(employee) );
            cout << "\nEnter another? (Y/N): ";
            cin >> ch;
        }
    }while((ch == 'y') || (ch == 'Y'));
}


void enter_data(Data& x)
{
    cout << "\nEnter first_name: ";
    cin >> x.first_name;
    cout << "Enter surname: ";
    cin >> x.surname;
    cout << "Enter age: ";
    cin >> x.age;
    cout << "Enter salary: ";
    cin >> x.salary;
}
```

226

Program Analysis

```
#include <fstream.h>
```

After the comment block, the **#include** directive is used to include the header file, **FSTREAM.H**.

```
struct Data
{
    char first_name[15];
    char surname[25];
    int age;
    float salary;
};
```

The structure is then defined.

```
void enter_data(Data&);
```

The next statement is a function prototype, **enter_data**.

If you look ahead to the function definition, you will see that the **enter_data()** function is called to prompt the user to enter the information which is placed in the structure variable, **employee**.

```
void main()
```

The program enters **main()**.

```
Data employee;
```

A structure variable, **employee**, is declared.

```
ofstream employ_record("a:\\file5.dat", ios::binary);
```

An **ofstream** object, **employ_record**, is declared and initialized with the file **A:\FILE5.DAT**. The **ios::binary** flag is also passed to the open function. The initialization opens the disk file in binary mode.

```
    if(!employ_record)
        cout << "\nCould not open file\n";
```

An **if** statement is used to check that the file has been correctly opened.

```
    char ch;
```

A character variable, **ch**, is declared.

```
    do{
        if(employ_record)
        {
            enter_data(employee);
            employ_record.write((char *) &employee, sizeof(employee) );
            cout << "\nEnter another? (Y/N): ";
            cin >> ch;
        }
    }while((ch == 'y') || (ch == 'Y'));
```

An **if** statement is used to check that the end-of-file marker has not been encountered and that no other errors have occurred. Provided this is correct, the statements in the braces of the **if** statement are executed.

A **do-while** loop is entered. The user is asked in the loop if another record is to be entered. If the user enters **Y** or **y** at the keyboard, the loop is re-entered to enable another record to be added.

```
void enter_data(Data& x)
{
    cout << "\nEnter first_name: ";
    cin >> x.first_name;
    cout << "Enter surname: ";
    cin >> x.surname;
    cout << "Enter age: ";
    cin >> x.age;
    cout << "Enter salary: ";
    cin >> x.salary;
}
```

The function **enter_data()** is called to prompt the user to enter the data. This data is stored in the **Data** variable, **employee.**

The write() function

The contents of the structure variable, **employee**, are written to the file, using the **write()** function. This function takes two arguments: the address of the variable to be written using the address of operator, **&**, and the size of the variable in bytes. The **sizeof** keyword is used to find the size of the variable. As this function has been defined as follows:

```
ostream& write ( const signed char*, int n );
ostream& write ( const unsigned char*, int n );
```

the address of the variable must be cast to be a pointer to **char**.

The user is asked if another record is to be written. The answer given by the user determines whether the loop continues.

Reading From the File

To work correctly, a program that reads data from a file written by the above program must work with the same type of variable. Therefore, a program written to read from the file, created by the above program, must use the same structure. If, for example, two programs thought the surname field was a different length neither could read a file generated by the other. The data must have the same format.

Reading the data back from the file requires the use of the **read()** function which takes the same arguments as the **write()** function. Again the address of the variable must be specifically cast to be a pointer to **char**.

The read() Function - An Example

The program which follows illustrates the use of the **read()** function. The program is similar to the last example and you should have no difficulty in understanding what the program does.

```cpp
/* *************************************************************
 *     file6.cpp                                              *
 *     Ian M Wilks                                            *
 ************************************************************ */
#include <fstream.h>

struct Data
{
    char first_name[15];
    char surname[25];
    int age;
    float salary;
};

void display_data(Data&);

void main()
{
    Data employee;
    ifstream employ_record("a:\\file5.dat", ios::binary);

    //check for errors
    if(!employ_record)
        cout << "\nCould not open file\n";

        while(employ_record)
        {
            employ_record.read((char *) &employee, sizeof(employee) );

            //to prevent last record being output twice
            if(!employ_record.eof())
                display_data(employee);
        }
}

void display_data(Data& x)
{
    cout << endl << x.first_name << " " << x.surname << endl
        << "aged " << x.age << "  Annual Salary £" << x.salary  << endl;
}
```

Program Analysis

```
#include <fstream.h>
```

After the comment block, the **#include** directive is used to include the header file, **FSTREAM.H**.

```
struct Data
{
    char first_name[15];
    char surname[25];
    int age;
    float salary;
};
```

The structure is then defined. This is the same structure that was used in the last program.

```
void display_data(Data&);
```

The next statement is a function prototype, **display_data**.

If you look ahead to the function definition, you will see that the **display_data()** function is called to display the information on the screen.

```
void main()
```

The program then enters **main()**.

```
Data employee;
```

A structure variable, **employee**, is declared.

```
ifstream employ_record("a:\\file5.dat", ios::binary);
```

An **ifstream** object, **employ_record,** is declared and initialized with the file **A:\FILE5.DAT**. the **ios::binary** flag is also passed to the open function. The initialization opens the disk file in binary mode.

```
        if(!employ_record)
             cout << "\nCould not open file\n";
```

An **if** statement is used to check that the file has been correctly opened.

```
        while(employ_record)
        {
             employ_record.read((char *) &employee, sizeof(employee) );
             if(!employ_record.eof())
                  display_data(employee);
        }
```

A **while** loop is entered and is used to test that no errors have occurred and that the end-of-file marker has not been detected - i.e. a non-zero value has been returned.

In the while loop the **read()** function is used to read a record which is stored in the structure variable **employee.**

```
        if(!employ_record.eof())
```

An **if** statement is used to check that the end-of-file marker has not been encountered to prevent the last record from being displayed twice.

```
        display_data(employee);
```

The **display_data()** function is used to display the record(s) on the screen.

File Pointers

Each file object has two integer values associated with it. These are called:

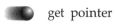 get pointer

  put pointer

These values signify the location, specified in bytes, where reading or writing will occur. (Note - the term pointer in this context does not refer to the normal C++ pointers used as address variables.)

What are they used for? The default actions allow an existing file to be read from the beginning continuing to the end. When writing to a file, the default action deletes any existing contents and starts writing from the beginning. Alternatively, if the file is opened with the **ios::app** flag the existing contents will not be deleted and writing to the file will start at the end.

However, there are times when you will want to control the file pointers so that they can read from and write to any location in the file. The **seekg()** and **tellg()** functions allow the programmer to set and examine the get pointer, and the **seekp()** and **tellp()** functions do the same for the put pointer.

File Pointers - An Example

Look at the following example:

```
/* ***********************************************************
 *     file7.cpp                                            *
 *     Ian M Wilks                                          *
 ************************************************************ */
#include <fstream.h>

struct Data
{
    char first_name[15];
    char surname[25];
    int age;
    float salary;
};

void display_data(Data&);

void main()
{
    Data employee;
    int number;

    ifstream employ_record("a:\\file5.dat", ios::binary);

    //check for errors
    if(!employ_record)
        cout << "\nCould not open file\n";

    employ_record.seekg(0, ios::end);
    int endOfFile = employ_record.tellg();
    int NoOfRecords = endOfFile / sizeof(employee);

    cout << "\n\nThere are " << NoOfRecords << " in the file.\n";
    cout << "Enter person number: ";
    cin >> number;
```

```
    int position = (number - 1) * sizeof(employee);
        employ_record.seekg(position);

        employ_record.read((char *) &employee, sizeof(employee) );
        display_data(employee);
    }

    void display_data(Data& x)
    {
        cout << endl << x.first_name << " " << x.surname << endl
            << "aged " << x.age << "  Annual Salary £" << x.salary << endl;
    }
```

Program Analysis

Read through the code to ascertain what the program is doing. Run the program as this will assist you.

You have encountered most of this code earlier in the chapter and these notes will only relate to code you have not previously seen.

As you can see, this program uses the `seekg()` function and the `tellg()` function. The `seekg()` function can be used in two ways. The first is where a single argument represents a position in the file. The start of the file is byte 0.

The second is using the `seekg()` with two arguments. The first argument represents an offset from a specific location in the file, and the second stipulates the location from where the offset is measured. There are three possibilities for the second argument, `beg` is the beginning of the file, `cur` is the current pointer position, and `end` is the end of the file. For example, the statement:

```
seekg(-20, ios::end);
```

will set the get pointer to 20 bytes before the end of the file.

This program uses the two-argument version of `seekg()` to find a particular employee record in the file and to display that data.

```
employ_record.seekg(0, ios::end);
```

The program does this by first calculating how many records are in the file. It does this by using the statement to position the get pointer at the end of the file.

```
int endOfFile = employ_record.tellg();
int NoOfRecords = endOfFile / sizeof(employee);
```

The program uses the `tellg()` function to return the pointer position at the end of the file - this is the length of the file in bytes. The program calculates how many records are in the file, by dividing by the size of the variable employee.

```
int position = (number - 1) * sizeof(employee);
employ_record.seekg(position);

employ_record.read((char *) &employee, sizeof(employee) );
display_data(employee);
```

The program then moves to the specified person object by using this code. It then reads one record of data starting from this point and displays the result.

Using a Program to Read and Write to a File

In the examples that we have looked at, the programs have created file objects that were either for input or output. However, sometimes you will want a file that can be read from and written to. This requires a slightly different approach.

The following code creates a file object that can be used for both input and output:

```
fstream employ_record;
```

The file object is created in the above statement but the file has not been specified or opened. To open the file we have to use the `open()` function:

```
employ_record.open("a:\\file5.dat", ios::app | ios::in | ios::out);
```

As you can see, three mode bits are included to specify certain aspects of the file object. The table below shows the possibilities.

Mode Bit	Result
in	open for reading (default for ifstream)
out	open for writing (default for ofstream)
app	start reading or writing at end of file (APPend)
ate	erase file before reading or writing (truncATE)
nocreate	error when opening if file does not already exist
noreplace	error when opening for output if file already exists, unless ate or app is set
binary	open file in binary (not text) mode

If the contents of the file are to be preserved **ios::app** is used. That means the program can write to the file and whatever is written will be at the end of the file. **ios::in** and **ios::out** would be used if the file is to be used both for input and output. The vertical bars between the flags cause the bits representing the flags to be logically **'OR'ed'** together, so several flags can be used simultaneously.

Using the File Object for both Input and Output

The file can then be used:

```
//check for errors
if(!employ_record)
    cout << "\nCould not open file\n";


employ_record.write((char *) &employee, sizeof(employee) );


employ_record.seekg(position);
employ_record.read((char *) &employee, sizeof(employee) );


employ_record.seekp(0);
while(employ_record)
{
    employ_record.read((char *) &employee, sizeof(employee) );
    if(!employ_record.eof())
        display_data(employee);
}
```

Putting It All Together

The example program that we have looked at will either read or write to a file. In a normal situation your program will read and write to a file depending on the options selected. It is likely that you will write functions to do various things - add records, read all the records, read a specific record and so on.

We will write some functions for a program which you can finish.

Writing a Program to Display a Menu with Options

This program will display a menu on the screen giving the user various options. The options will be:

- Add a Record
- Read a Record
- Read all Records
- Exit from the Program

There will be an initial message that says how many records are in the file. The user will press a number between 1 and 4. This value will be returned to **main()** to be used with a switching variable.

For example:

```
menu_option = menu();
```

In writing the function, we will need to open the file which we will assume is FILE5.DAT. This file is a binary file and in this function we need to read from it:

```
employ_record.open("a:\\file5.dat", ios::in | ios::binary);
```

As normal we will check that there are no errors.

```
if(!employ_record)
    cout << "\nCould not open file\n";
```

We now want to calculate the number of records in the file so that a suitable message can be displayed.

```
employ_record.seekg(0, ios::end);
endOfFile = employ_record.tellg();
NoOfRecords = endOfFile / sizeof(employee);
```

After the function has obtained the information that is needed from the file, we will close the file. The user may want to exit from the program immediately.

The Menu() Function

We should now be able to write the **menu()** function. Have a go.

```
int menu()
{
    int select;            //variable used to select option

    //open file and check for errors
    employ_record.open("a:\\file5.dat", ios::in | ios::binary);
    if(!employ_record)
        cout << "\nCould not open file\n";

    //calculate number of records in file
    employ_record.seekg(0, ios::end);
    int endOfFile = employ_record.tellg();
    int NoOfRecords = endOfFile / sizeof(employee);

    //output appropriate message
    cout << "At the present time there are " << NoOfRecords
        << " records in the file.\n";

    //display menu
    cout << "\n\t\tDo you wish to\n"
        << "\t1\tAdd a Record\n" << "\t2\tRead a Record\n"
        << "\t3\tRead all Records\n"
        << "\t4\tExit from the Program\n"  << "\nEnter number: ";

    //obtain user's selection
    cin >> select;

    //close the file
    employ_record.close();

    //return selection
    return(select);
}
```

The add_record() Function

The next function we will consider is the **add-record()** function. However, this function will use the **enter_data()** function which has to be slightly modified so that it can write the values into the variable **employee**. The **enter_data()** function is shown below. Basically the variable will be passed by reference.

```
void enter_data(Data& x)
{
    cout << "\nEnter first name: ";
    cin >> x.first_name;
    cout << "Enter surname: ";
    cin >> x.surname;
    cout << "Enter age: ";
    cin >> x.age;
    cout << "Enter salary: ";
    cin >> x.salary;
}
```

We will need to open the file so that records can be added at the end of the file. We will also check for errors.

```
employ_record.open("a:\\file5.dat",ios::app | ios::out |ios::binary);
//check for errors
if(!employ_record)
    cout << "\nCould not open file\n";
```

A call to the **enter_data()** function will prompt the user to enter the appropriate data.

The record will then be written to the file.

```
employ_record.write((char *) &employee, sizeof(employee) );
```

The file should again be closed.

Have a go at writing this function. In case you have any problems a suggested function is shown after the programming exercises.

The read_record() Function

The next function we will consider is the **read_record()** function. This function will read one of the records in the file. It makes use of the **display_data()** function which we have seen previously. The **display_data()** function has to be modified slightly so that the record can be passed as an argument.

```
void display_data(Data& x)
{
        cout << endl << x.first_name << " " << x.surname << endl
               << "aged " << x.age << "  Annual Salary £" << x.salary
               << endl;
}
```

The read_record() function will open the file and check for errors.

```
employ_record.open("a:\\file5.dat", ios::app |ios::out | ios::binary);
//check for errors
if(!employ_record)
        cout << "\nCould not open file\n";
```

The user will be asked to specify the record number. You could consider checking that the answer is greater than 0 and less than or equal to the number of records.

The program will have to move to the appropriate record.

```
position = (record - 1) * sizeof(employee);
employ_record.seekg(position);
```

Then the record can be read and the data can be displayed on the screen.

There is a function called **getch()** which will halt the program until a key is pressed. It would be useful to use this function so that the user can read the information on the screen and then press a key when ready to continue. You will have to include the header file **CONIO.H**.

Remember to close the file after you have finished.

Have a go at writing this function. A suggested answer is at the end of the chapter.

The read_all() Function

You should also write a function that displays all the records on the screen. You will have to modify the **read_record()** function.

Putting the Functions Together

Now that all the functions have been written you should write a program that uses a switch statement to call the functions. A skeleton may be like the following:

```
int menu_item = menu();
switch(menu_item)
{
    case 1:
            add_record();
            break;
    case 2:
            read_record();
            break;
    case 3:
            read_all();
            break;
    case 4:
            cout << "The program is now ending.";
            break;
    default:
            cout << "The number should be between 1 and 4."
                << " Try again.";
            sleep(6);          //waits on screen for 6 seconds
}                              //needs header file dos.h
```

Sending Output to the Printer

Sending data to the printer is similar to writing data to a file. The following example program demonstrates how to do this.

```
/* ***********************************************************
*     printer.cpp                                          *
*     Ian M Wilks                                          *
************************************************************ */
#include <fstream.h>        //header file for file i/o
#include <stdlib.h>         //header file for exit()

void main()
{
    const int MAX = 80;

    char * Message1 = "Instant C++ Programming";
    char * Message2 = "Scrape by in C++";
    char * Message3 = "Published by Wrox Press";

    char buffer[MAX];          //to store line of text read from input file
    char ch;                   //to store a character from input file

    ofstream printer("PRN");        //file object defined and initialized
```

241

```
    //output above strings
    printer << Message1 << endl << Message2 << endl << Message3 << endl;

    printer << endl << "Now from a file" << endl;

    //open file to read text from
    ifstream infile("a:\\file1.txt");

    if(!infile)
    {
        cout << "Unable to access file\n";
        exit(1);                    //exit from program if file error
    }


    while(infile)
    {
        //get a line of text
        infile.getline(buffer, MAX);
        if(!infile.eof())          //to avoid printing last line twice
            printer << buffer << endl;
    }

    infile.close();                    //close file

    printer << endl << "Now from the file again" << endl;

    //open input file
    infile.open("a:\\file1.txt", ios::in);

    while(infile.get(ch) != 0)              //get character one at a time
    {                                   //until end-of-file marker
        printer.put(ch);
    }
}
```

Program Analysis

```
#include <fstream.h>        //header file for file i/o
#include <stdlib.h>         //header file for exit()
```

After the comment block the **#include** directive is used to include the header file **FSTREAM.H** needed for file input/output routines and the header file **STDLIB.H** needed for the function **exit()**.

```
void main()
```

The program then enters **main()**.

```
const int MAX = 80;

char * Message1 = "Instant C++ Programming";
char * Message2 = "Scrape by in C++";
char * Message3 = "Published by Wrox Press";
char buffer[MAX];        //to store line of text read from input file
char ch;                 //to store a character from input file
```

A constant integer is declared followed by three character pointers initialized to hold messages. A character string is declared to be used as a buffer to hold a line of text and a character variable is declared to hold a single character.

```
ofstream printer("PRN");       //file object defined and initialized
```

A file object, **printer**, is defined and initialized using the DOS filename **PRN**.

```
printer << Message1 << endl << Message2 << endl << Message3 << endl;
```

The three character strings are sent to the printer using this statement:

```
printer << endl << "Now from a file" << endl;
```

Another message is sent to the printer.

```
ifstream infile("a:\\file1.txt");
```

A file object, **infile**, is declared and initialized. This opens the file for reading.

```
if(!infile)
    {
        cout << "Unable to access file\n";
        exit(1);                 //exit from program if file error
    }
```

An **if** statement is used to test for errors. If there is an error, for example if the file is not in the specified directory, a message will be displayed and the **exit()** function will cause the program to terminate.

```
while(infile)
{
    //get a line of text
    infile.getline(buffer, MAX);
    if(!infile.eof())          //to avoid printing last line twice
        printer << buffer << endl;
}
```

A **while** loop is then used to check if the end-of-file marker is encountered. Until the marker is encountered the statements between the braces will be executed.

You have seen this code before and should be able to see what is happening. The while loop is testing whether the end-of-file marker has not been reached and while the marker is not encountered the **getline()** function is used to read the characters on a line until the **\n** character is encountered, placing the characters in the string supplied as an argument to the function. The maximum size of the string is given as the second argument.

```
printer << endl << "Now from the file again" << endl;
```

The program then writes the string to the printer.

```
infile.close();
```

The file is then closed.

```
infile.open("a:\\file1.txt", ios::in);
```

Another message is output to the printer, then the file is opened again.

```
while(infile.get(ch) != 0)              //get character one at a time
{                                       //until end-of-file marker
    printer.put(ch);
}
```

This time another while-loop is used to obtain a single character from the file and output it to the printer.

244

The statement **infile.get(ch)** means that the program is getting a character from the file in the while-loop 'test'. This character is tested to see that it is not equal to 0. If it was equal to 0 it would mean that the end-of-file marker had been encountered. While the marker is not detected the character is output to the printer and the loop is re-entered.

Command Line Arguments

Most people will be familiar with command line arguments, used when invoking a program from DOS. It is fairly common to pass an argument to a program when the program is invoked from the command line. They are typically used to pass the name of a data file to an application.

For example, if you are using the WordPerfect word-processing program you might invoke it with the command:

```
wp  cppayf09.doc
```

In this case you are passing the name of a document, **CPPAYF09.DOC**, to the program, **WP**, as a command line argument.

Information about command line arguments is passed by the operating system to the entry function of the program. In the case of a C++ program the command line argument(s) would be passed to **main().**

To make use of these arguments **main()** needs to be told how many arguments there are and where to find them. This is achieved by giving **main()** two arguments. Traditionally they are normally called **argc** and **argv**.

For example:

```
void main(int argc, char * argv[])
{
    ...
}
```

- **argc** is an integer variable used to record the number of arguments

- **argv** is an array of character pointers.

Command Line Arguments - An Example

Consider the following example:

```
//testprog.cpp
#include <iostream.h>

void main(int argc, char *argv[])
{
    cout << "\nargc = " << argc;
    for (int i = 0; i < argc; i++)
        cout << "\nArgument " << i << " = " << argv[i];
}
```

Compile the program and then run it from the command line with two or three arguments.

Sample output from the program would be:

```
testprog Wrox Press

argc = 3
Argument 0 = testprog.exe
Argument 1 = Wrox
Argument 2 = Press
```

The first command line argument is always the program. The remaining command line arguments are those typed by the user, separated by the space characters.

The command line arguments are stored in an array of pointers to characters - they are stored as strings. The strings are accessed through the appropriate pointer, so the first string is **argv[0]**, the second is **argv[1]**, etc.

The arguments are accessed in turn and displayed in a **for** loop that uses **argc**, the number of command-line arguments, as its upper limit.

If you write a program that accepts three command line arguments, for example **copy file1.cpp file2.cpp**, then you can test that the correct number of arguments have been given using a statement like,

```
if (argc != 2)
{
    cout << "\nFormat: copy source-file destination-file";
    exit(-1);
}
```

Programming Exercises

1 Write a program that opens a text file and writes your name, address, age, and telephone number to the file.

2 Write a program that opens the text file you created in Question 1, read the information and display it on the screen.

3 Write a program that opens the text file you created in Question 1 and write your date of birth and occupation to the file.

Use the program you created in Question 2 to check you have written to the file correctly.

4 Repeat Questions 1, 2 and 3 but this time use a binary file.

5 Write a program that outputs the text file to the printer.

Now write another program that outputs the binary file to the printer.

6 Write a program called **SIZE** which takes the name of a file as a command line argument and writes to the screen the size of that file in bytes.

7 Write a file that imitates the DOS print command.

The following function is a possible solution for the **add_record()** function.

```
void add_record()
{
        employ_record.open("a:\\file5.dat",ios::app | ios::out |
                           ios::binary);
        //check for errors
        if(!employ_record)
            cout << "\nCould not open file\n";

        enter_data(employee);
        employ_record.write((char *) &employee, sizeof(employee) );
        cout << endl << endl << "Press a key to continue ...";
        employ_record.close();
        getch();
}
```

The following function is a possible solution for the **add_record()** function.

```
void add_record()
{
    employ_record.open("a:\\file5.dat", ios::in |
                            ios::binary);
    //check for errors
    if(!employ_record)
        cout << "\nCould not open file\n";
    cout << "Which record do you wish to read? ";
    cin >> record;
    cout << endl << endl;
    position = (record - 1) * sizeof(employee);
    employ_record.seekg(position);
    employ_record.read((char *) &employee, sizeof(employee) );
    display_data(employee);
    cout << endl << endl << "Press a key to continue ...";
    employ_record.close();
    getch();            //this function will cause the program to
}                //wait until a key is pressed
```

The following function is a possible solution for the **read_all()** records function.

```
void read ()
{
    employ_record.open("a:\\file5.dat", ios::in | ios::binary);
    //check for errors
    if(!employ_record)
        cout << "\nCould not open file\n";
    employ_record.seekg(0, ios::beg);
    while(employ_record)
      {
        employ_record.read( (char *) &employee, sizeof(employee) );
          if(!employ_record.eof() )    //to prevent last record
          display_data(employee);      //being output twice
      }
    cout << endl << << "Press a key to continue ...";
    employ_record.close();
    getch();
}
```

Chapter

Overloading

Overloading functions is one of the most powerful features in C++. In simple terms, when you overload a function, or indeed an operator, you define multiple versions of it. The elegance of multiple functions isn't initially obvious.

C++ distinguishes between functions of the same name with a simple method - if you want to use the same name, the **type** of the function has to be different in each case. You might ask why not just define the return type differently for each version? You can't, because it would appear as a simple re-declaration error. The compiler needs to be able to match the number and the type of the arguments involved in the function. This isn't a drawback, because if you have these parameters to play with, you can vary the number and type of arguments, or vary the argument and the return type. This gives you dynamic and flexible control over functions in your program, and can help you to extend existing code.

This chapter covers:

- Function overloading
- Operator overloading
- Readable code using overloading
- Binary and unary overloading

Function Overloading

C++ allows you to define two or more functions with the same name, providing that either their number of arguments or their argument type differs.

Your First Overloaded Function - An Example

Look at this example:

```
/* ************************************************************
 *    disp_num.cpp                                           *
 *    Ian M Wilks                                            *
 ************************************************************ */
#include <iostream.h>          //header file for input/output


//function prototypes
void display_num(int i);            //function 1
void display_num(float f);          //function 2


void show_num(float f1);            //function 3
void show_num(float f1, float f2); //function 4


void main()
{
    int integer = 10;
    float fl_number1 = 3.14, fl_number2 = 9.81;

    cout << "\n\tA Program to Demonstrate Overloaded Functions.\n\n";

    display_num(integer);
    display_num(fl_number1);

    show_num(fl_number1);
    show_num(fl_number1, fl_number2);
}


void display_num(int i)                     //function 1
{
    cout << "\n\n\tThis function display_num() takes an integer argument.\n"
         << "\tThe integer number passed to the function is " << i << endl;
}

void display_num(float f)                   //function 2
{
    cout << "\n\n\tThis function display_num() takes a float argument.\n"
         << "\tThe real number passed to the function is " << f << endl;
}

void show_num(float f1)                     //function 3
{
```

```
        cout << "\n\n\tThis function show_num() takes a single float argument.\n"
            << "\tThe real number passed to the function is " << f1 << endl;
}

void show_num(float f1, float f2)        //function 4
{
        cout << "\n\n\tThis function show_num() takes two float arguments.\n"
            << "\tThe real numbers passed to the function are " << f1
              << " and " << f2 << endl;
}
```

Program Analysis

```
void display_num(int i);           //function 1
void display_num(float f);         //function 2

void show_num(float f1);           //function 3
void show_num(float f1, float f2); //function 4
```

Four function prototypes are declared: two of them are called
display_num(),and the other two are called show_num().

The display_num() functions differ as to their argument *types*. One of them
takes an integer as an argument, and the other takes a float.

The show_num() functions differ as to the *number* of arguments they take. One
of them takes a single float argument, and the other takes two float arguments.

```
void main()
```

The program enters main().

```
    int integer = 10;
    float fl_number1 = 3.14, fl_number2 = 9.81;
```

An integer and two float variables are declared and initialized.

```
    cout << "\n\tA Program to Demonstrate Overloaded Functions.\n\n";
```

The cout statement is used to display a message.

```
display_num(integer);
```

The function **display_num()** is called with an integer argument. The compiler can distinguish between the two **display_num()** functions because of the different argument types.

The function labeled **function 1** is called, and the program produces the following output:

```
This function display_num() takes an integer argument.
The integer number passed to the function is 10
```

```
display_num(fl_number1);
```

The function **display_num()** is called with a float argument.

The function labeled **function 2** is called and the program produces the following output:

```
This function display_num() takes a float argument.
The real number passed to the function is 3.14
```

```
show_num(fl_number1);
```

The function **show_num()** is called with a single float argument.

The compiler can distinguish between the two **show_num()** functions because of the different number of arguments that each function takes. Therefore, the function labeled **function 3** is called and the program produces the following output:

```
This function show_num() takes a single float argument.
The real number passed to the function is 3.14
```

```
show_num(fl_number1, fl_number2);
```

The function **show_num()** is called with a two float argument.

The function labeled **function 4** is called and the program produces the following output:

```
This function display_num() takes two float arguments.
The real numbers passed to the function are 3.14 and 9.81
```

Function Overloading - Example 2

Look at the following example:

```cpp
/* ************************************************************
 *    do_it.cpp                                              *
 *    Ian M Wilks                                            *
 ************************************************************ */
#include <iostream.h>

//function prototypes
int do_it(int i);
float do_it(float f);
int do_it(float f1, float f2);

void main()
{
    int i_number = 5;
    float f_number1 = 6.5, f_number2 = 7.9;

    cout << "\n\n\tThis Program Demonstrates Function Overloading.\n";

    cout << "\n\tThe integer version: " << i_number << " squared = "
        << do_it(i_number) << endl;

    cout << "\n\tThe float version: " << f_number1 << " doubled = "
        << do_it(f_number1) << endl;

    cout << "\n\tThe version which takes two arguments, returning an int: "
        << "\n\tTakes " << f_number1 << " and " << f_number2
        << " and returns " << do_it(f_number1, f_number2) << endl;
}


int do_it(int i)
{
    return(i*i);
}


float do_it(float f)
{
    return(f+f);
}


int do_it(float f1, float f2)
{
    int i1 = (int) f1, i2 = (int) f2;
    return((i1*i1*i1) - (i2+i2));
}
```

In this case there are three functions called `do_it()`. These functions differ as to the type or number of their arguments.

253

At this stage, you should have no difficulty in understanding what's happening, and no further explanation should be needed.

Standard Library Functions

Defining several functions with the same name is *technically* known as overloading. Besides functions written by you the programmer, standard functions can also be overloaded.

For example:

```
double sqrt(double arg);

int sqrt(int arg);
```

The first function is the normal library function. You have to supply the second version. The compiler decides which version to use, by looking at the argument *types* in the call.

Converting Function Types

The integer version of the function `sqrt()` would be useful if you were writing a program that made several calls to this function. As this function would only use integer arithmetic, it can be faster than the standard function.

Newton-Raphson Function

How would we write the integer version of the `sqrt()` function? A formula based on the Newton-Raphson iteration function (well known in numerical analysis circles!) is shown below:

```
(x + A/x)/2
```

This formula is applied iteratively until a solution to the required degree of accuracy is achieved.

An Example

How to find +8 using this formula.

Start with an initial estimate of 1 as being the square root, and then apply the formula:

```
(1     + 8/1  )/2  = 9/2     = 4.5
(4.5   + 8/4.5)/2   = 6.28/2  = 3.138
(3.138 + 8/3.138)/2 = 5.697/2 = 2.844
(2.844 + 8/2.844)/2 = 5.657/2 = 2.828
(2.828 + 8/2.828)/2 = 5.657/2 = 2.828
```

This gives an answer of 2.828, which is correct to three decimal places.

We can, therefore, write the integer version of the function.

```
int sqrt (int arg)
{
    int prev_x, z, x = 1;

    do
    {
        z = arg/x;
        prev_x = x;
        x = (x + z)/2;
    }while(x != prev_x && x != z);
    return(x);
}
```

Function Taken to Integer - An Example

Your custom function can then be utilized at full speed. We've installed it into the next example program:

```
/* ************************************************************
 *    sqrt.cpp                                               *
 *    Ian M Wilks                                            *
 ********************************************************** */
#include <iostream.h>         //header file for i/o
#include <math.h>             //header file for standard sqrt()

int sqrt( int);

void main()
{
    const int MAX = 5000;
    int i_number1 = 25, i_number2 = 300, i_root;
    float f_number1 = 25.00, f_number2 = 300.00, f_root;
```

```
        cout << "\n\n\tThis Program Demonstrates Overloaded Functions.\n\n"
             << "\tThe program will compute the square root of 25 and 300\n"
             << "\tusing both functions 5000 times to see which is quicker.\n\n";

        for (int i = 0; i < MAX; i++)
            i_root = sqrt(i_number1);              //our version of sqrt()
        cout << "The integer square root of " << i_number1 << " is "
             << i_root << endl << endl;

        for (i = 0; i < MAX; i++)
            f_root = sqrt(f_number1);              //library version of sqrt()
        cout << "The square root of " << f_number1 << " is "
             << f_root << endl << endl;

        for (i = 0; i < MAX; i++)
            i_root = sqrt(i_number2);              //our version of sqrt()
        cout << "The integer square root of " << i_number2 << " is "
             << i_root << endl << endl;

        for (i = 0; i < MAX; i++)
            f_root = sqrt(f_number2);              //library version of sqrt()
        cout << "The square root of " << f_number2 << " is "
             << f_root << endl << endl;
}


int sqrt (int arg)
{
        int prev_x, z, x = 1;

        do
        {
                z = arg/x;
                prev_x = x;
                x = (x + z)/2;
        }while(x != prev_x && x != z);
        return(x);
}
```

Program Analysis

You'll see that the function we wrote is used when the program calls **sqrt()** with an integer argument.

Operator Overloading

In our earlier section on function overloading, we saw that for the compiler to be able to identify a function, not only is its name required, but the number and type of its arguments are also required. In order to use operators with user-defined data types, we can also overload most, though not all, of the existing C++ operator set.

You have to overload the operator for it to effect your newly defined data type. For example, the division operator / performs integer arithmetic if its two operands are both integers. It will perform floating-point arithmetic if at least one of the operands has floating-point type.

Usable Operators

You've seen that a standard function, like **sqrt()**, can be overloaded. Operator overloading works in a similar way. Although you can define operators to work with user defined data types, overloading can only be done with the following existing operators:

+ -	*	/	%	^	& |	~	!	=	<
> +=	-=	*=	/=	&=	^=	&=	|=	<<	>>
>>=	<<=	==	!=	<=	>=	&&	||	++	--
,									
->*	->	()	[]	new	delete				

The precedence of the operators can't be changed. For example, if you define the operators + and * for use on your data, the precedence of * will be higher than +.

> The four operators: * , & , + , - , may be used in either binary or unary forms - depending on where they are placed in an expression

Overloading Operator Syntax

To overload an operator you use the following syntax:

```
type operator opr (arguments);
```

type represents a user-defined type.

This is followed by the operator keyword, the operator itself, and the arguments to be passed to the overloaded operator.

Practical Operator Overloading

To discuss operator overloading we'll use a structure called **point** which is defined as follows:

```
struct point
{
    int x, y, z;
};
```

This may represent a point on a three-dimensional graph. We can add the points together as follows:

```
point p1 = {1,2,3}, p2 = {2,3,4), p3;
p3.x = p1.x + p2.x;
p3.y = p1.y + p2.y;
p3.z = p1.z + p2.z;
```

It would be simpler if we could use the statement **p3 = p1 + p2;**.

Overloading the + Operator - An Example

The following program will overload the addition operator **+** for points so that we can use the statement **p3 = p1 + p2;**.

```
/* ***********************************************************
 *    operator.cpp                                          *
 *    Ian M Wilks                                           *
 *********************************************************** */
#include <iostream.h>


struct point
{
    int x, y, z;
};
```

```
point operator+(point &a, point &b);

void main()
{
    point p1 = {2, 3, 4}, p2 = {4, 5, 6}, p3;

    p3 = p1 + p2;              //p3 should equal 6, 8, 10

    cout << "Point p3 = {" << p3.x << ", " << p3.y << ", " << p3.z
        << "} " << endl;
}


point operator+ (point &a, point &b)
{
    int ax = a.x, bx = b.x, ay = a.y, by = b.y, az = a.z, bz = b.z;
    point t = {ax + bx, ay + by, az + bz};
    return(t);
}
```

Program Analysis

Setting the Prototype

```
struct point
{
    int x, y, z;
};
```

The structure **point** is declared. The structure contains three integer variables, **x**, **y**, and **z**, which could represent the coordinates in a three-dimensional graph.

The following statement occurs:

```
point operator+(point &a, point &b);
```

This is a new statement. It's the prototype for the definition which is at the end of the program.

Look ahead to the definition:

```
point operator+ (point &a, point &b)
{
    int ax = a.x, bx = b.x, ay = a.y, by = b.y, az = a.z, bz = b.z;
    point t = {ax + bx, ay + by, az + bz};
    return(t);
}
```

In this case there are two arguments (both point variables). You can visualize the arguments as **a + b**, where the first parameter is on the left-hand side of the operator, and the second parameter is on the right. (At this point, you should note that when we move to object-oriented programming there are some differences - Appendix B has further information on this).

As you can see, the overloaded operator function declares six integer variables which are initialized to the values held in the point variables.

```
ax + bx, ay + by, az + bz.
```

A point variable is declared and initialized to hold the values above.

This variable is then returned to the calling function - **main()**.

Definition Details

You should note that the first line of the definition (and the prototype) has almost the same form as

```
point add(point &a, point &b)
```

which is of a function **add()**, and which could have been defined instead. In that case, you would have used the statement

```
p3 = add(p1, p2);
```

instead of the more convenient statement

```
p3 = p1 + p2;
```

Returning to Program Analysis

```
void main()
```

The program enters **main()**.

```
point p1 = {2, 3, 4}, p2 = {4, 5, 6}, p3;
```

Three point variables are declared and two of them are initialized.

```
p3 = p1 + p2;            //p3 should equal 6, 8, 10
```

p3 is then assigned the value produced by the expression **p2 + p3**.

```
cout << "Point p3 = {" << p3.x << ", " << p3.y << ", " << p3.z
     << "} " << endl;
```

The values of the variable **p3** are displayed.

Readable Code Using Overloading

When we looked at Structures in Chapter 7, we considered an example program where two **yardsFeetInches** variables were added together. We developed the following function.

```
yardsFeetInches add_measure(yardsFeetInches mm1,
                            yardsFeetInches mm2)
{
    yardsFeetInches ans;
    ans.yards = mm1.yards + mm2.yards;
    ans.feet = mm1.feet + mm2.feet;
    ans.inches = mm1.inches + mm2.inches;

    while (ans.inches > 12 )
    {
        ans.inches -= 12;
        ans.feet++;
    }

    while (ans.feet > 3 )
    {
        ans.feet -= 3;
        ans.yards++;
    }

    return(ans);
}
```

261

In that example you were asked to alter the program. In *this* case, we've altered it to incorporate an overloaded operator. This means that instead of using the statement:

```
m3 = add_measure(m1, m2);
```

we can use the statement

```
m3 = m1 + m2;
```

Overloading for Readability - An Example

Look at the example program:

```
/* *********************************************************
 *     over14.cpp                                          *
 *     Ian M Wilks                                         *
 ********************************************************* */
#include <iostream.h>          //header file for input/output

struct yardsFeetInches
{
    int yards;
    int feet;
    float inches;
};

yardsFeetInches operator+(yardsFeetInches mm1, yardsFeetInches mm2);

void out_measure(yardsFeetInches m);

void main()
{
    yardsFeetInches m1, m3, m2 = {2, 2, 9.75};

    cout << "This Program Demonstrates Overloading Operators.\n\n"
         << "Please enter yard, feet and inches: ";
    cin >> m1.yards >> m1.feet >> m1.inches;

    m3 = m1 + m2;

    out_measure(m1);
    cout << " + ";
    out_measure(m2);
    cout << " = ";
    out_measure(m3);
}

void out_measure(yardsFeetInches m)
{
    cout << m.yards << "yd " << m.feet << "ft " << m.inches << "in";
}
```

```
yardsFeetInches operator+ (yardsFeetInches mm1, yardsFeetInches mm2)
{
    yardsFeetInches ans;

    ans.yards = mm1.yards + mm2.yards;
    ans.feet = mm1.feet + mm2.feet;
    ans.inches = mm1.inches + mm2.inches;

    while (ans.inches > 12 )
    {
        ans.inches -= 12;
        ans.feet++;
    }

    while (ans.feet > 3 )
    {
        ans.feet -= 3;
        ans.yards++;
    }

    return(ans);
}
```

Program Analysis

```
struct yardsFeetInches
{
    int yards;
    int feet;
    float inches;
};
```

A structure specifier is declared for the structure **yardsFeetInches** which has three simple variables - **int yards**, **int feet** and **float inches**.

```
yardsFeetInches operator+(yardsFeetInches mm1, yardsFeetInches mm2);

void out_measure(yardsFeetInches m);
```

There are then two function prototypes: the overloaded operator + and **out_measure()**.

The overloaded function is very similar to the initial version of **add_measure()**. Note how the **while** statement is used to check if **m3.inches** is greater than 12. If it *is* greater than 12, **m3.inches** is reduced by 12 and **m3.feet** is incremented. A similar procedure is used to check if **m3.feet** is greater than 3.

Why is a **while** loop used? In this example, an **if** statement would have sufficed. (Why don't you alter all the example programs as an experiment and see?) You may have a value such as 13 yards 17 feet 39 inches before the **while** loop. If an **if** statement is used it would alter the value to 14 yards 15 feet 27 inches when, in fact, the value should be 19 yards 2 feet 3 inches.

Therefore, the **while** loop has been used in case this happens, and you have several **yardsFeetInches** variables being added together.

```
void main()
```

The program enters **main()**.

```
    yardsFeetInches m1, m3, m2 = {2, 2, 9.75};
```

yardsFeetInches variables are defined: **m1**, **m3** and **m2**.

```
        m2 = {2, 2, 9.75}
```

m2 is initialized to hold the values **2 yards 2 feet 9.75** inches using the expression.

```
        cout << "This Program Demonstrates Overloading Operators.\n\n"
             << "Please enter yard, feet and inches: ";
```

cout is used to display a message on the screen and asks the user to enter some data.

```
        cin >> m1.yards >> m1.feet >> m1.inches;
```

cin is used to store the data in **m1**.

```
        m3 = m1 + m2;
```

m1 and **m2** are added together and the answer is stored in **m3**.

```
    out_measure(m1);
    cout << " + ";
    out_measure(m2);
    cout << " = ";
    out_measure(m3);
```

The values and the answer are then displayed on the screen.

Binary and Unary Overloading

Nearly all the operators can be altered. Binary operators have a left and a right side operand (as in addition and subtraction operations). When the compiler defines and overloads our functions, it makes use of the left and right side operands when forming its arguments. The arguments it generates (to pass to overloaded components) will be in direct relation to the operands that are active at that point in the evaluation

Binary and Unary Overloading - An Example

The next example returns to the structure **point**. As well as overloading the operator **+** in this example, we also overload the **binary minus** operator and the **unary minus** operator.

```
/* ***********************************************************
 *    oper.cpp                                              *
 *    Ian M Wilks                                           *
 *********************************************************** */
#include <iostream.h>

struct point
{
    int x, y, z;
};

point operator+(point &a, point &b);
point operator-(point &a, point &b);
point operator-(point &b);

void display(point &a);

void main()
{
    point p1 = {2, 3, 4}, p2 = {4, 5, 6}, p3, p4, p5;

    p3 = p1 + p2;           //p3 should equal {6, 8, 10}
    p4 = p3 - p2;           //p4 should equal {2, 3, 4}
    p5 = -p2;          //p5 should equal {-4, -5, -6}
```

```
        cout << "\nPoint p3 =";
        display(p3);
        cout << "\nPoint p4 =";
        display(p4);
        cout << "\nPoint p5 =";
        display(p5);
    }

    void display(point &a)
    {
        cout << " {" << a.x << ", " << a.y << ", " << a.z << "} " << endl;
    }


    point operator+ (point &a, point &b)
    {
        int ax = a.x, bx = b.x, ay = a.y, by = b.y, az = a.z, bz = b.z;
        point t = {ax + bx, ay + by, az + bz};
        return(t);
    }

    point operator- (point &a, point &b)
    {
        int ax = a.x, bx = b.x, ay = a.y, by = b.y, az = a.z, bz = b.z;
        point t = {ax - bx, ay - by, az - bz};
        return(t);
    }

    point operator- (point &b)
    {
        int bx = b.x, by = b.y, bz = b.z;
        point t = {-bx, -by, -bz};
        return(t);
    }
```

Program Analysis

Initial Program Declarations

```
    struct point
    {
        int x, y, z;
    };
```

The structure **point** is declared. The structure contains three integer variables, **x, y,** and **z**.

```
point operator+(point &a, point &b);
point operator-(point &a, point &b);
point operator-(point &b);
```

Three overloaded operator function prototypes are declared. These are explained below.

Binary Overloaded Operator

Look ahead to the definitions. The operator **+** function is defined as before. This type of operator is known as a binary operator because it has two operands associated with it; that is, **operand1 + operand2**.

The **operator -** function, which has two arguments, is also a binary operator. It's defined in a similar way to the **operator +** function, except that the following statement is obviously different:

```
point t = {ax - bx, ay - by, az - bz};
```

Unary Overloaded Operator

The other **operator -** function only takes one argument. This is a unary operator because it only has one operand, the **- operand**. When this operator is applied using the statement:

```
p5 = -p2;
```

the values that were stored in **p2**, that is, **{4, 5, 6}**, are transformed to **{-4, -5, -6}**.

The prototype for the function **display()** is then declared. This function simply displays the values stored in the point variables on the screen.

Final Program Analysis

```
void main()
```

The program enters **main()**.

```
point p1 = {2, 3, 4}, p2 = {4, 5, 6}, p3, p4, p5;
```

Five point variables are declared, and two of these are initialized.

267

```
p3 = p1 + p2;          //p3 should equal {6, 8, 10}
```

p3 is then assigned the value produced by the expression **p2 + p3**.

```
p4 = p3 - p2;          //p4 should equal {2, 3, 4}
```

p4 is then assigned the value produced by the expression **p3 - p2**.

```
p5 = -p2;       //p5 should equal {-4, -5, -6}
```

p5 is then assigned the value produced by the expression **-p2**.

```
cout << "\nPoint p3 =";
display(p3);
cout << "\nPoint p4 =";
display(p4);
cout << "\nPoint p5 =";
display(p5);
```

The values of the variables **p3, p4**, and **p5** are then displayed on the screen.

Passing By Reference

You will have noticed that the arguments to the overloaded operators have been passed by reference. It isn't necessary to do this, but it can be a good idea. As you'll recall, an argument passed by value generates a copy of itself in the function to which it's passed. In a large program, a lot of memory can be wasted because of this. Values passed by reference don't generate copies, and therefore help to save memory.

Summary

This chapter has introduced you to a very powerful C++ feature - overloading. We've seen how readable code can be created using this technique. You've seen how both functions and operators can be overloaded. In the next chapter we'll discuss the importance of testing your programs and making them work before we move on to object-oriented programming.

Programming Exercises

1 Write a program that has three functions called **add()**. One of the functions is to add integers, one is to add floats, and one is to add doubles.

2 Write a program that has four functions called **what_is_it()**. The functions make no return but will output to the screen a message saying what type of variable has been passed to the function and the value of the variable.

The functions should identify integer values, float values, characters, and strings.

3 Use the program that contains the **yardsFeetInches** structure, **OVERL4.CPP**, and create an overloaded operator- for the binary operator used in subtractions.

Create additional variables by subtracting one from the other. What will you do if you have to subtract 1 yard 2 feet 3 inches from 4 yards 1 feet 6 inches?

yards	feet	inches
4	1	6
1	2	3
2	2	3

4 Use the program that contains the **yardsFeetInches** structure, **OVERL4.CPP**, and create an overloaded operator – for the unary operator.

Create additional variables such that **var3 = -var2**.

Chapter

Making Programs Work

In this chapter we'll look at a few areas that need to be covered before we move on to object-oriented programming.

This chapter covers:

- Program testing
- Top-down and bottom-up testing
- Syntax errors
- Run-time errors
- Logic errors
- Organization of memory
- Testing to check if allocation is successful
- Linked lists
- The terseness of C++

Defensive Programming

What is defensive programming? It's where the programmer takes responsibility for ensuring that incorrect or bad data doesn't cause a problem. The main idea is that if a function or routine is passed incorrect or bad data the program ensures that nothing is damaged.

The best form of defensive programming is ensuring that there are no errors (bugs) in the code.

A good program will ensure that if the user enters incorrect data, or garbage, then an error message is issued. This means that the program should ensure that input data is in the allowable range, numeric values are within thresholds. Function arguments should be checked to ensure that they are in the correct range. Array bounds should be checked. Return values from functions should be tested.

The aim of defensive programming is to guard against unexpected errors and to prevent data loss.

Testing

Once your program is written you'll need to test the program and, if errors are found, debug it. There will be errors (bugs) in your early programs. All programmers accept this fact.

Before you can debug your programs you have to know that there are bugs. You must test all the programs you write.

Why do we have to do this? Most people consider that it's to prove that the program works correctly.

You should create a suite of test data that is drawn up to test the functions and routines to the limit. You want enough data to ensure that every line of code is tested. You need to test every possible path through a program and every boundary - maximum and minimum. You should test with the wrong type of data, as this is what the user may well do the first time they use your program.

How do we test? When you look in manuals on software engineering you'll often read about bottom-up testing **and** top-down testing.

If you're using a modular method of programming, that is, you've broken the program down into functions, you can test each function as you write it. This method of testing is bottom-up testing. You start at the lowest level of your program and work your way up through the levels, testing at each stage.

Although bottom-up testing is efficient because it proves that the individual functions in your program are working correctly and there are no bugs in them, it's not very good at testing whether the program has been designed properly. To do this you need to reverse the method of testing and test from the top-down.

Top-down testing is a fairly involved process. Basically, the top-level control functions are tested. You do this by substituting lower level functions with dummy functions providing enough support to allow the higher level functions to work.

For example, suppose that your **main**() function calls the **menu**() function that returns values in the range from 1 to 4. You'd replace the **menu**() function with a dummy that would not display a menu or request an input. The dummy function would simply return a preset value to test the higher level function. You could experiment with this method, using the program you may have written in Chapter 9 that included a **menu**() function.

This method of testing then continues by testing all the functions at a higher level before going down through the levels, testing all functions at each stage.

Your testing will discover three types of errors:

- Syntax errors
- Run-time errors
- Logic errors

Syntax Errors

Syntax errors arise when the rules of the programming language have been disobeyed, when keywords have been mis-typed or omitted, or punctuation has been misused.

They are the easiest type of error to find as the computer warns you of their existence. They aren't, however, always easy to put right.

Let's have a look at a few of the more frequent mistakes of this type.

Missing Semi-Colon

This is probably the most common mistake and is often made by experienced programmers. The compiler will usually spot this error, although it may indicate the line after the missing semi-colon.

Errors will be of the kind:

```
cout << "This is obviously a mistake\n"
```

Semi-Colon in the Wrong Place - An Example

This is a harder mistake to find as the compiler may not regard this as an error.

```
//fault1.cpp
#include <iostream.h>

void main()
{
    cout << "\t\tTest program.\n\n\t\tfor-loop starting\n";
    for(int i = 0; i < 10; i++);
        cout <<"\n\t\tInside for-loop";
}
```

Program Analysis

Read through the code - what will happen? Run the program to see if you're right or not.

The expected output is:

```
Test Program

for-loop starting

inside for-loop
inside for-loop
inside for-loop
inside for-loop
inside for-loop
inside for-loop
inside for-loop
inside for-loop
inside for-loop
inside for-loop
```

However, the resulting output is:

```
Test Program

for-loop starting

inside for-loop
```

The actual **for** loop is a loop that does nothing, and these loops are allowed.

Similar errors can occur with other loops and conditional statements.

Braces

Braces can be another source of error. If you omit an opening or closing brace the compiler may flag this as an error.

However, you normally use the brace to group two or more statements together so they can be treated as a single statement.

One problem in C++ is that braces are not always required in certain positions. For example:

```
if(number < MAX)
    number++;
```

and

```
if(number < MAX)
{
    number++;
}
```

are both correct. As you know, if there's more than one line of code to be performed after a test, then it must be in braces.

```
if(number < MAX)
{
    number++;
    do_it();
}
```

The following is valid code but isn't what was intended.

```
while(i < MAX)
    array[i] = function1();
    i++;
```

Assignments or Equality

The C++ test for equality is **==** and the C++ assignment operator is **=**. It's easy to enter:

```
if(number = MAX)
```

when what should have been entered was this:

```
if (number == MAX)
```

This is, of course, a legal statement in C++. It will be true provided **MAX** does not equal **0**.

Run-Time Errors

These come to light when the program has been compiled and is running. They are due to correct commands that breach some mathematical or logic rule; for example, in a program that tries to divide a number by zero.

These types of errors will appear when you're testing the program. For example, the formula   **f'(x0) = [f(x0 + h) - f(x0 - h)]/2h** is a formula for calculating the approximate value of the derivative of a numerical function at one point.

Run-Time Errors - An Example

The program that follows would calculate approximate values. Read through the program to see if you can spot the error. It may not be obvious at first.

```
//num_meth.cpp
#include <iostream.h>
#include <math.h>

void main()
{
    double h = 1;
    double x = 0;

    //function prototype
    double f(double );

    do
    {
        h -= 0.1;
        cout << "f'(0) = " << (f(x + h) - f(x - h))/(2 * h)
            << endl;
```

```
    }while (h != 0);
}

double f (double x)
{
    return (exp (x));
}
```

Did you see the error?

You'll see that **h** is reduced on each pass through the loop. Eventually, **h** will equal **0.** What will happen?

When **h** is equal to zero it will be used to do a division which will cause the program to crash. A simple **if** statement prior to the division should prevent this error.

Logic Errors

These arise when the program has been poorly designed. It might branch off at the wrong place. It may appear to run correctly but give incorrect results.

These problems will only come to light when you're testing the program. You must perform tests that will generate a value you can check.

These errors are harder to find. You may have to check on the values of variables at various points in the program.

Debugging

Debugging occurs as a result of testing. Once the program has been compiled, (you've cured the syntax problems) you can run the program with some test data. You must compare the actual results with the expected results.

If the actual results differ from the expected results can you identify the reason? It may be a trivial error where a typing error has resulted in you entering a value for the constant PI as 2.14159... instead of 3.14159...!
Remember that you're trying to discover the errors.

You should keep the following in mind when trying to debug a program:

 The error may temporarily disappear when you correct another error.

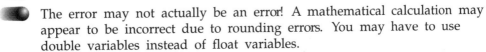 The error may not actually be an error! A mathematical calculation may appear to be incorrect due to rounding errors. You may have to use double variables instead of float variables.

277

Is a function altering the copy of an argument rather than the original argument? Alternatively, is a function altering the original variable when it should be working with a copy?

It's not possible to give a detailed list of instructions for you to follow to be able to debug a program.

You'll find that at times reading through the code and looking at the output produced with test data is not enough to find the error. A useful technique is to include statements in your program that display important data values at various points in the program. When you examine the output and compare the values of the variables you should be able to locate an area in the program that needs further investigation.

If necessary you can continue with this technique until the debugging information is displayed after each statement in the source code.

Debugging Tools

It may be that your compiler comes with debugging tools, like the debugger supplied with Borland C++. If your compiler does have debugging tools you're advised to learn how to use them.

Good debugging tools allow you to set breakpoints so that execution pauses when a certain line is reached. They allow the program to be stepped through line-by-line and data values can be examined.

Dynamic Memory Allocation

All of the variables we've been using in our programs have been declared in the source code. As programmers, we have to know what variables we want to use and what size the arrays should be.

This chapter looks at variables that were not declared in the source code. They are created by the program when it's running. This is known as dynamic memory allocation.

With these techniques we can create as many variables as we need, use them, and de-allocate their space for use by other variables.

Memory Management

The ability to manage memory from inside your program, to grab sections of free memory, use them for storing data and then to release that memory, is one of the stronger facets of C++.

It's important that you understand some of the concepts behind these facilities.

When a program is compiled certain memory locations will be allocated. These will vary according to a number of factors - one of which is the memory model you are compiling under. Basically, memory is divided into four areas.

The first region is the memory that holds the program code. The next section is the region where global variables are stored. The stack is used for many things while the program executes. It holds the return address of function calls, arguments to functions, and local variables. The heap is a region of free memory which the program can use for dynamic allocation.

Memory Management - An Example

Consider the program that follows. When you look at the source code see how many variables are declared for use within the program. Remember that a structure specifier doesn't reserve space for the storage of variables.

```
/* **********************************************************
 *    dynam1.cpp                                            *
 *    Ian M Wilks                                           *
 ********************************************************** */
#include <iostream.h>        //header file for i/o
#include <string.h>          //header file for string operations

struct Data
{
    char first_name[15];
    char surname[25];
    int age;
    float salary;
};

void display_data(Data *);

void main()
{
    Data *employee1, *employee2, *employee3;
    employee1 = new Data;   //reserve memory dynamically
```

```
        //insert some data
        strcpy(employee1->first_name, "Ian");
        strcpy(employee1->surname, "Wilks");
        employee1->age = 39;
        employee1->salary = 15000;


        employee2 = employee1;  //employee2 now points to the above data

        //employee1 can be re-used
        employee1 = new Data;          //reserve memory space dynamically

        strcpy(employee1->first_name, "Susan");
        strcpy(employee1->surname, "Wilks");
        employee1->age = 38;
        employee1->salary = 12500;


        employee3 = new Data;          //reserve memory space dynamically

        strcpy(employee3->first_name, "Chris");
        strcpy(employee3->surname, "Smyth");
        employee3->age = 27;
        employee3->salary = 20000;

        //display results
        display_data(employee1);
        display_data(employee2);
        display_data(employee3);

        employee1 = employee3;

        delete(employee2);
        delete(employee3);
   //   delete(employee1):                     //cannot be done.
    }

    void display_data(Data * x)
    {
        cout << x->first_name << " " << x->surname << endl
            << "Aged " << x->age << "  salary £" << x->salary << endl;
    }
```

Program Analysis

Read through the source code and run the program to help you understand
what's happening.

There are only two new statements in the code.

```
#include <iostream.h>        //header file for i/o
#include <string.h>          //header file for string operations
```

After the comment block the **#include** directive is used to include the header files **IOSTREAM.H**, for input/output operation, and **STRING.H**, for string handling.

```
struct Data
{
    char first_name[15];
    char surname[25];
    int age;
    float salary;
};
```

A structure is then defined. This is the structure we've been using in some of the previous examples and should present us with little difficulty.

```
void display_data(Data *);
```

A function prototype is declared. We've used this before and should be familiar with it.

```
void main()
{
```

The program then enters **main()**.

```
Data *employee1, *employee2, *employee3;
```

Three pointers to the structure are declared. You'll notice that no variables of this type are defined elsewhere in the program. Apparently, there's nothing to store data in.

In order to do anything the programmer needs some variables, so they are created dynamically.

Dynamic Memory Allocation

```
employee1 = new Data;    //reserve memory dynamically
```

The statement **employee1 = new Data**; follows. This is a statement that we haven't seen before. It's assigning something to the pointer **employee1.**

We introduce **new** as the dynamic memory allocation operator. This will allocate a piece of memory on the heap that is the size of the type that follows the operator. Sufficient memory is needed to store a Data variable and the compiler is told this in the statement - **new Data**. If space was needed for an integer array then the code would have been:
employee1 = new int[MAX];.

Basically, the new operator is asking the system for a block of memory of the size specified. When the block is allocated, the pointer points to the first element of the block.

Analysis Continued

```
strcpy(employee1->first_name, "Ian");
strcpy(employee1->surname, "Wilks");
employee1->age = 39;
employee1->salary = 15000;
```

The next four lines of code simply assign some data to the structure. You'll notice that the memory block is used in exactly the same way as a pointer to a structure variable would be used.

```
employee2 = employee1;  //employee2 now points to the above data
```

In the next statement, the value of **employee1** is assigned to **employee2**. This creates no new data nor any additional memory space. The program simply has two pointers to the same memory location.

Since **employee2** is pointing to the structure, **employee1** can be re-used to get another dynamically allocated structure.

```
employee1 = new Data;
```

employee1 is again used to point to another block of memory. **employee2** could have been used just as easily.

**Dynamic Memory
Allocation**

```
strcpy(employee1->first_name, "Susan");
strcpy(employee1->surname, "Wilks");
employee1->age = 38;
employee1->salary = 12500;
```

The next four lines of code simply assign data to the structure.

```
employee3 = new Data;

strcpy(employee3->first_name, "Chris");
strcpy(employee3->surname, "Smyth");
employee3->age = 27;
employee3->salary = 20000;
```

employee3 is then used to point to another block of memory and this is filled with data.

```
display_data(employee1);
display_data(employee2);
display_data(employee3);
```

The function, **display_data()**, is then used to display all the data.

```
employee1 = employee3;
```

The pointer **employee1** is assigned the value of **employee3.** In doing this, the block of memory that **employee1** was pointing to is effectively lost since there is now no pointer pointing to that area of memory.

This means that the block of memory that was previously pointed to by **employee1** can't be referred to, changed, or disposed of. From this point on that block of memory on the heap is wasted.

This isn't something that a programmer would purposely do, except, as in this case, for illustration.

```
delete(employee2);
delete(employee3);
```

The operator **delete** is then used to delete that data and release the space on the heap. It is used by calling it with the appropriate pointer being in brackets.

Therefore, the memory blocks pointed to by the pointers **employee2** and **employee3** are de-allocated. The program has now lost access to the data generated earlier.

There's still one block of memory on the heap but there's no pointer to it as we lost the address earlier. Trying to free the memory location pointed to by **employee1** would result in an error as it's already been de-allocated by the use of **employee3**.

When the program finishes and control returns to the operating system, the entire heap will be disposed of with no regard for what was stored in it. However, while the program is running, that block of memory can't be used until the program terminates.

Success or Failure

How do you know if your request to the system to allocate a block of memory has been successful?

If the request was successful, that is, if there's memory to grab, the pointer will point to the address at the start of the allocated block.

If the request was unsuccessful (usually due to insufficient memory) then the pointer will return to **0**.

This means that it's possible to test whether the allocation request was successful. The code below illustrates this.

```
employee1 = new Data;          //reserve memory dynamically

//check that memory has been allocated

if(employee1 == NULL)
{
    cout << "Insufficient Memory - Program terminating\n";
    exit(1);
}
else
    cout << "\t\tMemory allocated.\n\n";
```

Success or Failure - An Example

The following example program illustrates this point:

```
/* ***********************************************************
 *    dynam2.cpp                                            *
 *    Ian M Wilks                                           *
 ********************************************************** */
#include <iostream.h>          //header file for i/o
#include <string.h>            //header file for string operations
#include <stdlib.h>            //header file for exit()

struct Data
{
    char first_name[15];
    char surname[25];
    int age;
    float salary;
};

void display_data(Data *);

void main()
{
    Data *employee1;
    employee1 = new Data;    //reserve memory dynamically
    //check that memory has been allocated
    if(employee1 == NULL)
    {
        cout << "Insufficient Memory - Program terminating\n";
        exit(1);
    }
    else
        cout << "\t\tMemory allocated.\n\n";
    //insert some data
    strcpy(employee1->first_name, "Ian");
    strcpy(employee1->surname, "Wilks");
    employee1->age = 39;
    employee1->salary = 15000;
    //display results
    display_data(employee1);
    delete(employee1);
}

void display_data(Data * x)
{
    cout << x->first_name << " " << x->surname << endl
         << "Aged " << x->age << "  salary £" << x->salary << endl;
}
```

Program Analysis

Read through the code and run the program to help you understand what's happening.

There are no new statements in this code.

As you'll see, the program is a shorter version of the first example and after the request to the system to allocate some memory, a check is made to see if the allocation has been made.

Linked Lists

One of the problems that programmers have to contend with is what to do when they have a quantity of data to handle but don't know the extent of that data prior to the program being run.

A data structure which is often used to deal with this problem is the linked list.

The following figure shows the basic structure of a linked list.

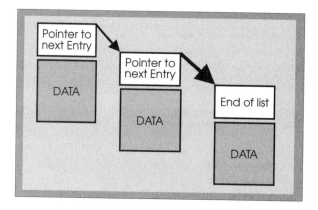

A linked list is a set of data elements which are linked together. The location of only one element in the list is known to the program. Other elements are accessed by reference to information as to their location which is held in the list.

The simplest form of a linked list is the one-way linked list. In this, each element of the list consists of two parts - a data element, which holds the data contained in that element, and a pointer, which gives the address of the next list element.

Practical Linked List - An Example

Consider the example:

```
/* ***********************************************************
 *    dynam2.cpp                                            *
 *    Ian M Wilks                                           *
 ********************************************************** */
#include <iostream.h>      //header file for i/o
#include <string.h>        //header file for string operations
#include <stdlib.h>        //header file for exit()

struct Data
{
    char first_name[15];
    char surname[25];
    int age;
    float salary;
    Data * next;           //pointer to another structure of this type
};

void display_data(Data *);

void main()
{
    const int MAX = 5;
    int index;
    Data *point, *start, *prior;

    //insert data into first record - a special case
    start = new Data;

    strcpy(start->first_name, "Ian");
    strcpy(start->surname, "Wilks");
    start->age = 39;
    start->salary = 15000;
    start->next = NULL;

    prior = start;



    //now use a loop to create and fill other records
    for(index = 0; index < MAX; index++)
    {
        point = new Data;
        strcpy(point->first_name, "Chris");
        strcpy(point->surname, "Jones");
        point->age = 27 + index;
        point->salary = 6000 * (index + 1);
        prior->next = point;           //put address of this record into
                                       //last records next field
        point->next = NULL;            //set this records next field to NULL
        prior = point;                 //this is now prior record
    }
```

```
        //Display data
        point = start;                    //first block of group
        do
        {
              prior = point->next;
              display_data(point);
              point = point->next;
        }while(prior != NULL);

        //free dynamically allocated memory
        point = start;                    //first block of group
        do
        {
              prior = point->next;        //next block of data
              delete(point);              //free present block
              point = prior;              //point to next
        }while(prior != NULL);       //quit when next is NULL
}

void display_data(Data * x)
{
    cout << x->first_name << " " << x->surname << endl
         << "Aged " << x->age << "  salary £" << x->salary << endl;
}
```

Program Analysis

```
#include <iostream.h>
#include <string.h>
#include <stdlib.h>
```

After the comment block the **#include** directive is used to include three header files:

IOSTREAM.H for input/output operations

STRING.H   for string operations

STDLIB.H   for exit()

```
struct Data
{
    char first_name[15];
    char surname[25];
    int age;
    float salary;
    Data * next;
};
```

The structure is then defined. You'll see that although the structure is like the one we've been using in previous programs, it now has an extra field - **Data * next;** which is a pointer to another structure of this type. This field will be used to point to the next element in the list.

```
void display_data(Data *);
```

The function prototype for **display_data()** is defined. This is the function we've been using in the previous examples.

```
void main()
```

The program then enters **main()**.

```
const int MAX = 5;
int index;
Data *point, *start, *prior;
```

Variables are then declared; a constant integer **MAX** and an integer index which will both be used in the **for** loops. There are also three pointers to the structure.

```
start = new Data;
```

A block of memory is then allocated using the statement **start = new Data;**.

```
strcpy(start->first_name, "Ian");
strcpy(start->surname, "Wilks");
start->age = 39;
start->salary = 15000;
start->next = NULL;
```

The next five lines of code put data into the structure. The additional field, the pointer, is assigned the value **NULL**, which is used to indicate that this is the end of the list.

The pointer **start** will be left pointing at this structure so that it will always point to the first element in the list.

```
prior = start;
```

The pointer **prior** is assigned the value of **start**.

```
for(index = 0; index < MAX; index++)
{
       point = new Data;
       strcpy(point->first_name, "Chris");
       strcpy(point->surname, "Jones");
       point->age = 27 + index;
       point->salary = 6000 * (index + 1);
       prior->next = point;            //put address of this record into
                                       //last records next field
       point->next = NULL;             //set this records next field to NULL
       prior = point;                  //this is now prior record
}
```

A **for** loop is now used to quickly create and assign data to the other elements in the list.

The program executes the loop a number of times - equal to the value of the constant **MAX**, defined at the beginning of the program.

```
point = new Data;
```

Memory is allocated each time through the loop.

The first four fields are filled with illustrative data. The pointer in the previous record is given the address of the new record.

```
prior->next = point;
point->next = NULL;
```

Accordingly, the statement **prior->next = point;** gives the address of the newly filled record to the previous record. The pointer in the new record is assigned the value of **NULL.**

The pointer **prior** is given the address of the new record because the next time a record is created, this record will be the prior one at the time. That is **prior = point;**.

When the loop has been executed 5 times there will be a list of 6 structures. The list will have the following characteristics:

1   **start** points to the first structure in the list.

2   Each structure contains a pointer to the next structure.

3   The last structure has a pointer that points to **NULL** and can be used to detect the end of the list.

290

The following figure should illustrate the position.

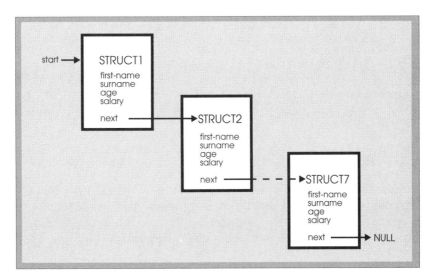

```
point = start;                      //first block of group
```

You should recognize that it's not possible to enter a structure that's in the middle of a list. You have to start at the beginning of the list and work through one record at a time.

```
do
{
      prior = point->next;
      display_data(point);
      point = point->next;
}while(prior != NULL);
```

A **do-while** loop is used to display the data.

The pointers are initialized and are used to go from record to record displaying the data. The loop terminates when the **NULL** in the last record is found. This means that the program doesn't need to know the number of elements in the list.

```
        point = start;                    //first block of group
        do
        {
                prior = point->next;      //next block of data
                delete(point);            //free present block
                point = prior;            //point to next
        }while(prior != NULL);            //quit when next is NULL
```

Finally, another **do-while** loop is used to 'delete' the entire list. You must take care to ensure that the last element is not deleted before the **NULL** is checked.

The Economy of C++

C++ can be a very terse language. As you read other books on C and/or C++ programming you'll find that a lot of programmers pride themselves on producing economical code. Sometimes, this can be a disadvantage, especially when we want to learn more about the language.

Let me demonstrate this.

Programming Exercise 1 in Chapter 8 says:

Write a function called **copy_string()** that takes two arguments, both being pointers to characters, and copies one string to the other. For example:

```
copy_string(char * source, char * dest);
```

Write a program to test this function.

I expect that you'll have written functions along the lines of:

```
void copy_string(register char * source, register char * dest)
{
    for (; *dest = *source; ++source, ++dest);
}
```

or

```
void copy_string(char * source, char * dest)
{
    while(*source != '\0')
    {
        *dest = *source;
        dest++;
        source++;
    }
    *dest = '\0';
}
```

Look at the above function and remember that in C++ **0** is taken as false and any other value as true.

Therefore: ***source != '\0'** is analogous with ***source** in the condition of the **while** loop.

Also, if the incremental operator **++** is being used as a suffix, then the expression
*dest++ = *source++; can be used.

A better version of the function would therefore be:

```
void copy_string(char * source, char * dest)
{
    while(*source)
          *dest++ = *source++;
    *dest = '\0';
}
```

This can also be shortened. You can substitute the while loop statement into the condition. Because the null character would be copied before the test to end the loop is made, we can omit the last statement in the function.

```
void copy_string(char * source, char * dest)
{
    while(*dest++ = *source++);
}
```

These functions have been tested in the following program.

Economical Code - An Example

Read through the source code to make sure you understand what's happening.

```
/* ************************************************************
 *    Chap8q1.cpp                                            *
 *    Ian M Wilks                                            *
 ************************************************************ */
#include <iostream.h>

void copy_string1(char * source, char * dest);
void copy_string2(char * source, char * dest);
void copy_string3(char * source, char * dest);

void main()
{
    char string1[] = "Instant C++ Programming";
    char string2[28];
    char * string3 = "Scrape By in C++";
    char string4[20];
```

```
        copy_string1(string1, string2);
        cout << "Using copy_string1()\n" << "string1:  " << string1 << endl
                << "string2:  " << string2 << endl;

        copy_string1(string3, string4);
        cout << "\nstring3:  " << string3 << endl << "string4:  " << string4
                << endl;

        copy_string2(string1, string2);
        cout << "\nUsing copy_string2()\n" << "string1:  " << string1 << endl
                << "string2:  " << string2 << endl;

        copy_string2(string3, string4);
        cout << "\nstring3:  " << string3 << endl << "string4:  " << string4
                << endl;

        copy_string3(string1, string2);
        cout << "\nUsing copy_string3()\n" << "string1:  " << string1 << endl
                << "string2:  " << string2 << endl;

        copy_string3(string3, string4);
        cout << "\nstring3:  " << string3 << endl << "string4:  " << string4
                << endl;
}


void copy_string1(char * source, char * dest)
{
    while(*source != '\0')
    {
        *dest = *source;
        dest++;
        source++;
    }
    *dest = '\0';
}


void copy_string2(char * source, char * dest)
{
    while(*source)              //*source != '\0' is identical to *source in test
        *dest++ = *source++;    //makes assignment, then increments
    *dest = '\0';
}


void copy_string3(char * source, char * dest)
{
    while(*dest++ = *source++);              //the null character is copied before
test
}
```

If you've read the source code and run the program you'll understand what
this program is doing. We won't therefore go into a full explanation of the
program as you should be able to follow it.

Summary

In this chapter we've looked at program testing (including top-down and bottom-up).and debugging. We've also given some guidelines on how to find different types of errors. We've looked at how to make the most of C++'s ability to manage memory through dynamic memory allocation, and you've seen how to use a linked list in the situation where you don't know the extent of your data prior to running the program. Finally, we've discussed making your code more economical and given you some hints on writing really terse code.

Programming Exercises

1 The following program has been written to calculate the volume and the surface area of a sphere using the formulae:

$$volume = \frac{4}{3}\ \Pi\ r^3$$

$$Surface\ Area = 4\ \Pi\ r^2$$

There are several errors in the program. Some of the errors are syntax errors (that is, the program breaks some rules of C++) and some are semantic errors (that is, the program doesn't perform as expected).

Totally debug the program so that it compiles and performs as expected.

```
//prob.cpp
//This program calculates the volume and surface area of a sphere
#include <iostream.h>
void main()
{
    const float PI = 3.1415926;
    float radius, volume, surface_area;
    float cube(float );
    float square(float );

    cout >> "Enter the radius of the sphere: ";
    cin << radius;

    volume = 4 / 3 * PI * cube(radius);
    surface_area = 4 * PI * square(radius)
    cout << "\n\nThe surface area is " << volume
            << " and the volume is " << surface_area << endl;
}

float cube (float x)
{
    return(x*x);
}

float square (float y)
{
    return(y*y);
}
```

2 Re-write the program dealing with linked lists so that the program is modular. There should be functions to add records and to display the entries in the list. Use a **switch** statement and a menu function.

3 Modify the above program so you can delete a record from the list.

4 Modify the above program so you can add a record to the list.

5 Write your own linked list program to store a person's name, address and telephone number (including the area code).

6 Modify the program you wrote in question 5 so the records in the list can be saved to and loaded from a disk file.

Instant

Where Are We Now?

In the second section you have looked at several more example programs and you have now covered enough topics to enable you to use C++ at an advanced level in a traditional, procedural manner.

You have been introduced to the essentials of combining data that can be of the same or different types - structures and unions. Combining data into structures means that related items can be kept in a single entity. Structures are one of the two important building blocks in the understanding of objects and classes. As you will see, the syntax of the structure is almost identical to that of a class.

You have examined pointers and have seen that they are variables which hold addresses of data stored in the computer's memory. They can be used to access the variable to which they point. Pointers are basically a simple idea and are used for a number of reasons, including, array access and the creation of certain data structures.

File handling considered how to read from and write to disk files from within the program. Both text and binary files were considered. You saw that the printer is regarded as a file and were also introduced to command-line arguments.

You have been acquainted with the fundamentals of overloading - both of functions and operators. The compiler can distinguish between functions which have the same name, provided the arguments (either number or type) differ. Operator overloading allows user-defined types to look as if they are a natural part of the language.

Chapter 11 looked at three specific areas. The first area was program testing to discover syntax errors, run-time errors and logic errors. The second area was dynamic memory allocation. This allows for the allocation of memory as a program runs rather than pre-assigning memory when the program is compiled. We saw that the keyword **new** is used to dynamically allocate memory and the keyword **delete** is used to release the memory when it is no longer needed. The last area we considered was the terseness of the language.

You now have enough knowledge to write advanced programs. Unfortunately, this book hasn't looked at many of the functions that are built into the compiler's library. By using the library functions you will be saved from having to re-invent the wheel each time you need a special routine. C++ offers a lot of support for string handling, character conversion, and mathematical work. A lot of the standard library functions are portable from one computer to another and from one operating system to another.

You are, therefore, advised to read the manuals that came with your compiler so that you know where to locate these functions. Experiment with these functions and you will discover that they are as easy to use as the library functions we have considered in this book. You will find that these functions are extremely useful as you start to do more serious programming.

What We Have Omitted

Due to the scope of the book there are some specialized areas that we have deliberately omitted. These include the following.

Systems Resources

We have just discussed the C++ library functions that offer a lot of support for string handling, character conversion, and mathematical work. These functions are as close to a standard C++ as you can get.

Most compilers also provide functions that are not standardized but which are hardware and/or operating system dependent. Most compilers provide functions that allow you to access the software and hardware characteristics of the system you are working on.

For example, compilers that work on IBM-compatible computers under DOS will have header files called **BIOS.H** and **DOS.H**. The header file **BIOS.H** prototypes seven functions that allow immediate access to the BIOS (basic input and output services) built into IBM-compatible computers. The header file **DOS.H** prototype functions that allow access to DOS interrupt capabilities built into IBM-compatible computers.

Graphics

Most compilers also provide an extensive set of graphics routines. These routines normally contain primitives for drawing pixels, lines, rectangles, arcs, circles and so on. There may be more advanced functions that draw two or three-dimensional bars and pie slices.

You are advised to read the manuals that come with your compiler so that you know about these functions. Again, you should experiment with them.

Assembly Language

With some compilers it's possible to write assembly language code in your source file. This technique is ideal for simple assembly language routines. However, this code tends to become unmanageable and hard to understand as your program size grows. When you need more complicated assembly language routines you will probably find that it's better to write separate C++ and Assembly Language modules.

Putting It All Together - An Example

Let us look at a further example of the concepts we have been investigating.

Linked-Lists

In Chapter 11 we looked at an example of a linked-list. As you delve further into computer programming you will discover several data structures, of which the linked-list is one. The linked-list can access its storage in a random manner because each piece of information carries with it a link to the next item in the chain. Additionally, a linked-list retrieval operation doesn't remove and destroy an item from the list. A specific deletion operation is required. Linked-lists are used to create arrays of unknown size in memory and are also used in disk-file storage of databases.

Linked-lists can either have a single link, as we saw in our earlier example, or have a double link. A linked-list with a double link contains links to the previous element in the list and to the next element in the list.

The following example uses a double link:

```
/* *********************************************************
 *     address.cpp                                   *
 *     Ian M Wilks                            *
 ********************************************************* */
#include <fstream.h>
#include <stdio.h>
#include <stdlib.h>
#include <string.h>
#include <conio.h>
#define YES 1
#define NO 0

struct address
{
    char name[40];
    char street[40];
    char town[30];
    char county[30];
    char postcode[10];
    address * next;              //pointer to next entry
    address * previous;              //pointer to previous entry
};

address *start, *last;
fstream list_file;

address * find(char *);       //This is something new.
                       //Functions that return pointers are handled just
                       //like any other function.  Remember pointers to
                       //variables are not integers.  They are the memory
                       //addresses of a certain type of data.  The reason
                       //for the distinction is because pointer arithmetic
                       //is relative to its base type.  If a pointer is
                       //incremented it points to the next data item of its
                       //type.  If no match is found a pointer to null
                       //is returned.

void enter(), search(), save(), load(), list();

void delete_entry(address **, address **);          //this function takes a
pointer
                                        //to a pointer as arguments
void store(address *, address **, address **);
void display(address *);
int select_menu();

void main()
{
    int another_go = YES;
    start = last = NULL;                     //initialize first and last pointers

    while(another_go == YES)
    {
```

```
        switch(select_menu())
        {
                case 1:
                        enter();       //enter data into list
                        break;
                case 2:
                        delete_entry(&start, &last);
                        break;
                case 3:
                        list();        //list the data
                        break;
                case 4:
                        search();      //find a record
                        break;
                case 5:
                        save();        //save list to disc file
                        break;
                case 6:
                        load();        //load list from disc file
                        break;
                case 7:
                        another_go = NO;
                        break;
                default:
                        cout << "\n\nInternal Error\n\n";
        }                              //end of switch statement
    }                                  //end of while loop
}                                      //end of main()

int select_menu()
{
    int item;
    clrscr();
    cout << endl << "\t 1\tMake Entry\n" << "\t 2\tDelete Entry\n"
         << "\t 3\tList Entries\n" << "\t 4\tSearch\n"
         << "\t 5\tSave to File\n" << "\t 6\tLoad from File\n"
         << "\t 7\tExit from Program\n\n";
    do
    {
        cout << "\t\t\tEnter Choice:  ";
        cin >> item;
    }while(item < 0 || item > 7);
    return(item);
}

//Enter data into list
void enter()
{
    address * info;
    char again = 'Y';
    do
    {
        if(!(info = new address))
        {//check if memory allocated - if not terminate program
            cout << "\n\nMEMORY ALLOCATION ERROR";
```

303

```
                    exit(-1);
        }
        clrscr();
        cout << "\n\tEnter Name:  ";
        gets(info->name);
        cout << "\n\tEnter Street:  ";
        gets(info->street);
        cout << "\n\tEnter Town:  ";
        gets(info->town);
        cout << "\n\tEnter County:  ";
        gets(info->county);
        cout << "\n\tEnter Postcode:  ";
        gets(info->postcode);

        store(info, &start, &last);   //put data into list

        cout << "\n\n\nEnter another?  (Y/N)    ";
        cin >> again;
    }while( again == 'Y' || again == 'y');
}

//create linked list
void store(address * i, address ** start, address **last)
{
    if (*start == NULL)                    //first record has to be treated
    {                              //specially
        i->next = NULL;            //if first record - no next record
        i->previous = NULL;            //if first record - no previous
record
        *last = i;              //store details in last
        *start = i;             //store details in start
    }
    else                       //not first record
    {
        (*last)->next = i;
        i->next = NULL;
        i->previous = *last;
        *last = i;
    }
}

//remove entry from list
void delete_entry(address ** start, address ** last)
{
    address * info;
    char name[40];

    clrscr();
    cout << "\n\n\t\tEnter Name:  ";
    gets(name);
    info = find(name);                 //find record
    if(info)
    {
        if(*start == info)             //if start of list is to be deleted
        {                          //new start of list is needed
```

```
                              *start = info->next;
                              if(*start)
                                      (*start)->previous = NULL;
                              else
                                      *last = NULL;
                }
                else
                {
                        info->previous->next = info->next;
                        if(info != *last)
                                info->next->previous = info->previous;
                        else
                                *last = info->previous;
                }
                delete info;
        }
        else
                gotoxy(25, 25);
                cout << "Press a key to continue.";
                getch();
}

//find address
address * find(char * name)
{
        address * info;

        info = start;

        while(info)
        {
                if(!strcmp(name, info->name))
                        return(info);
                info = info->next;
        }
        cout << "\n\n\tName not found\n";
        return(NULL);
}

//display list
void list()
{
        address * info;
        int count = 0;

        clrscr();
        info = start;

        while(info)
        {
                count++;
                display(info);
                info = info->next;

                if ( (count % 4) == 0) //to prevent records scrolling off
```

```
                {                           //screen
                    gotoxy(25,25);
                    cout << "Press a key to continue";
                    getch();
                    clrscr();
                }
        }
    cout << endl << endl;
    gotoxy(25, 25);
    cout << "Press a key to continue.";
    getch();
}

//print list to screen
void display(address *info)                //Would an overloaded operator be
better
{
    cout << endl << "\t" << info->name << endl
         << "\t" << info->street << endl
         << "\t" << info->town << endl
         << "\t" << info->county
         << ", " << info->postcode << endl;
}


//look for name in list
void search()
{
    char name[40];
    address * info;

    clrscr();
    cout << "\n\nEnter name to find:   ";
    gets(name);

    info = find(name);

    if (info)
    {
        display(info);
        gotoxy(25, 25);
        cout << "Press a key to continue.";
        getch();
    }
    else
    {
        gotoxy(25, 25);
        cout << "Press a key to continue.";
        getch();
    }
}


//save list to disc
```

```
void save()
{
    address * info;

    rename("list.dat", "list.old");                    //create backup file
    list_file.open("list.dat",ios::out);
    if(!list_file)
    {
        cout << "\n\nCould not open file.";
        exit(-1);
    }
    cout << "\n\n\t\tSAVING FILE\n";

    info = start;
    while(info)
    {
        list_file << info->name << endl << info->street << endl
                << info->town << endl << info->county << endl
                << info->postcode << endl;
        info = info->next;
    }
    list_file.close();
}

//load from disc
void load()
{
    address * info;

    list_file.open("list.dat", ios::in);
    if(!list_file)
    {
        cout << "\n\nCould not open file.";
        exit(-1);
    }

    while(start)                        //delete any lists already in memory
    {
        info = start->next;
        delete info;
        start = info;
    }
    start = last = NULL;

    cout << "\n\n\t\tLOADING FILE\n";

    while(!list_file.eof())
    {
        info = new address;
        if(!info)
        {
            cout << "\n\n\t\tMEMORY ALLOCATION ERROR\n";
            exit(-1);
        }
        list_file.getline(info->name, 40);
```

```
            list_file.getline(info->street, 40);
            list_file.getline(info->town, 30);
            list_file.getline(info->county, 30);
            list_file.getline(info->postcode, 10);

            if(!( list_file.eof()))
            {
                    store(info, &start, &last);
            }
        }
    }
    list_file.close();
}
```

Program Analysis

Hopefully, the code shouldn't present any difficulties. There were two pieces of code that you haven't previously encountered but these were explained with comments in the code.

Well, what does the program do?

As you can see, this program is an address list which can be stored to and loaded from a disk file. If a disk file exists when you save an up-dated list, the old file is renamed and kept as a backup. The disk file is in ASCII form so that the addresses could be obtained via your word processing package.

Having two links instead of one means that the list can be read in either direction. This simplifies list management. In addition, if one of the links fail, the list can be reconstructed using the other.

The function **store()** needs to be considered. There are three ways that a new element can be inserted into the list - either as a new first element, a new last element or between two other elements. This functions puts new elements onto the end of the list.

It's possible to store elements in specific locations instead of always placing new elements at the end of the list, in other words the list could be sorted. This can happen to a linked-list with a single link or a linked-list with double links. The following, replacement, function would sort our list in ascending order:

```
void store(address * i, address ** start, address ** last)
{
    address * old,  * point;

    if(*last == NULL)                //first element in list
    {
```

```
            i->next = NULL;
            i->previous = NULL;
            *last = i;
            *start = i;
            return;
    }

    point = *start;                      //start at top of list

    old = NULL;

    while(point)
    {
        if(strcmp(point->name, i->name) < 0)
        {
            old = point;
            point = point->next;
        }
        else
        {
            if(point->previous)
            {
                point->previous->next = i;
                i->next = point;
                i->previous = point->previous;
                point->previous = i;
                return;
            }
            i->next = point;
            i->previous = NULL;
            point->previous = i;
            *start = i;
            return;
        }
    }
    old->next = i;
    i->next = NULL;
    i->previous = old;
    *last = i;
}
```

Replace the **store()** function in the program with the one above and see what happens. You should be able to follow what's happening. As the first or the last element in the list can change, this function updates pointers to start of the list and to the last element.

Retrieving a specific record is simply the process of following the links until the required element is found.

There are three cases to consider when deleting an element from the list: deleting the first item, deleting the last item or deleting an item from between two other elements. As the first or the last element in the list can be deleted, the **delete()** function updates pointers to the start of the list and to the last element.

You will see that we display the list on the screen using the **display()** function. Wouldn't it be better if we overloaded the **<<** operator? We could then say **cout << info;** instead of **display(info);**

Consider this function:

```
ostream& operator << (ostream& out, address* point)
{
    out << endl << "\t" << point->name << endl
        << "\t" << point->street << endl
        << "\t" << point->town << endl
        << "\t" << point->county
        << ", " << point->postcode << endl;
}
```

Can this function be altered so that the overloaded operator can be used to send the information to the disk file?

Remainder of the Book

The last part of this book will look at **object-oriented programming**. In object-oriented programming, your program will consist of a group of **objects**. These objects are controlled with **messages**. Object-oriented programs offer several benefits over procedural programs which we will now show you.

Chapter

Object-Oriented Programming

This book has introduced you to C++ concepts in a traditional, procedural way. In a typical procedural program there is a **main()** function and many additional functions (such as subroutines and procedures) that are called from **main()**. In this top-down approach, **main()** is usually a short function, with the majority of the work (processing) being performed in the other functions. As you've seen, program execution flows from the top of **main()** and usually terminates at the end of **main()**. This is a common technique among structured languages.

This chapter looks at the object-oriented approach, and covers:

 OOP - modularity, abstraction, and information hiding

 Classes and objects

 private, public and protected visibility

 Members

 Constructors

 Class specifiers

 Overloaded operators with classes

Object-Oriented Programming

The intention of object based programming is to create a model of the real world in a program. In the world of computer science, an object is an abstract concept used to represent the features of a real-world entity. Object-oriented design results in a design that combines data and the functions that operate on that data in a way that structures data and processing rather than data alone.

Programming methodology gave rise to the concept of object based programming, and isn't dependent upon one, single language. It pre-dates C++, and has been used in a number of languages such as Lisp, Fortran, and also in assembly language. It is unique because of its ability to build upon three key concepts:

- Modularity
- Abstraction
- Information hiding

Modularity

Software is divided into separately named and addressable elements, called **modules**. The most obvious example of modules that we have seen is functions.

Abstraction

When a modular solution to a problem is being considered, many levels of abstraction are suggested. At the highest level, a solution to a problem is stated in broad terms. At lower levels, abstraction highlights the procedures involved. And at its lowest level the solution will have been stated in such a way that it can be implemented.

Information Hiding

Modules should be designed so that the data and the functions that operate on that data is inaccessible to other modules which don't need to have access.

An object is a real world component, modeled into the program. Typical objects are files, menus, strings, and commands, as well as people, places, and any other entities. When the object is modeled it consists of a private data structure together with processes (functions) that can alter the data.

Data and its functions are said to be encapsulated into a single entity.

The following figure illustrates an object, in this case a course, which is to be modeled in a program.

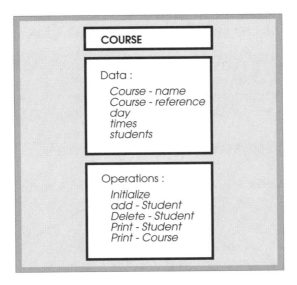

The illustration shows a private data structure and related operations. The data to be stored in the object is as follows:

Data Fields	Private Data Structure
course_name	Introduction to C++ Programming
course_reference	A36
Day	Thursday
Times	7pm - 9pm
Students	Name, age, address, telephone

The operations that can process this data are:

Operations	Data
initialize	Basic information - course name, course reference, days and times.
add_student	Student's details
delete_student	Remove student
print_students	Print names and details to either screen or printer
print_course	Print course name, references, days and times, to either screen or printer

Classes, Objects and Methods

In object-oriented programming, your program consists of **objects**. The C++ class is the basis of object-oriented programming, since a class provides a module to hold data and the operations (functions) that act *on* this data.

Classes are what makes C++ suitable for object-oriented programming. The class structure allows us to create objects. A class is a structure that can have functions as members, as well as data elements. In object-oriented programming terminology, these member functions are called **methods**.

The Difference Between Objects and Classes

The difference between objects and classes can be unclear to new programmers.

Objects

An object is a variable of the data-type defined by the class. The C programming language has used the word object to refer to the memory location set aside to store an item of data. For example:

```
int number;
```

Historically, the memory area reserved for data storage (referred to by the identifier **number**) has been known as an object. The keyword **int** is the type specifier. It tells the compiler to reserve two bytes of memory. You can think of **int** as being a template.

Classes

If a type specifier can be considered a template for a variable, a class is a template for an object. This is because the class specifier, like a structure specifier, doesn't set aside memory for the storage of data - it's simply a template. Only objects (the actual variables), also known as **instances** of classes, actually have memory storage reserved.

Consider the following class declaration:

```
class coordinate
{
    int x, y;

public:
    void print();
};
```

314

This declares a new type, in the same way as a structure declaration. The new type can be used in a similar way to the standard, built-in types: **int**, **float**, and **char**. No memory space has been reserved as a result of the class declaration.

An object can be created from class **coordinate** by using the statement:

```
coordinate point1;
```

This statement sets aside enough storage space for the object **point1**. Classes are user-defined data types. Objects are variables.

Messages

In the class declaration for coordinate, **print()** is a method. It's a function that is a member of the class. A call to this function is referred to as **sending a message**. A message can be sent to an object.

If you want to see the contents of object **point1**, you send the **print()** message to the object:

```
point1.print();
```

Declaring a Class

A class specifier is similar to a structure specifier. The specifier starts with the keyword **class**, followed by the class name. Like a structure, the body of a class is contained within braces and the specifier is terminated with a semicolon.

The following figure illustrates the general syntax of a class specifier.

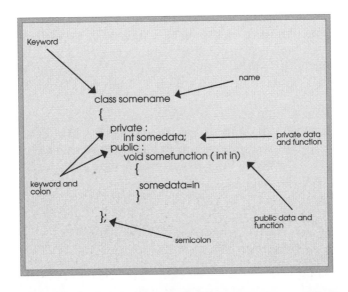

315

The following is the specifier for a class called `rectangle`:

```
class rectangle
{
private:
    int length, width;

public:
    rectangle(int l = 0, int w = 0)
    {
        length = 1;
        width = w;
    }

    void print_info()
    {
        cout << "\nLength = " << length << "  Width = " << width
            << endl << "Area = " << length * width
            << "  Perimeter = " << (2 * length) + (2 * width)
            << endl;
    }

    void set_length(int);          //modify length variable
    void set_width(int);           //modify width variable
};
```

private, public, and protected Visibility

There are three three levels of visibilty for C++ classes:

- If a member is **private**, it can only be used by member functions and friends of the class in which it is declared. Members of a class are private by default.

- If a member is **public**, it can be used by any function.

- There are also **protected** members (they're not illustrated in the figure or the example). If a member is protected, its access is the same as it is for private. In addition, the member can be used by member functions, as well as friends of classes derived from the declared class.

Usually, the data within a class is private and the functions are public (the example shows this). The data is hidden so that it's safe from accidental manipulation, while the functions are public so they can be accessed from outside the class. However, there is no reason why data can't be public and the functions private.

Friend Keyword

You will have noticed that we have referred to **'friends of the class'**. What is a friend?

A class, or a function, declared to be a friend of another class, has access to the private, protected, and public members of the other class, and to the private, protected, and public members of any class from which it's derived.

Member Functions

The class rectangle has four member functions. Member functions can be declared and defined inside the class (as with `rectangle()` and `print_info()`) or they can be declared in the class and defined outside of the class.

Constructors

The function `rectangle()` is a special kind of function called a **constructor**. A constructor allows the object to initialize itself when it's created, without the need to make a separate function call.

In basic terms, a constructor determines how the objects of a class are created, initialized or copied. Constructors are member functions which have the same name as the class to which they belong. As with other member functions, they can either be declared and defined inside the class, or they can be declared in the class and defined outside of the class. You should note that constructors have no return values, not even void. It would be an error to declare a constructor as having any return type.

You don't need to define a constructor unless you need one. If you *don't* define a constructor, the compiler will automatically generate a default constructor (that is, one that takes no arguments). If a class has one or more constructors, one of them is invoked each time you define an object of the class.

As the class has been defined, the private components of the class can only be accessed by the member functions of the class.

The Class Rectangle - An Example

Let's now consider an example program that uses the **class rectangle**.

```cpp
/* ************************************************************
 *     OOP1.CPP                                              *
 *         Ian M Wilks                                       *
 ************************************************** */
#include <iostream.h>

class rectangle
{
private:        //If a member is private, it can only be used by member
                //functions and friends of the class in which it is declared.
                //Members of a class are private by default.

    int length, width;              //the data are called "data members"

public:     //If a member is public, it can be used by any function.
                //the functions are called "member functions"

    rectangle(int l = 0, int w = 0)             //constructor
    {
        length = 1;
        width = w;
    }

    void print_info()                       //output information
    {
        cout << "\nLength = " << length << "  Width = " << width
             << endl << "Area = " << length * width
             << "  Perimeter = " << (2 * length) + (2 * width) << endl;
    }
    void set_length(int);                       //modify length variable
    void set_width(int);                        //modify width variable
};

void rectangle::set_length(int l)
{
    if (l > 0)
        length = 1;
}

void rectangle::set_width(int w)
{
    if (w > 0)
        width = w;
}

void main()
{
    cout << "\n\t\tClass demonstration program\n\n";
    rectangle oblong(4,5);
    rectangle square(6,6);
```

318

```
        rectangle un_init;
        cout << "\t\tThree rectangle objects created\n";
        un_init.set_length(3);
        un_init.set_width(4);
        cout << "\t\tun_init's length and width set\n";
        cout << "\nThe information about oblong:\n";
        oblong.print_info();
        cout << "\nThe information about square:\n";
        square.print_info();
        cout << "\nThe information about un_init:\n";
        un_init.print_info();
}
```

Program Analysis

```
class rectangle
{
private:        //If a member is private, it can only be used by member
                //functions and friends of the class in which it is declared.
                //Members of a class are private by default.

    int length, width;          //the data are called "data members"

public:     //If a member is public, it can be used by any function.
                //the functions are called "member functions"
```

The class specifier, **rectangle**, follows. **rectangle** is a user-defined, composite data type, that contains a private and a public section. The components of the private section, **length** and **width**, can be accessed by the member functions, but not by any other function.

```
    rectangle(int l = 0, int w = 0)             //constructor
    {
        length = l;
        width = w;
    }
```

The function **rectangle()** is a constructor. It will be executed automatically each time an instance of the class is created, that is, rectangle box.

Constructors can be designed to accept arguments, and default values can be given (as they were in this case). If a **rectangle** is defined without arguments, default values of **0** are assigned to **length** and **width**. If a **rectangle** *is* defined with arguments, the first argument will be assigned to the **length** and the second argument will be assigned to the **width** - that is, rectangle box(7,9); will assign **7** to **box.length** and **9** to **box.width**.

```
void print_info()                         //output information
{
    cout << "\nLength = " << length << "  Width = " << width
         << endl << "Area = " << length * width
         << "  Perimeter = " << (2 * length) + (2 * width) << endl;
}
```

As you can see, the definition for the function **print_info()** is given within the class specifier. Member functions can be declared and defined inside the class, or they can be declared in the class and defined outside of the class.

If the function definitions are long then a function definition would be given outside the class specifier.

```
void set_length(int);                     //modify length variable
void set_width(int);                      //modify width variable
```

The functions **set_length()** and **set_width()** are given outside of the specifier. Note that the class name and the scope resolution operator, **::**, are placed between the type specifier and the function name (see below):

```
void rectangle::set_length(int 1)
{
    if (1 > 0)
        length = 1;
}
```

Without the class name and the scope resolution operator, the compiler wouldn't know of the connection between the functions and the class.

```
void main()
```

The program enters **main()**.

```
cout << "\n\t\tClass demonstration program\n\n";
```

A **cout** statement is used to output a message to the screen.

```
        rectangle oblong(4,5);
        rectangle square(6,6);
        rectangle un_init;
```

The next three lines define **rectangle** variables, objects, or instances of the class.

In the case of **oblong** and **square**, these objects are initialized to have the values that were passed as arguments. In the case of **un_init**, as no arguments were given the default value of **0** is assigned to the **un_init.length** and **un_init.width.**

```
        un_init.set_length(3);
        un_init.set_width(4);
        cout << "\t\tun_init's length and width set\n";
        cout << "\nThe information about oblong:\n";
```

The **set_length()** and **set_width()** functions are then used to assign values for **un_init.length** and **un_init.width.**

```
        oblong.print_info();
        cout << "\nThe information about square:\n";
        square.print_info();
        cout << "\nThe information about un_init:\n";
        un_init.print_info();
```

The values of the three objects are then displayed using the **print_info()** function.

Accessing Class Components

In the chapter on structures we saw that structure components can be accessed by using the syntax

```
        struct_name.struct_component.
```

We can now see that a class's components, be they public or private, can be accessed by member functions by specifying the component name alone (look at the function definitions). Non-member functions can access the public components of a class by using the dot operator:

```
        square.print_info();
```

The following figure shows how memory is used to store objects.

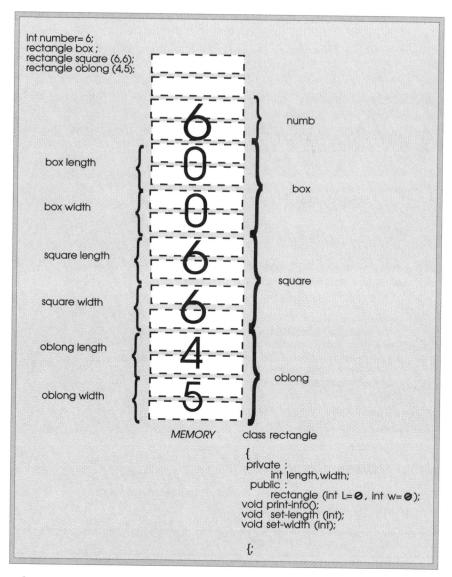

```
int number= 6;
rectangle box ;
rectangle square (6,6);
rectangle oblong (4,5);
```

numb — 6

box length — 0
box width — 0
box

square length — 6
square width — 6
square

oblong length — 4
oblong width — 5
oblong

MEMORY   class rectangle

```
class rectangle
{
private :
    int length,width;
public :
    rectangle (int L=0, int w=0);
void print-info();
void  set-length (int);
void set-width (int);
{;
```

In the chapter on file handling we considered example programs that used a structure, **Data**. The structure is reproduced below:

```
struct Data
{
    char first_name[15];
    char surname[25];
    int age;
    float salary;
};
```

Two functions were used to enter the data and display the data. These are also shown:

```cpp
void display_data(Data& x)
{
    cout << endl << x.first_name << " " << x.surname << endl
         << "aged " << x.age << "  Annual Salary £" << x.salary
         << endl;
}

void enter_data(Data& x)
{
    cout << "\nEnter first name: ";
    cin >> x.first_name;
    cout << "Enter surname: ";
    cin >> x.surname;
    cout << "Enter age: ";
    cin >> x.age;
    cout << "Enter salary: ";
    cin >> x.salary;
}
```

We'll now write a class called **employee** that has the same data items as in the structure, and we'll incorporate the two functions as member functions of the class. See if you can write out the class specifier for **employee**. As well as changing the keyword from struct to class, you have to create a private section for the data and a public section for the functions. This is shown below:

```cpp
class employee
{
private:
    char first_name[15];
    char surname[25];
    int age;
    float salary;
public:
    void enter_data();
    void display_data();
};
```

The functions now need to be defined. Have a go - define the function **enter_data()**.

Not much work here, is there? Remember that the class name and the scope resolution operator, **::**, have to be placed between the type specifier, void, and the function name, **enter_data**. As this function will only work on objects of the class **employee**, there's no need to pass any arguments to the function.

```
void employee::enter_data()
{
    cout << "\n\tEnter first name: ";
    cin >> first_name;
    cout << "\tEnter surname: ";
    cin >> surname;
    cout << "\tEnter age: ";
    cin >> age;
    cout << "\tEnter salary: ";
    cin >> salary;
    cout << endl;
}
```

Similarly, the other function presents no problems either.

```
void employee::display_data()
{
    cout << "\n\tName: " << first_name << " " << surname << endl
         << "\tAged: " << age << "  Salary: £" << salary << endl;
}
```

Class Specifier

Class Specifier - An Example

The next example program uses this class specifier.

```
/* *************************************************************
 *    oop2.cpp                                                 *
 *    Ian M Wilks                                              *
 ************************************************************* */
#include <iostream.h>

class employee
{
private:
    char first_name[15];
    char surname[25];
    int age;
    float salary;
public:
    void enter_data();
    void display_data();
};

void employee::enter_data()
{
    cout << "\n\tEnter first name: ";
    cin >> first_name;
    cout << "\tEnter surname: ";
```

```
    cin >> surname;
    cout << "\tEnter age: ";
    cin >> age;
    cout << "\tEnter salary: ";
    cin >> salary;
    cout << endl;
}

void employee::display_data()
{
    cout << "\n\tName: " << first_name << " " << surname << endl
        << "\tAged: " << age << "  Salary: £" << salary << endl;
}

void main()
{
    employee Wilks;
    Wilks.enter_data();
    Wilks.display_data();
}
```

Program Analysis

```
    employee Wilks;
    Wilks.enter_data();
    Wilks.display_data();
```

There are only three statements in **main()**.

1   The first statement declares a variable of the class (an object).

2   The second statement calls the member function so that data can be stored in the variable.

3   The third statement displays that data on the screen.

Let's use this class specifier and alter one of example programs from the chapter on file handling. Look back to the example program **FILE7.CPP** and read the analysis of that program.

The following program is very similar to **FILE7.CPP**. It's a copy of that program, amended to use the class specifier **employee**. Read through the code - notice that apart from the specifier, there's very little difference.

You'll recall that in the chapter on file handling (Chapter 9) we said the data structures used to read from a file must have the same format as the data structure that was used to write to the file.

325

If you look at the original structure, you'll see that the size of the variable is 46 bytes. This is made up of the following:

```
first_name     15 bytes
surname        25 bytes
age             2 bytes
salary          4 bytes
```

Class Specifier Compatibility

If you look at the class you'll see that the fields are exactly the same. When an object is saved to a file, only the data elements are saved. The functions aren't saved. As the two data structures are equivalent, a program using the class specifier can read from a file that was written by a program using the original structure. Similarly, a program using the original structure can read from a file that was written by a program using the class specifier. Run the program using the same binary file that was created when you ran the original program. This will confirm it. Also, look at the output.

Class Specifier Compatibility - An Example

```
/* *************************************************************
 *    oop3.cpp                                                 *
 *    Ian M Wilks                                              *
 ************************************************************* */
#include <fstream.h>

class employee
{
private:
    char first_name[15];
    char surname[25];
    int age;
    float salary;

public:
    void enter_data();
    void display_data();
};


void employee::enter_data()
{
    cout << "\n\tEnter first name: ";
    cin >> first_name;
```

```
        cout << "\tEnter surname: ";
    cin >> surname;
    cout << "\tEnter age: ";
    cin >> age;
    cout << "\tEnter salary: ";
    cin >> salary;
    cout << endl;
}


void employee::display_data()
{

    cout << "\n\tName: " << first_name << " " << surname << endl
        << "\tAged: " << age << " Salary: £" << salary << endl;
}

void main()
{
    employee person;
    int number;

    ifstream employ_record("a:\\file5.dat", ios::binary);

    //check for errors
    if(!employ_record)
        cout << "\nCould not open file\n";

    employ_record.seekg(0, ios::end);
    int endOfFile = employ_record.tellg();
    int NoOfRecords = endOfFile / sizeof(person);

    cout << "\n\nThere are " << NoOfRecords << " in the file.\n";
    cout << "Enter person number: ";
    cin >> number;

    int position = (number - 1) * sizeof(person);
    employ_record.seekg(position);

    employ_record.read((char *) &person, sizeof(person) );
    person.display_data();
}
```

Program Analysis

When you run the program you'll see that the output is exactly the same as the one you got when you ran the program **FILE7**. Did you spot the difference in the code? The obvious change is that we're now using the class specifier with two member functions instead of the structure with two separate functions.

The other changes are:

```
employee person;
```

We're now declaring the variable (the object) with the statement **employee person**. The only reason for this is that the class is called **employee**. If we had named the class **Data** we could have retained the same statement. As a result of the change of name, we now refer to the variable as **person** instead of **employee**.

```
person.display_data();
```

In this program the data is displayed on the screen using the statement - **person.display_data();**. In the original program the statement was a 'traditionally' styled function call - **display_data(employee);**.

When using objects, the dot operator is used to call a member function associated with a specific object. As **display_data()** is a member function of the employee class, it must be called in connection with an object of this class. It wouldn't make sense to call **display_data();** by itself, as a member function is always called to act on a *specific* object, not on the class in general.

Overloaded Operators With Classes

Overloaded Operators - An Example

We considered overloaded operators in Chapter 10. However, we'll now consider how they work with classes. Consider the following example:

```
/* ****************************************************************
 *    OOP14.CPP                                                  *
 *    Ian M Wilks                                                *
 **************************************************************** */
#include <iostream.h>

class rectangle
{
private:
    int length, width;
public:
    rectangle(int l = 0, int w = 0)
    {
        length = l;
```

```
            width = w;
    }

    void print_info()
    {
            cout << "\nLength = " << length << "  Width = " << width
                << endl << "Area = " << length * width
                << "  Perimeter = " << (2 * length) + (2 * width) << endl;
    }

    void set_length(int);               //modify length variable
    void set_width(int);                //modify width variable
    friend rectangle operator+(rectangle a, rectangle b);    // Add two
rectangles
    friend rectangle operator+(int a, rectangle b);    // Add constant to
rectangle
    friend rectangle operator*(int a, rectangle b);    // Multiply by constant
};

void rectangle::set_length(int l)
{
    if (l > 0)
        length = l;
}

void rectangle::set_width(int w)
{
    if (w > 0)
        width = w;
}

rectangle operator+(rectangle a, rectangle b)    // Add two together
{
    rectangle temp;
    temp.length = a.length + b.length;
    temp.width = a.width + b.width;
    return(temp);
}

rectangle operator+(int a, rectangle b)    // Add a constant to rectangle
{
    rectangle temp;
    temp.length = a + b.length;
    temp.width = a + b.width;
    return(temp);
}

rectangle operator*(int a, rectangle b)    // Multiply a rectangle by a
constant
{
    rectangle temp;
    temp.length = a * b.length;
    temp.width = a * b.width;
    return(temp);
}
```

```
void main()
{
    cout << "\n\t\tClass demonstration program\n\n";
    rectangle oblong(4,5);
    rectangle square(6,6);
    cout << "\t\tTwo rectangle objects created\n";
    cout << "\nThe information about oblong:";
    oblong.print_info();
    cout << "\nThe information about square:";
    square.print_info();

    //add two rectangles
    rectangle add;
    add = oblong + square;
    cout << "\nThe information about add:";
    add.print_info();

    //add a constant to a rectangle
    rectangle constant;
    constant = 5 + oblong;
    cout << "\nThe information about constant:";
    constant.print_info();


    //multiply a rectangle by a constant
    rectangle mult;
    mult = 5 * oblong;
    cout << "\nThe information about mult:";
    mult.print_info();
}
```

Program Analysis

This example program shows examples of operator overloading.

> Operator overloading allows us to redefine the normal operators so that they can be used with the objects. The end result is that objects of the new class can be used in as natural a manner as the pre-defined types. They seem to be a part of the language rather than an add-on created by the programmer.

When you run the program you will obtain the following output:

```
Class demonstration program

Two rectangle objects created

The information about oblong:
Length = 4  Width = 5
Area = 20  Perimeter = 18
```

```
The information about square:
Length = 6  Width = 6
Area = 36  Perimeter = 24

The information about add:
Length = 10  Width = 11
Area = 110  Perimeter = 42


The information about constant:
Length = 9  Width = 10
Area = 90  Perimeter = 38

The information about mult:
Length = 20  Width = 25
Area = 500  Perimeter = 90
```

In this case we overload the **+** operator and the ***** operator with the declarations:

```
friend rectangle operator+(rectangle a, rectangle b);
friend rectangle operator+(int a, rectangle b);
friend rectangle operator*(int a, rectangle b);
```

and with the definitions shown below.

```
rectangle operator+(rectangle a, rectangle b)
{
    rectangle temp;
    temp.length = a.length + b.length;
    temp.width = a.width + b.width;
    return(temp);
}
```

The first function enables us to add two rectangle objects together using the expression **object1 + object2**.

```
rectangle operator+(int a, rectangle b)
{
    rectangle temp;
    temp.length = a + b.length;
    temp.width = a + b.width;
    return(temp);
}
```

The second function allows us to add a constant to the object's **length** and **width**.

```
rectangle operator*(int a, rectangle b)
{
    rectangle temp;
    temp.length = a * b.length;
    temp.width = a * b.width;
    return(temp);
}
```

The third function allows an object to be multiplied by a constant.

```
object1.operator+(object2)
```

The methods are declared as friend functions, so we can use the double parameter functions as listed. If we didn't use the friend keyword, the function would be a member of one of the objects, and that object would be the object to which the message was sent. We'd then have to use the following syntax (rather than the more 'natural' expression):

```
object1  +  object2
```

Additionally, without the friend keyword we couldn't use an overloading with an integer variable for the first parameter because we can't send a message to an integer variable such as int.operator+(object). Two of the three operator overloadings use an integer for the first parameter, so you must declare them as friend functions.

```
rectangle operator+(rectangle a, rectangle b)    // Add two together
rectangle operator+(int a, rectangle b)    // Add a constant to rectangle
```

The first function header illustrates how the + operator is overloaded by giving the return type, followed by the keyword operator and the operator we wish to overload. The two formal arguments are listed in the brackets, and the normal function operations are given in the definition. There's nothing unusual about this implementation, and I'm sure you understand it (we gave the program some math to do, for purposes of illustration).

I'm sure you understand the other overloaded operator functions which follow this format.

In the program, the expression **constant = 5 + oblong;** asks the system to add an integer to an object of class **rectangle**, so the system finds the second overloading of the **+** operator to enable it to perform this operation.

> You should note that it would be illegal to attempt to use the **+** operator the other way around, namely **constant = oblong + 5;**. This is because we haven't defined a method which uses the two types in that order. Another overloading could be given with reversed types, and we could use the reverse order in a program.

```
rectangle mult;
mult = 5 * oblong;
cout << "\nThe information about mult:";
mult.print_info();
```

In the program the expression **mult = 5 * oblong;** asks the system to use the ***** operator to multiply an integer and an object of class **rectangle** together, which it satisfies by finding the overloaded **operator ***. As before, it would be illegal to attempt to use the *** operator** the other way around.

When we use operator overloading in this way, we make the class we've defined look as if it's a natural part of the language, since it integrates well into the program. This shows that C++ is an extendible language and can be fashioned to deal with problems as they arise.

The overloading of operators is only available for structures and classes as you can't redefine the operators for the pre-defined simple types. You'll have noticed that when using operator overloading, we're also using function name overloading, since some of the function names are the same.

Summary

This has been the briefest of tours around the possibilities of OOP. The subject justifies a book all of its own, but I hope that I've whetted your appetite to develop your interest in this fascinating topic.

Programming Exercises

1   Look at the example program **OOP14.CPP** and overload the binary (subtraction operator) so that you can create a new rectangle object which is equal to **object1** - **object2**.

2   Write a class called **Square** which has private data elements of int **length, width**. There should be public methods:

```
Square(int l = 0, int w = 0);
```

Use **print_info();**   which returns the size of **length** and **width**. It should also return the perimeter size and area.

Use **set_size();**   which sets the **length** and **width**.

Create some objects and test that the class and methods work correctly

3   Use the program that you wrote in question 2 and overload the following operators:

+ (binary - to add to squares together)
+ (binary - to add a constant to a square)
- (binary - to subtract two squares)
- (binary - to subtract a constant from a square)
* (binary - to multiply a square by a constant).

4   Return to the example program OOP14.CPP. Overload the following operators:

+ (binary - so that the following would be correct: **rect1 - 6;**)
* (binary - so that the following would be correct: **rect1 * 5;**).

334

Chapter

Inheritance And Polymorphism

Inheritance is the process of creating new classes, called **derived** classes from existing or **base** classes. The derived class inherits some or all of the base class's features and allows you to add new ones as you need to.

Virtual methods have made another feature of OOP possible - **polymorphism**. This allows related classes to have functions that have the same name but which produce different results. Imagine you created a base class called **home** and then derived **house** and **tent** from it. You could then create a function, **build_home**, to build them. Even though building these two types of homes is quite different, with polymorphism with this one **build_home** function you could build either. This is obviously a powerful feature which we will explain in more detail later in the chapter.

This chapter covers:

- Derived classes
- Base classes
- public and private inheritance
- Constructors
- Multiple inheritance
- Polymorphism
- Virtual functions

Inheritance

OOP's great strength and use lies in the ability of one class to inherit functionality from another. You will find that often when you need to create a new class, an object already exists that resembles the one you need. With **inheritance** you can simply derive a new object which inherits the existing object's member functions and data fields. Let's see how this works.

Associating Extra Characteristics

Let's consider the class **employee**. Every **employee** has a first name, surname, age and salary. Depending on what we want to use the application for we may wish to associate a set of actions with **employee**s, such as printing the details, modifying a name, salary, and so on. In some cases we may want to associate extra characteristics, such as hours of a part-time worker, overtime rate, additional responsibilities, or something else.

Based on our earlier specification of **employee** let's think about **part_timer**.

```
class part_timer: public employee
{
private:
    int hours;

public:
    void enter_data();
    void display_data();
};
```

The syntax is different to what we've already seen:

```
class derived_class_name : public base_class_name
{
...
};
```

This establishes a new class of objects, **derived_class_name**, based on an existing class, **base_class_name**, that inherits the private and public members from the base class.

For example, **first_name**, **surname**, **age**, **salary**, and **hours** are the data members of the class **part_timer**.

Derived Classes

The member functions are defined as follows:

```
void part_timer::enter_data()
{
    employee::enter_data();
    cout << "\tEnter number of hours worked each week: ";
    cin >> hours;
}
```

The member function **enter_data()** has the same name as a member function in its base class. Entering the data for a **part-timer** involves entering the inherited **employee** data, using the inherited function **enter_data()**, and then entering **hours**. The scope resolution operator allows the **enter_data()** function from the base class to be called first.

To clarify the situation, the statement **employee::enter_data();** calls the original function from the base class for entering the first name, surname, age and salary. The remaining two statements prompt the user to enter hours and store this in the appropriate data member using the **cin** statement.

Similarly, the other function is as follows:

```
void part_timer::display_data()
{
    employee::display_data();
    cout << "\tPart-time employee.  Works " << hours
         << " hours per week.\n\n";
}
```

Derived Classes - An Example

Look at the following example program. This is a similar program to **OOP2.CPP**. This time an object of the class **employee** and an object from the class **part_timer** are both filled with data and then displayed on the screen.

Read through the program to see what's happening. Run the program to make things clearer.

```
/* ***********************************************************
 *    oop4.cpp                                              *
 *    Ian M Wilks                                           *
 ********************************************************* */
#include <iostream.h>

class employee
{
private:
    char first_name[15];
    char surname[25];
    int age;
    float salary;
public:
    void enter_data();
    void display_data();
};

class part_timer: public employee
{
private:
    int hours;
public:
    void enter_data();
    void display_data();
};

void employee::enter_data()
{
    cout << "\n\tEnter first name: ";
    cin >> first_name;
    cout << "\tEnter surname: ";
    cin >> surname;
    cout << "\tEnter age: ";
    cin >> age;
    cout << "\tEnter salary: ";
    cin >> salary;
}

void employee::display_data()
{
    cout << "\n\tName: " << first_name << " " << surname << endl
         << "\tAged: " << age << "  Salary: £" << salary << endl;
}

void part_timer::enter_data()
{
    employee::enter_data();
    cout << "\tEnter number of hours worked each week: ";
    cin >> hours;
}
```

```
void part_timer::display_data()
{
    employee::display_data();
    cout << "\tPart-time employee.  Works " << hours << " hours per
week.\n\n";
}
void main()
{
    employee Smyth;
    part_timer Wilks;
    Smyth.enter_data();
    Wilks.enter_data();
    Smyth.display_data();
    Wilks.display_data();
}
```

Program Analysis

```
#include <iostream.h>
```

After the comment block the **#include** directive is used to include the header file **IOSTREAM.H** which is needed for the input and output routines.

```
class employee
{
private:
    char first_name[15];
    char surname[25];
    int age;
    float salary;
public:
    void enter_data();
    void display_data();
};
```

The class **employee** is then declared. This class has four member data items and two member functions. The member functions are defined after the specifier for the class **part_timer**.

```
class part_timer: public employee
{
private:
    int hours;
public:
    void enter_data();
    void display_data();
};
```

The class **part_timer** is then declared. Its member functions are defined immediately after the member functions for **employee**.

```
employee Smyth;
part_timer Wilks;
Smyth.enter_data();
Wilks.enter_data();
Smyth.display_data();
Wilks.display_data();
```

The program then enters **main()**. There are six statements in **main()**. The first statement declares an object of **employee**, and the second statement declares an object of **part_timer**. The next two statements call the **enter_data()** functions for each object. The last two statements call the **display_data()** functions for each object.

Designing Classes

In C++ you'll design classes to perform certain tasks. You will probably start with an indistinct notion of class specifications, filling in more and more components as the project develops. You may find that you finish up with two or more classes that have similarities. To avoid duplicating code in these classes, you could split up the classes, putting the common features in a base class, and using derived classes for the separate entities. Classes that are made only for sharing code in derived classes are known as **seed** classes.

For example, consider the following classes:

```
class bicycle
{
private:
    int wheels;
    float weight;
public:
    void init(int wheels_inp, float weight_inp);
    int return_wheels(void);
    float return_weight(void);

};
```

```
class car
{
private:
   int wheels;
   float weight;
   int pass_capacity;
public:
   void init(int wheels_inp, float weight_inp, int people = 4);
   int return_wheels(void);
   float return_weight(void);

   int passengers(void);
};
```

```
class lorry
{
private:
   int wheels;
   float weight;
   int pass_capacity;
   float carry_capacity;
public:
   void init_lorry(int wheels_inp, int weight_inp,
                      int how_many = 2, float max_load = 24000.0);
   int return_wheels(void);
   float return_weight(void);

   float efficiency(void);
   int passengers(void);
};
```

As you can see, each of these classes have common data members - **wheels**
and **weight**. They also all have common methods - **return_wheels()**, and
return_weight().

Creating Base Classes

It's possible to create a base class that contains the common elements and then
use derived classes for particular entities.

The following base class has been created:

```
class vehicle
{
protected:
   int wheels;
   float weight;
public:
   void init(int wheels_inp, float weight_inp);
   int return_wheels(void);
   float return_weight(void);

};
```

341

Creating Derived Classes Using Base Classes

Instead of creating a bicycle class, we can create a general vehicle class. This base class can be used to declare variables, like bicycle. It can also be used to create derived classes as shown below:

```
class car : public vehicle
{
private:
    int pass_capacity;
public:
    void init(int wheels_inp, float weight_inp, int people = 4);
    int passengers(void);
};
```

```
class lorry : public vehicle
{
private:
    int pass_capacity;
    float carry_capacity;
public:
    void init_lorry(int how_many = 2, float max_load = 24000.0);
    float efficiency(void);
    int passengers(void);
};
```

This base class and the derived classes are then used in the next example.

Using Base and Derived Classes

One reason to use inheritance is that it allows you to reuse code from an earlier program as well as enabling you to slightly modify the source code if this doesn't do what you want. At times, it won't make sense to start a new project from scratch, as some code may be repeated in several programs. It makes sense to attempt to build on what you've previously done.

A second reason for using inheritance is if the project requires the use of several classes which are very similar but do have slight differences.

C++ allows you to inherit all or part of the methods of a class, modify some, and add new ones which aren't available in the parent class. You have complete flexibility, and as usual C++ results in the most efficient code execution.

Using Base and Derived Classes - An Example

Look at the following example:

```
/* ***********************************************************
 *    oop11.cpp                                              *
 *    Ian M Wilks                                            *
 ************************************************************ */
#include <iostream.h>

class vehicle
{
protected:
    int wheels;
    float weight;
public:
    void init(int wheels_inp, float weight_inp);
    int return_wheels(void);
    float return_weight(void);

};


class car : public vehicle
{
private:
    int pass_capacity;

public:
    void init(int wheels_inp, float weight_inp, int people = 4);
    int passengers(void);
};


class lorry : public vehicle
{
private:
    int pass_capacity;
    float carry_capacity;
public:
    void init_lorry(int how_many = 2, float max_load = 24000.0);
    float efficiency(void);
    int passengers(void);
};

void main()
{
vehicle bicycle;
    bicycle.init(2, 27.5);
    cout << "The bicycle has " << bicycle.return_wheels() << " wheels.\n"

        << "The bicycle weighs "
        << bicycle.return_weight() << " pounds.\n\n";
```

```
    car saloon;
        saloon.init(4, 3500.0, 5);
        cout << "The saloon carries " << saloon.passengers() <<  " passengers.\n"
             << "The saloon weighs " << saloon.return_weight() << " pounds.\n"


    lorry flatback;
        flatback.init(6, 12500.0);
        flatback.init_lorry();
        cout << "The flatback lorry weighs " << flatback.return_weight()
             << " pounds.\nThe lorry's efficiency is "
             << 100.0 * flatback.efficiency() << "%.\n";
}

/* *************************** Vehicle ***********************************
*/
// initialize
void vehicle::init(int wheels_inp, float weight_inp)
{
    wheels = wheels_inp;
    weight = weight_inp;
}


//return number of wheels
int vehicle::return_wheels()
{
    return(wheels);
}


// return weight of vehicle
float vehicle::return_weight()
{
    return(weight);

}


/* ****************************** Car *********************************
*/
//initialize
void car::init(int wheels_inp, float weight_inp, int people)
{
    pass_capacity = people;
    wheels = wheels_inp;
    weight = weight_inp;
}

//return passengers
int car::passengers(void)
{
    return(pass_capacity);
}
/* ************************** lorry *****************************************
*/
```

```
//initialize
void lorry::init_lorry(int how_many, float max_load)
{
    pass_capacity = how_many;
    carry_capacity = max_load;
}

float lorry::efficiency(void)
{
    return(carry_capacity / (carry_capacity + weight));
}

int lorry::passengers(void)
{
    return(pass_capacity);
}
```

Program Analysis

Read through the source code and run the program to help you understand what's happening.

The output produced by the program is shown below:

```
The bicycle has 2 wheels.
The bicycle weighs 27.5 pounds.

The saloon carries 5 passengers.
The saloon weighs 3500 pounds.

The flatback lorry weighs 12500 pounds.
The lorry's efficiency is 65.753425%.
```

Look at the class, **vehicle**. It consists of three simple methods which can be used to manipulate data pertaining to our vehicle. The **init()** method assigns the values, which are input as parameters, to the **wheels** and **weight** variables. There are methods to return the number of wheels and the weight, and there is a method that does a calculation to return the loading on each wheel.

The **vehicle** class is used to declare a variable **bicycle**. You should have no problem understanding what the program does with this variable.

The next class is **car**. The **vehicle** class is inherited to this class because of the expression **;public vehicle** added to **class car**. The **car** class is composed of all of the information included in the **vehicle** class plus its own additional information.

This program demonstrates that although the **vehicle** class is being used as a base class, it can also be used as a normal class in the same program.

When considering object-oriented programming, a class that inherits another one is called a **subclass**, but the proper term as defined for C++ is a **derived class**. As both terms are descriptive most programmers are inclined to use the terms synonymously.

As you can see, the **vehicle** class can be used to declare objects that represent bicycles or any other type of vehicle. The **car** class should only be used to declare an object that is of type **car** because the data that can be used with it has been limited. The **car** class is, therefore, more specific than the **vehicle** class.

We could get even more specific. We could define a subclass of **car** named **estate_car** and include information such as **load_capacity**, although this would be silly for a sports car. Therefore, there's nothing, preventing us from using the **car** class as a subclass and as a base class at the same time.

The next class that's defined is also derived from **vehicle** class and is called **lorry**. As we saw with the **car** class, **lorry** inherits all the information included in the **vehicle** class and adds its own additional information.

Remember that the **car** class and the **lorry** class have nothing to do with each other. They only happen to be derived classes of the same base class, or parent class as it's sometimes called.

You'll see that both the **car** and the **lorry** classes have methods named **passengers()** but this doesn't cause any problems and is allowed. If classes are related in some way, as you would expect if they're both derived from the same base class, you would expect them to be performing similar tasks. In these circumstances there's a distinct possibility that a method name would be repeated in both the derived classes.

You shouldn't have any difficulty in understanding the rest of this program.

public or private Inheritance

You'll probably have noticed that we haven't yet discussed the keyword **public** which we've used in the derived class declarations.

```
class derived_class_name : public base_class_name
{
    ...
};
```

What's the effect of the **public** keyword? The keyword **public** specifies that objects of the derived class are able to access public member functions of the base class. The keyword **private** can be used as an alternative.

```
class derived_class_name : private base_class_name
{
    ...
};
```

If the keyword **private** is used, objects of the derived class can't access public member functions of the base class. As objects can't access **private** or **protected** members of a class, then no members of the base class are accessible to objects of the derived class.

How to Declare Member Functions

You'll have noticed that the function definitions account for a lot of the code in the previous example. As you have seen, functions can be defined in the class specifier. For example:

```
class vehicle
{
protected:
    int wheels;
    float weight;
public:
    void init(int wheels_inp, float weight_inp);
    int return_wheels(void) { return(wheels);}
    float return_weight(void) { return(weight);}
    float load_per_wheel(void) { return(weight/wheels);}
};
```

Similarly:

```
class car : public vehicle
{
private:
    int pass_capacity;
public:
    void init(int wheels_inp, float weight_inp, int people = 4);
    int passengers(void) { return(pass_capacity);}
};
```

Try rewriting the above example program so that the smaller functions are defined within the class specifier.

Constructors in Derived Classes

Let's examine another example of inheritance. Look at the following class specifiers.

```
class bookcase
{
private:
    int colour, width, height, shelves, material;
public:
    bookcase(int c, int w, int h, int s, int m)
    {
        colour = c;
        width = w;
        height = h;
        shelves = s;
        material = m;
    }

    int report_colour()    {return(colour);}
    int report_width()     {return(width);}
    int report_height()    {return(height);}
    int report_shelves()   {return(shelves);}
    int report_material()  {return(material);}
};
```

```
class desk
{
private:
    int colour, width, height, drawers, material;
public:
    desk(int c, int w, int h, int d, int m)
    {
        width = w;
        height = h;
        colour = c;
        shelves = s;
        material = m;
    }

    int report_colour()    {return(colour);}
    int report_width()     {return(width);}
    int report_height()    {return(height);}
    int report_drawers()   {return(drawers);}
    int report_material()  {return(material);}
};
```

Look at the above two classes. You'll see that they have several features in common. The common features could be extracted and placed in a parent or base class.

```
class furniture
{    //parent or base class
private:
    int colour, width, height, material;

public:
    furniture(int c, int w, int h, int m)
    {
        colour = c;
        width = w;
        height = h;
        material = m;
    }

    int report_colour()   {return(colour);}
    int report_width()    {return(width);}
    int report_height()   {return(height);}
    int report_material() {return(material);}
};
```

As you've seen, once we have defined the base class we can then define the derived classes. Consider the class **bookcase**. What needs to be done?

Look at the definition below:

```
class bookcase : public furniture
{
private:
    int shelves;
public:
    bookcase(int c, int w, int h, int s, int m) :
                                    furniture(c, w, h, m)
    {
        shelves = s;
    }
    int report_shelves() {return(shelves);}
};
```

This class should be simpler now we're using a base class. The class **bookcase** inherits all public variables and functions. We therefore have access to **report_colour()**, **report_width()**, **report_height()**, and **report_material()**. Remember that we don't have any access to **colour**, **width**, **height**, or **material**. To store values in these variables we use the **bookcase** constructor which calls, and passes arguments to the base class constructor:

```
bookcase(int c, int w, int h, int s, int m) : furniture(c, w, h, m)
{ ... }
```

If we wanted to have an additional member function of **bookcase** which outputs details, we could define it as follows:

```
void bookcase::display_bookcase()
{
    cout << "The bookcase is made from " << report_material()
         << ".  It is " << report_colour() << ".\nThe width is "
         << report_width() << " and the height is "
         << report_height() << ".  It has " << report_shelves()
         << " shelves.\n\n";
}
```

You'll see that as material and color are stored as integer values these would need to be translated from integers to appropriate string values.

In a similar way the **desk** class can become a derived class. This has been left for you to do as an exercise.

Multiple Inheritance

In C++ a class isn't limited to having only one base class. A class can have many base classes and inherit properties from each of these. The general syntax is:

```
class derived_class: public A, public B, public C, ...
{
private:
    ...
public:
    ...
};
```

The derived class inherits the members of all its base classes.

Let's have a look at the following classes:

```
class van
{
protected:
    int wheels;
    float weight;
    float mpg;
    int carry_capacity;
public:
    void init(int wheels_inp, float weight_inp,
                        float mpg_in, float carry_inp);
    int return_wheels(void) { return(wheels);}
    float return_weight(void) { return(weight);}
```

350

```
    float return_mpg(void) { return(mpg);}
    float load_per_wheel(void) { return( weight/wheels);}
    float efficiency(void)
              {return carry_capacity/(carry_capacity + weight);}
};
```

```
class driver
{
protected:
    float hourly_pay;
public:
    void init(float pay) {hourly_pay = pay; };
    float cost_per_mile(void) {return(hourly_pay / 50.0); } ;
    //cost_per_mile = hourly pay/ average number of miles per hour
};
```

If we used these classes as base classes we could create a derived class as follows:

```
class driven_van : public van, public driver
{
public:
    void init_all(int wheels_in, float weight_in,
                  float mpg_in, float carry_in, float pay)
        {
             wheels = wheels_in;
             weight = weight_in;
             mpg = mpg_in;
             carry_capacity = carry_in;
             hourly_pay = pay;
        };

    float cost_per_day(float cost_fuel)
        {
        return( 8.0 * hourly_pay + 8.0 *
                             (cost_fuel / mpg) * 50.0);
        };
};
```

This code fragment illustrates the mechanics of the use of multiple inheritance. In order to keep the code as simple as possible, all of the member methods are defined in the class so that the code for the member functions is easy to find and study.

All variables in both base classes are declared to be protected so they will be available for use in any class which inherits them. The code for each class is kept very simple so you can concentrate on studying the techniques rather than spending time trying to understand intricate code.

We define the derived class. In the previous example we considered how to inherit a single base class into another class. As you can see, to use two or more base classes we employ the same technique. The only difference is that we use a list of inherited classes separated by commas.

The two base classes are normal classes and can be used to define and manipulate objects in a program.

Now try writing a program that uses these three classes.

Polymorphism

Polymorphism describes the capability of C++ code to behave in different ways depending on run-time conditions. Polymorphism can be defined more simply as similar. Objects are polymorphic if they have some similarities remain distinct.

Consider the ways an article can be used in real life. You can:

- Clean it
- Move it
- Repair it
- Paint it

These actions are generic because you don't know what kind of article you're working with. For example, to move house requires a completely different set of actions than those needed to move a cup. We can only associate the verb with a set of actions once we know what the article is.

Similarly, in C++, when we have some polymorphic functions, we don't know which function will be called until the object is specified.

We've looked at operator and function overloading which might be considered a novice type of polymorphism. Remember to refer to two things with a single entity is polymorphism in action.

Using Virtual Functions

Virtual functions can be a great aid in programming some types of project.

Virtual Functions - An Example

Take a look at the example program named **OOP18.CPP**. This is the basic program we'll use for this illustration.

```
/* *************************************************************
 *    oop18.cpp                                               *
 *    Ian M Wilks                                             *
 ********************************************************* */
#include <iostream.h>
class vehicle
{
    int wheels;
    float weight;
public:
    void message(void)
    {
        cout << "Message from the vehicle class\n";
    }
};

class car : public vehicle
{
    int pass_capacity;
public:
    void message(void)
        { cout << "Message from the car class\n"; }
};

class lorry : public vehicle
{
    int pass_capacity;
    float carry_capacity;
public:
    int passengers(void) {return pass_capacity;}
};

class boat : public vehicle
{
    int pass_capacity;
public:
    int passengers(void) {return pass_capacity;}
    void message(void)
        { cout << "Message from the boat class\n"; }
};

void main()
{
    vehicle bicycle;
    car hatchback;
    lorry flatback;
    boat dinghy;
```

```
        bicycle.message();
        hatchback.message();
        flatback.message();
        dinghy.message();
    }
```

Program Analysis

You'll see that some functions that were in the earlier programs have been dropped and a new function, **message()**, has been added to the base class. We'll be considering the operation of **message()** in the base class and the derived classes. For that reason, there is a function **message()** in both the **car** class and the **boat** class.

You'll also have noticed that there's a lack of a function named **message()** in the **lorry** class. Remember that the function **message()** from the base class is available in the **lorry** class, because the function is inherited from the base class due to the keyword **public** in the expression:

```
class lorry : public vehicle
```

You should also notice that the use of the keyword **public** means the specifiers for the other derived classes actually do nothing because the only function available in this class, because it is inherited from the base class.

In **main()**, one object of each of the classes is declared and **message()** is called once for each object.

The output from the program is shown below:

```
Message from the vehicle class
Message from the car class
Message from the vehicle class
Message from the boat class
```

As you can see, in the case of the **lorry** class, the function named **message()** from the base class is called. The message displayed on the screen indicates that this has happened.

The Keyword Virtual - An Example

Consider the following example:

```
/* ************************************************************
 *    oop19.cpp                            *
 *    Ian M Wilks                          *
 ************************************************************ */
#include <iostream.h>
```

```
class vehicle
{
    int wheels;
    float weight;
public:
    virtual void message(void)
    {
            cout << "Message from the vehicle class\n";
    }
};

class car : public vehicle
{
    int pass_capacity;
public:
    void message(void)
            { cout << "Message from the car class\n"; }
};


class lorry : public vehicle
{
    int pass_capacity;
    float carry_capacity;
public:
    int passengers(void) {return pass_capacity;}
};


class boat : public vehicle
{
    int pass_capacity;
public:
    int passengers(void) {return pass_capacity;}

    void message(void)
            { cout << "Message from the boat class\n"; }
};


void main()
{
    vehicle bicycle;
    car hatchback;
    lorry flatback;
    boat dinghy;

    bicycle.message();
    hatchback.message();
    flatback.message();
    dinghy.message();
}
```

Program Analysis

You should notice that there's only one change. The keyword **virtual** has been added to the declaration of **message()** in the base class.

This program operates no differently than the last example program and this is confirmed by the output, which is shown below:

```
Message  from  the  vehicle  class
Message  from  the  car  class
Message  from  the  vehicle  class
Message  from  the  boat  class
```

Nothing different has happened, so what is a virtual function?

A virtual function is a member function that is invoked through a pointer to a public base class. The member function invoked is decided by the class type of the actual object that is addressed by the pointer.

Invoking Virtual Functions

For example, consider a graphics program that includes a number of different shapes - say, triangle, circle, square and so on ... Each of these classes has a member function **display()** that draws the appropriate shape on the screen. If you were going to create a screen image composed of a number of these elements grouped together, you could create an array that holds pointers to all the different objects in the program. You could define the array with the following statement:

```
shape * point_array[20];
```

If you insert pointers to all the objects in the array, you can use a simple loop to create the screen image. For example:

```
for (int i = 0; i < number; i++)
    point_array[i]->display();
```

You can use the above loop to execute completely different functions. If the pointer in **point_array** points to a rectangle, the function that displays the rectangle is called. However, two conditions must be met for this to work:

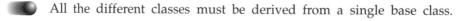 All the different classes must be derived from a single base class.

The member function in the base class must be declared to be virtual.

Virtual Functions Exhibiting Polymorphism - An Example

The next example program illustrates a virtual function that operates as a virtual function exhibiting polymorphism. This is in the example program OOP23.CPP.

```
/* ***********************************************************
 *    oop23.cpp                                             *
 *    Ian M Wilks                                           *
 *********************************************************** */

#include <iostream.h>

class vehicle
{
    int wheels;
    float weight;
public:
    virtual void message(void)
    {
        cout << "Message from the vehicle class\n";
    }
};

class car : public vehicle
{
    int pass_capacity;
public:
    void message(void)
    {
        cout << "Message from the car class\n";
    }
};

class lorry : public vehicle
{
    int pass_capacity;
    float carry_capacity;
public:
    int passengers(void) {return pass_capacity;}
};

class boat : public vehicle
{
    int pass_capacity;
public:
    int passengers(void) {return pass_capacity;}

    void message(void)
    {
        cout << "Message from the boat class\n";
    }
};
void main()
```

```
{
    vehicle *  any_vehicle;

    any_vehicle = new vehicle;
    any_vehicle->message();
    delete any_vehicle;

    any_vehicle = new car;
    any_vehicle->message();
    delete any_vehicle;

    any_vehicle = new lorry;
    any_vehicle->message();
    delete any_vehicle;

    any_vehicle = new boat;
    any_vehicle->message();
    delete any_vehicle;
}
```

Program Analysis

```
virtual void message(void)
```

As you can see, the keyword `virtual` is still added to the function `message()` but only in the base class.

```
void main()
{
    vehicle *  any_vehicle;

    any_vehicle = new vehicle;
```

The `main()` function declares a pointer to the base class. Since we've only declared a pointer and no variables we need to dynamically allocate memory to store the objects before using them. Dynamic memory allocation occurs by using the `new` operator.

Using a Pointer

As you've seen, only a single pointer is declared to a class and the pointer is pointing to the parent class of the class hierarchy. We use this pointer to refer to each of the four classes in turn and this is used to examine the output of `message()`.

How can we use a pointer to one class to refer to another class? If, when chatting with our neighbor, we referred to a vehicle, we could be referring to a car, a lorry, a motorcycle, or any other kind of vehicular transport. This is because we are referring to a general form. If, however, we were to refer to a car, we're excluding all other kinds of transport.

The same mechanism can be applied in C++. If we have a pointer to a vehicle, we can use that pointer to refer to any of the more specific objects. In a similar manner, if we have a pointer to a car, we can't use that pointer to reference any of the other classes, including the base class, because the pointer to the **car** class is too specific and not allowed to be used on any of the other classes.

We can use a pointer to a base class to point to an object of a derived class of that base class. However, we can't use a pointer to a derived class to point to the base class or, to any of the other derived classes of the base class.

In this program we can therefore declare a pointer to the **vehicle** class, which is the base class, and use that pointer to refer to either the base class or any of the derived classes.

As you can see, this is what has been done in **main()**.

The program frees memory after use.

The output from the program is:

```
Message from the vehicle class
Message from the car class
Message from the vehicle class
Message from the boat class
```

message() is declared to be a virtual function in the base class. So, when we call this function with a pointer to the base class, we actually execute the function associated with one of the derived classes, if a function is available in the derived class to which the pointer is actually pointing.

Remember that the structure of the virtual function in the base class, and each of the derived classes is identical. The return type and the number and types of the arguments must be identical for all, since a single statement can be used to call any of them.

Summary

In this chapter we've looked at inheritance and how to derive a class (derived class) from a base class. We've covered public and private inheritance and seen how constructors are used in derived classes. We've examined multiple inheritance, seeing how classes can inherit properties from many base classes and then moved on to polymorphism and virtual functions.

Programming Exercises

1   Consider the example program **OOP14.CPP** which we saw in the previous chapter. Rewrite your **Square** class (from question 2 in the previous chapter) so that it is a derived class of **rectangle**.

2   Now alter the program you wrote in question 1 and add the class **Triangle** which should be derived from **rectangle**.

3   Experiment with overloaded operators. Can you inherit the friend functions from the base class? Do they work correctly with **Square** and/or **Triangle** objects? Do you need to re-write the overloaded functions for each derived class?

4   From question 2, use the **Triangle** class as a base class and derive two more classes - **Equilateral** and **Isosceles**. Remember, an equilateral triangle is one which has all its sides equal in length and an isosceles triangle is one which has two sides equal in length.

5   Use the program you wrote in question 4, and make the **print_info()** function virtual. Experiment with polymorphism. Do the correct functions get accessed for the classes **Equilateral** and **Isosceles**? Do you have to make the **print_info()** function in **Triangle** virtual?

Chapter

Object-Oriented Design

The title of this chapter says we are going to look at object-oriented design. We will, but first we must set the scene and consider design in a procedural program. This then naturally leads on to OOP as you will find there is some similarity between the object and procedural design in that the scoping of elements comes into play early. After we have looked at design we will look at a larger object-oriented program and see how it all fits together.

In this chapter we cover:

- Procedural program design
- Object-Oriented program design
- Defining classes
- How an OO program is made up

Program Design

In Chapter 1 we looked at the basics of program design and said that this is normally broken down into two areas:

- Problem analysis
- Code design

When you are designing a procedural program you would normally write out the requirements in English. You would then look at the poignant verbs, which would give some indication to the pattern of actions. Finally, some of these same verbs may become the names of functions in your program.

A typical specification may develop as follows:

- Input the data, checking that the data is within the required range.
- The data will then be processed (which would identify the process or processes that will be applied to the data).
- Then the results would be output to the screen.

You would probably decide on the following functions:

```
input()
process()
output()
```

You would probably then sub-divide the **input()** function so that it was comprised of two other functions, namely **getdata()** and **checkdata().**

Your program would then be on the following basis:

```
void main()
{
    input();
    process();
    output();
}

void input()
{
    getdata();
    checkdata();
}
```

This book isn't intended to be a detailed guide to program design and you are advised to read other books on this subject.

Object vs Procedural Programming

You may be wondering when it is better to use either object-oriented or procedural programming. With an object-oriented program you have to identify the objects that you will use in your program and this is actually easier than deciding on the functions to include in a procedural program.

For example, you are going to write a procedural program that gives the user a graphical user interface. What functions do you need? This isn't easy to answer without a lot of thought.

Now, consider the problem again. You are going to write an object-oriented program gives that user a graphical user interface (GUI). What objects will you need? This is easier to answer. You will work with the following: window, menu, mouse, button, etc.

What you are in fact doing, is looking at the nouns in your specification. The nouns will indicate the objects that you will need. After you have identified the objects, you'll then look at the verbs to see what actions operate on the objects. These actions will become your member functions.

Object-Oriented Design

There are several formal approaches to object-oriented design. In his book, *Object-Oriented Design, CRD Software Engineeering Guidelines,* W Lorensen suggested the following approach.

1   Identify the data abstractions for each subsystem. These data abstractions will be the classes for the program. Working from the specification, the abstraction is performed top-down where possible.

2   Identify the attributes for each abstraction. The attributes become the members for each class.

3   Identify the operations for each abstraction. The operations are the member functions for each class. Some functions will access and update data members whilst others execute specific operations for that class.

4   Identify the communication between objects. This is to define the messages that objects send to each other. You are attempting to define an association between the functions and the messages that invoke the functions.

5   Test the design. Test the design's ability to match the specification.

6   Apply inheritance where appropriate. If step 1 is performed top-down then inheritance can be found there. However, if abstractions are created bottom-up (possibly because the specification directly names the abstractions) apply inheritance here.

These steps are applied at each level of abstraction. This will continue until a point is reached where the abstraction corresponds to a primitive element in the design.

An OOP Structure

Let's look at how we would create an object-oriented program.

Defining Classes

Classes are typically defined in a number of files. These would normally comprise:

A header file, `<classname>.h` This file contains only declarations for the data type. It is the file that a user of the class will include in the application program.

An implementation file, `<CLASSNAME>.CPP`. This file holds the code that implements the class methods. The user will normally not be given this file but would be given a pre-compiled object code version instead.

A suite of test programs, `TST<CLASSNAME>.CPP`, or a suite of application programs. These files are either for the developers benefit only - used to test the implementation of the class before its release to users. Otherwise they will be the application that a user has developed.

We will create a class **IntSet** which is used to create sets of integers. Accordingly, our definition of **IntSet** will require the production of 3 files: `intset.h`, `INTSET.CPP`, `TSTINTSE.CPP`.

These files are compiled together. If you are using Borland C++ or Turbo C++, you will use the project menu to put both the files having the extension `CPP` into the project. You should refer to your manuals for further details.

The Internal Implementation

The integer sets will be designed using an array cleed **data_items** and two integer values: **numberIn**, which represents the number of members in the set, and **max**, which represents the size of the array.

The Header File - An Example

We will now look at the header file, **intset.h**, to see the class specifier.

```
/* ****************************************************************
 *          intset.h                                             *
 *          Header file for integer sets                         *
 **************************************************************** */
#ifndef INTSET                  //to prevent multiple declarations
#define INTSET

#include <iostream.h>           //as iostream.h is included here, it is
                                //not needed in the main program


//class definition
class IntSet
{
public:
    //default constructor
    IntSet() : numberIn(0), max(10), data_items(new int[10]) {return;}
    IntSet(int s)   : numberIn(0), max(s), data_items(new int[s]) {return;}
    IntSet ( IntSet& );             // copy constructor
    IntSet ( int , int* );          // type coercion function
    ~IntSet() { delete data_items; }    //destructor

    //member functions
    void Add( int x);
    int NumberIn() { return numberIn; }
    int Empty() { return numberIn == 0; }
    int In ( int x );
    void Display(ostream& out);

    //friend functions
    friend IntSet operator* (IntSet& A, IntSet& B); // INTERSECTION
    friend IntSet operator+ (IntSet& A, IntSet& B); // UNION
    friend IntSet operator- (IntSet& A, IntSet& B); // DIFFERENCE
    friend int    operator== (IntSet& A, IntSet& B);// EQUALITY

private:
    int numberIn;
    int *data_items;
    int max;
};                              //End of definition
```

```
// overload the stream operator<< for convenience

inline ostream& operator<< (ostream& out, IntSet& A)
{
     A.Display(out);
     return out;
}

#endif
```

Header File Analysis

Constructors

```
     IntSet() : numberIn(0), max(10), data_items(new int[10]) {return;}
     IntSet(int s)    : numberIn(0), max(s), data_items(new int[s]) {return;}
```

There are four constructors in the **IntSet** class in the header file declarations.

The first two constructors (shown above) are a little different to other member functions or constructors that you have seen so far. As you are aware constructors have no return type. This is because the name of the function is the name of the class. However, the main difference is that between the function specification and the braces (which is the function body), is a list of data members looking like function calls, preceded by a colon. This is the initialization list.

The items in the initialization list are calls to constructors to initialize the individual data members. Therefore, in the default constructor, **numberIn** is set equal to 0, **max** is set equal to 10, and the pointer **data_items** is used to dynamically allocate memory for an integer array holding ten elements using the operator **new.**

```
     IntSet ( IntSet& );      // copy constructor
```

The next constructor is a copy constructor. A constructor with the specification **classname(const classname &)** or **classname(classname &)** is usually called a copy constructor. The constructor takes a reference to an object of the same type to do the initialization.

```
        IntSet ( int , int* );          // type coercion function
```

The next constructor is a type coercion function, `IntSet(int,int*);`. This is a coercion that doesn't require a fundamental change of type. Accordingly, a coercion from **name** to **const name** or to **name &** are trivial coercions, changing trivial properties of type rather than the type itself.

Destructors

```
        ~IntSet() { delete data_items; }    //destructor
```

The next statement that you haven't seen before is `~IntSet();`. This is known as a destructor. As you have seen a constructor is called to initialize the members of a newly created variable. When the variable comes to the end of its 'life', a destructor is called to do any necessary tidying up.

For example, if the constructor switched the screen to graphics mode the destructor would be used to reset the screen to text mode. In this case, the constructor dynamically allocates memory and the destructor deallocates the memory.

There are five member functions. There are four overloaded operator functions which are declared to be friends of the class.

The Implementation File - An Example

The next file we will examine is **INTSET.CPP**.

```
/* **************************************************************
 *     intset.cpp                                 *
 *     implementation file for Integer sets             *
 ********************************************************* */
#include "intset.h"
const INCREASE = 50;

IntSet::IntSet( IntSet& A )                  //copy constructor
{
    max = A.max;
    numberIn = A.numberIn;
    data_items = new int [max];
    for (int i = 0; i < numberIn ; i++ )
        data_items[i] = A.data_items[i];
}
```

```
IntSet::IntSet( int n, int *Array )              // type coercion function
{
    max = n;
    numberIn = n;
    data_items = new int [max];
    for (int i = 0; i < max ; i++ )
            data_items[i] = Array[i];
}



// add an element to an existing set, if not already present, and
// expand the array if it is full.
void IntSet::Add( int x )
{
    if (! In(x)  )
    {
            if (numberIn < max)
                    data_items[numberIn++] = x;
            else
            {
                    int newsize    = max + INCREASE;      //create new array
                    int *newarray = new int[ newsize ];
                    for (int i = 0; i < max; i++)         //copy old array into
                            newarray[i] = data_items[i]; //new array
                    delete data_items;                    //delete old array
                    data_items = newarray;            //assign new array to
                    max = newsize;                        //IntSet
                    data_items[numberIn++] = x;        //add item to IntSet
            }
    }
}

int IntSet::In( int x )                       //check if integer is member of set
{
    for ( int i = 0 ; i < numberIn ; i++ )
            if ( data_items[i] == x )
                    return(1);
    return(0);
}

void IntSet::Display(ostream& out )               //display set on stream out
{
    if (numberIn == 0)
            out << "{}";
    else
    {
            out << "{ ";
            for (int i = 0; i < numberIn; i++)
            {
                    out << data_items[i];
                    if(i != numberIn - 1)
                            out << ", ";
            }
            out << " }" ;
    }
}
```

370

```
IntSet operator+ (IntSet& A, IntSet& B)  //return UNION of two sets
{
    int i;
    IntSet Union( A.numberIn + B.numberIn );

    for (i = 0; i < A.numberIn ; i++ )  //union contains all items in A
        Union.Add( A.data_items[i] );

    for (i = 0; i < B.numberIn; i++)    //plus those in B that aren't in A
        if ( ! Union.In(B.data_items[i]) )
            Union.Add( B.data_items[i] );

    return(Union);
}


//Intersection
//Iterate through items in A and check if the item is also in B
//If it is in both we add it to the intersection.  The size of
//the intersection is the largest of A and B


IntSet operator* (IntSet& A, IntSet& B)
{
    IntSet intersection( (A.numberIn > B.numberIn) ? A.numberIn : B.numberIn
) ;
    for (int i = 0 ; i < A.numberIn ; i++ )
        if ( B.In( A.data_items[i] ) )          //item is in A and B
            intersection.Add( A.data_items[i] ); //add intersection
    return(intersection);
}


// check if two sets contain the same elements and are the same size
int operator== (IntSet& A, IntSet& B)
{
    if ( A.numberIn != B.numberIn )     //if not same size then not equal
        return(0);
    else
    {
        for (int i = 0 ; i < A.numberIn ; i++ )
            if(!B.In( A.data_items[i]))  //if in A but not B
                return(0);              //return false
        return(1);                      //sets contain same elements
    }
}
```

```
//Set Difference operator - removes from A items in B
IntSet operator- ( IntSet& A, IntSet& B )
{
    IntSet difference;                    // start with empty set

    for (int i = 0 ; i < A.numberIn ; i++ )
        if ( ! B.In( A.data_items[i]) )
            difference.Add( A.data_items[i] );
    return(difference);
}
```

Implementation File Analysis

Let's explain implementing **Add()**. The inadvisable route would be to compose the class, with the sets having a fixed size - we need a dynamic container for some operations. We require dynamic memory allocation.

```
const setincrement = 100;

// add an element to an existing set, if not already present, and
// expand the array if it is full.
void IntSet::Add(int x)
{
    if (! In(x)  )
    {
        if (numberIn < max)
            data_items[numberIn++] = x;
        else
        {
            int newsize   = max + setincrement; //create new array
            int *newarray = new int[ newsize ];
            for (int i = 0; i < max; i++)         //copy old array into
                newarray[i] = data_items[i];  //new array
            delete data_items;                                      //
delete old array
            data_items = newarray;                                  //assign
new array to
            max = newsize;
//IntSet
            data_items[numberIn++] = x;          //add item to IntSet
        }
    }
}
```

As a result of dynamically allocating memory, **data_items** has to be a pointer to an integer - this enables it to point to the array elements. The new operator returns a pointer to the beginning of allocated memory. When using **new** to dynamically allocate memory for the array, we need to supply the type of array and its size using the statement: **data_items = newint[20]**. This means, if we run out of space in the array we can dynamically increase its size. The data member **numberIn** always indicates the position of the next empty slot in the array and changes as items are added to the set. The data member, **max,** indicates the number of slots in the array. When **numberIn==max,** the array is full and no further items can be added to the set However, by using arrays created on the heap we can simply create a new, larger, array when one array is full and copy the contents of the old array across to the new array. The new array is then allocated to **data_items**. Finally, we dispose of the old array using the **delete** operator.

This means that we can expand the size of our sets automatically whenever it is required.

```
int IntSet::In( int x )
{
    for ( int i = 0 ; i < numberIn ; i++ )
        if ( data_items[i] == x )
            return(1);
    return(0);
}
```

The function **In()** tests for membership of the set. As items can be added in any order, we must search through the array until either the member we are searching for is found or we reach the end of the array. Remember true is represented by 1 and false by 0.

```
void IntSet::Display(ostream& out )
{
    if (numberIn == 0)
        out << "{}";
    else
    {
        out << "{ ";
        for (int i = 0; i < numberIn; i++)
        {
            out << data_items[i];
            if(i != numberIn - 1)
                out << ", ";
        }
        out << " }" ;
    }
}
```

The function **Display()** steps through the set outputting the members on the given output stream.

```
IntSet operator+ (IntSet& A, IntSet& B) //return UNION of two sets
{
    int i;
    IntSet Union( A.numberIn + B.numberIn );

    for(i = 0; i < A.numberIn ; i++ )   //union holds all items in A
        Union.Add( A.data_items[i] );

    for (i = 0; i < B.numberIn; i++)    //plus those in B not in A
        if ( ! Union.In(B.data_items[i]) )
            Union.Add( B.data_items[i] );

    return(Union);
}
```

The binary operators: **+** (union), ***** (intersection), **-** (difference), and **==** (equality) are declared to be friend functions.

The Test Program - An Example

We will now look at the test program which is contained in the file **TSTINTSE.CPP**.

You must include test cases for all the operations you have currently coded. You will normally extend the test program as more operations are implemented until you have completely tested the class.

```
/* ************************************************************
 *    tstintse.cpp                                           *
 *    test file for Integer sets                             *
 ************************************************************ */
#include <conio.h>
#include "IntSet.h"

void main()
{
    clrscr();
    cout << " This is a test program for the classIntSet\n"
         << " The operations defined in the class will be\n"
         << " tested in turn.\n\n"
         << " Please add to this program as you develop \n"
         << " more operations.\n\n";

    IntSet A;
    IntSet B(25);

    cout << " A.Empty() returns - " << A.Empty() << "\n";
    cout << " cout << A returns - " << A << "\n";
    cout << " A's size  is      - " << A.NumberIn() << "\n";
    cout << " A.In(5) returns   - " << A.In(5) << "\n\n";
    getch ();//to stop info scrolling off the screen
```

```
// make A = { 5, 12, 13 }
// make B = { 12, 13, 14, 15, 16 }
    A.Add(5);  A.Add(12); A.Add(13);
    B.Add(12); B.Add(13); B.Add(14); B.Add(15); B.Add16);

    cout << " A's value is now " << A << "\n\n";

    cout << " B's value is  " << B
         << " It's size is  " << B.NumberIn() << "\n"
         << " Empty returns " << B.Empty() << "\n\n";

    cout << " A.In(1) returns  " << A.In(1)
         << " A.In(13) returns " << A.In(13) << "\n\n";

    IntSet C = A + B ;  // union of two sets

    cout << " C is UNION of A and B \n"
         << " it should be { 5, 12, 13, 14, 15, 16 } \n"
         << " The size of C is " << C.NumberIn()
         << "\n" << " C = " << C << "\n\n";

    IntSet D;   // {15, 16, 17, 18 }
    D.Add(15); D.Add(16); D.Add(17); D.Add(18);

    IntSet E = C * D;  // should be {15, 16 }
    cout << " E is INTERSECTION of C and D \n"
         << " E should be {15, 16 } \n\n" << " D = " << D << "\n"
         << " E = " << E << "\n\n";

    IntSet F = D - E; // should be { 17, 18 }
    cout << " F is the DIFFERENCE of D and E \n"
         << " it should be { 17, 18 }\n" << " F = " << F << "\n\n";

    int test[4] = { 19,11,54,94 };
    IntSet G (4, test );
    cout << " G = " << G << "\n\n";
}
```

If you examine, the three files and then compile and run the program you will be able to understand what is actually happening. Through designing, writing, compiling and then running OO programs you will soon get to grips with how they work. Practice is certainly the best teacher, so try doing the programming exercises at the end of this chapter!

Summary

This chapter has looked at procedural design and how that compares to object-oriented design. We saw how to define classes and how to design an object-oriented program. We looked at header files, implementation files and test suites, all of which make up object-oriented programs. So now you have a general picture of what object-oriented programs are and how they work. You need to try writing more programs to really see how powerful this can be.

Programming Exercises

1   Add the following function to the `IntSet` class and test that it is correctly implemented. `IntSet Delete( int i);`.

The function should remove an item from an `IntSet`. For example, if `A = { 1, 2, 3}` then `A.Delete(2) = { 1, 3}`.

2   Add the following function to the `IntSet` class and test that it is correctly implemented. `IntSet Universal (int start, int finish);`.

This function will create a set containing all the integers between start and stop. For example, `Universal(1,4) = {1, 2, 3, 4}`.

3   Add the following function to the `IntSet` class and test that it is correctly implemented. `IntSet FromFile(char * filename);`.

This function creates a set by reading integers contained in a file.

4   Write the following function (not a member function of `IntSet`) and test that it is correctly implemented.

```
void ToFile (IntSet I, char * filename);
```

This function will create a file containing the values in `IntSet I`.

Instant

C++

Hints To Programming Exercises

Chapter 2

1 Experiment with the **cout** statement to display your name and address. Try using the special character \t at the start of your string to put your details in different positions.

2 No explanation should be needed. Simply change the **cout** statement in **WELCOME.CPP**.

3 Same as for question 2.

4 You will need to modify the **WELCOME.CPP** file as follows:

Declare three variables - one of type **char**, one of type **int**, and one of type **float**.

Output a message to the screen asking the user to enter the letter '**A**'.

Use **cin** to read the character from the keyboard and store it in the appropriate variable. Then repeat the process for 21 and 3.142.

Now display the variables on the screen.

5 Prompt the user to enter the radius of the circle which should be stored in an appropriate variable. Declare other variables to store the answers in, and perform the calculations.

Chapter 3

1 Simply modify the program **OPERAT1.CPP** to do these two calculations. You can either put the values in appropriate variables and then do the calculation, or you can use a statement such as

```
int ans = 46/11;
```

2 Look at the example programs for ideas.

3 This is to give you some experience of interpreting error messages given by the compiler.

4 Similar to earlier exercises in the book.

5 Similar to earlier exercises in the book.

Chapter 4

1 Read through the source code. Look up any of the syntax you don't remember. Run it on the computer to see if you were correct. You will need to alter the **for** loop so that only a maximum of 20 integers can be displayed.

2 You have already got most of the code. This is to get you to experiment with the **while** loop.

3 You have already got most of the code. This is to get you to experiment with the **do while** loop.

4 Using a loop (try all of them) ask the user to enter a sequence of numbers. You will need to declare two variables.

One will be used to hold the character entered via the keyboard

The other will hold the largest number.

The one that will hold the largest number should be initialized to **0**.

Each character entered should be compared with the current largest number. If the character entered is larger, you will need to assign the character entered to the variable holding the largest number.

5 Similar to question 4.

6 Although this is a long question, it isn't complicated. Firstly, output the menu to the screen and ask the user to enter the appropriate letter. Depending on the letter entered, the appropriate help message should be displayed. What construct will you use? There *is* an obvious candidate.

Chapter 5

1 You do not need an array! This is to remind you to remember to loop.

2 As question 1.

3 You need to declare a variable to store the months. This is a two dimensional array of characters. You can then use a loop to enter the months - prompt user to enter month and store keyboard entry.

Declare the array as:

```
char array[12][10];
```

The **cin** statement will then be:

```
cin >> array[i];
```

4 No explanation needed.

5 No explanation needed.

6 All you really need to do is experiment with the relational operators.

Chapter 6

1   Simply alter one of the example functions you have seen to do this calculation. I'd alter **square()** from **SQUARE.CPP**.

2   As question 1, with some simple selection revision.

3   Look at the example given and consider the examples earlier in the text. You may need to experiment, but don't give up.

4   Earlier in the book you saw some example code which checked to see if the input was in the range **0** to **9**. You also saw some code that tested if a lowercase letter had been entered. You can use similar code now in a function.

If you know the ASCII codes you can work with these instead. The ASCII code is included in many computer manuals. If you don't have one, use the following code fragment to generate the ASCII code table:

```
for (int i = 32; i < 256; i++)
{
    if(i % 20 == 0)
    {
        cout << "\n\n\tPress any key to continue";
        getch();
        clrscr();
    }
    cout << "\t\t" << i << "\t\t" << (char) i << endl;
}
```

5   This is quite easy. Firstly, you need a variable to store the result which should be initialized to **1**. A **for** loop is needed that starts at **0** and goes to **p** to assign the product:

```
for(i = 0; i < p; i++)
    ans *= N;
```

The chapter shows you how to set a default argument.

Chapter 7

1   Simply define a structure point that contains three variables representing **X_Coordinate, Y_Coordinate,** and **Z_Coordinate.**

Look at the **yardsFeetInches** example programs.

2   Similar to the **add_measure()** function.

3   You have the code in the example program. Simply put the code into functions.

4   Define a suitable structure. Use your new type to define an array of structures which will hold your data. Personally, I'd use a loop to ask the user if they want to enter details. I'd also use a loop to view the records.

5   Very similar in concept to question 4.

Chapter 8

1   If all else fails see Chapter 11!

2   If the first argument is greater than the second, you need to use a temporary variable to store the data held in **var1**. Then assign the data in **var2** into **var1.** To complete the swap, assign the data in the temporary variable to **var2**.

3   You have the function from question 2, and now you have seen the other one!

Chapter 9

1 To do this you could open the file and use the `<<` operator to write to the stream.

2 Similarly, you can open the file and use the `>>` operator to store the information in variables. Display these variables to the screen in the normal way.

3 Append springs to mind here!

4 As for questions 1, 2 and 3 but use a binary file this time.

5 **PRINTER.CPP** should point you in the right direction.

6 File pointers come to mind. Look at **FILE7.CPP** to see how they can be used.

7 Again **PRINTER.CPP** should point you in the right direction. Will you read the file a character at a time, a word at a time, or a line at a time? Experiment!

Chapter 10

1 The functions should cause no problems - you can decide how many numbers you add together. You could use a loop and add all the numbers until a terminating character was entered.

2 This function takes a variable as an argument and then displays a message on the screen saying what type of variable it is - **char**, **int**, **float**, **double**. The variable should then be displayed.

3 Similar to **OVER14.CPP.**

4 Look at **OPER.CPP** for suggestions.

Chapter 11

1   This is for practice to see if you can find the errors. Read through the code first to find any obvious errors. Step through the program and watch the values being returned from functions and so on.

2   You have the code, now write the functions.

3   There are three cases:

Deleting the first item

Deleting the last item

Deleting an item in the middle.

The function should be sent pointers to the item to be deleted, the item before it in the chain, and the first and last item in the list. If the first item is to be deleted, the previous pointer must be null. The function should update the first and last item in the list if one of them is to be deleted.

4   There are two basic ways to build a linked list which only has a pointer to the next item in the list:

The first is to put each new item at the end of the list.

The other is to add items in specific places in the list - in some kind of sorted order.

How you build the list will determine how the this function will be coded, but adding items at the end will be simpler.

5   Now you have functions to work with, a linked list simply defines your own structure to hold the data and work with this.

6   Once the program in question 5 is working you only have to open a file, write the data to it and close the file. You will also have to open the file, read the information and re-create the list.

If all else fails look at the example of a linked list with two pointers which comes up next.

Chapter 12

1   Similar to the overloaded + operator.

2   Similar to the `rectangle` class.

3   Similar to the overloaded operator that work with the `rectangle` class.

4   Similar to the other overloaded operators in the file.

Chapter 13

1   Look at the examples of derived classes. You should then have no problems.

2   Simply derive another class.

3   This is the opportunity for you to experiment.

4   You should be getting the hang of this now.

5   This is another opportunity for you to experiment.

Chapter 14

1   Find the element in the array then use a loop to move all the other elements, in a higher position in the array, down by one item. You are effectively overwriting the item. Remember to reduce **numberIn** in the array by one.

2   A simple **for** loop can be used going from **start** to **finish** which calls the **add()** function.

3   Open the file - while not at the end of the file read each element in turn and pass to **add()** function.

4   This function needs to be a **friend.**

Open file and then use a loop to write the set to the file.

5   First you need some test functions - test if an add number, test if an even number, and so on.

The function you write will use a loop to test each item. Those that pass the test will be added to the set.

Best of Luck!

Appendix

Library Functions

With C++ life is made that much easier by use of the function libraries. With them, most of the drudgery of controlling basic elements in the program and the host computer is removed. Math and character strings have heavy support in your standard C++ compiler function library. Further details on extended libraries (for example, graphics and sound) are available from your compiler's manufacturer or in the commercial market. Most of the standard function library will port to other operating systems and computer types.

Header Files

Listed below are the commonly used header files available in the **include** subdirectory of your compiler. If you wish to start some customization, you will find they are in ASCII format. This should make it easy to utilize some of the function prototypes they contain in your own programs.

Header File	Use
bios.h	BIOS interupts
complex.h	Complex numbers in C++
conio.h	Port and console input/output
dos.h	DOS interupts
graphics.h	Simple graphic actions (with Borland compilers)
io.h	Low level input/output and file handling
iostream.h	Streaming routines in C++
math.h	Math functions
stdio.h	Streaming routines in C
stdlib.h	Standard library routines
string.h	String functions
time.h	Date and time routines

Standard Library Functions

Standard library functions (**stdlib.h**) used for memory allocation, data conversion and so on.

Library Functions	Use
_exit	Program termination
_lrotl	Rotates an unsigned long to the left
_lrotr	Rotates an unsigned long to the right
_rotl	Rotates an unsigned integer to the left
_rotr	Rotates an unsigned integer to the right
abort	Program aborts
abs	Absolute integer value
atexit	Registers termination function
atof	String to float conversion

Library Functions	Use
atoi	String to integer conversion
bsearch	Binary search of an array
calloc	Allocation of main memory
div	Divide integer types
ecvt	Float to string conversion
exit	Program termination
fcvt	Float to string conversion
free	Releases memory for usage
gcvt	Float to string conversion
getenv	Gets a string from the environment
itoa	Integer to string conversion
labs	Absolute long value
ldiv	Divides two longs
lfind	Linear search
lsearch	Linear search
ltoa	Long to string conversion
malloc	Memory allocation
putenv	Puts a string into the environment
qsort	Quick sort
rand	Random number generator
realloc	Reallocates main memory
srand	Random number generator initialised
strtod	String to double conversion
strtol	String to long conversion
strtoul	String to unsigned long conversion
swab	Swaps bytes from s1 to s2
system	Invokes DOS command.com
ultoa	Unsigned long to string conversion

An important group of functions, described in **stdlib.h** are the data conversion functions. These functions convert data from one format to another. For example **atof()** will convert string information to a string.

The syntax for some of these functions is shown in the following prototypes:

```
double atof (const char *s )
int atoi (const char *s)
long atol (const char *s)
char *ecvt (double value,int n, int *dec,int *sign)
```

Some of the other functions are shown below:

Abort or End

`void   abort(void)`	Returns an exit code of 3`
`int   atexit(atexit_t   func)`	Calls the function before an exit
`void   exit(int   status)`	Returns 0 for a normal exit
`int   system(const   char*command)`	Command in DOS command
`void_exit(int   status)`	Terminates without an action

Math

`div_t   div(int   numer,int   denom)`	Divides and returns quotient and remainder in **div_t**
`int   abs(int   x)`	Absolute value of x
`long   labs(long   x)`	Absolute value of x
`idiv_t   ldiv   (long   numer,long   denom)`	Similar to **div** but with longs
`int   rand(void)`	Calls random number generator
`void   srand(unsigned   seed)`	Seeding of RNG

Character Functions

Characters are defined as single byte values in ASCII. The macros and functions prototyped in **ctype.h** will accept integer arguments. Auto type conversion will often allows character arguments to be passed. The available macros and functions are listed opposite.

Character Functions	Use
isalnum	Validates for alpha-numeric character
isalpha	Validates for alpha character
isascii	Validates for ASCII character
iscntrl	Validates for control character
isdigit	Validates for digit (0-9)
isgraph	Validates for a printable character (no space)
islower	Validates for lowercase character
isprint	Validates for printable character
ispunct	Validates for punctuation character
isspace	Validates for whitespace character
isupper	Validates for uppercase character
isxdigit	Validates for hexadecimal digit
toascii	Converts a character into its ASCII equivalent
tolower	Converts character from upper to lowercase
toupper	Converts character from lower to uppercase

Validating for ASCII Values/Letters/Numbers

These macros allow a check on ASCII values. Zero returned for false, non zero for true.

Macro	Use
int isalnum(ch)	Validates for alphanumeric values: A to Z / a-z / 0-9 - *ch* is to be integer
int isalph(ch)	Validates for alpha values: A_Z / a-z - *ch* is to be integer
int isascii(ch)	Validates for ASCII values: 0 - 127 (0 - 7Fh) - *ch* is to be integer

Validating for Control/Whitespace/Punctuation/Printable Characters

These macros allow a check on ASCII values. Zero returned for false, non zero for true.

Macro	Use
int iscntrl(ch)	Validates for a control character
int isdigit(ch)	Validates for digits 0 - 9
int isgraph(ch)	Validates for printable characters (no space)
int islower(ch)	Validates for lowercase a-z
int isprint(ch)	Validates for printable character
int punct(ch)	Validates for punctuation
int isspace(ch)	Validates for whitespace
int isupper(ch)	Validates for uppercase A-Z
int isxdigit(ch)	Validates for hexadecimal value 0 - 9/a-f of A-F

Converting to ASCII/Lowercase/Uppercase

These macros allow conversion of ASCII values. The macro toascii converts ch to ASCII. The functions **tolower** and **toupper**, convert the character value to a specified format. The macros **_tolower** and **_toupper** return identical resultants when given the proper ASCII values.

Macro	Use
int toascii(ch)	Converts to ASCII character
int tolower(ch)	Converts ch from uppercase to lower
int _tolower(ch)	Converts ch to lowercase
int toupper(ch)	Converts ch from lowercase to upper
int _toupper(ch)	Converts ch to uppercase

Memory and String Functions

In C++ you may consider strings to be one dimensional character arrays, that are terminated with a null character. The string functions that are prototyped in **string.h** often use pointer arguments and consequently return pointer or integer values (your compiler's library reference will have details of the syntax for each command).

The following functions are available in normal Borland compatible compilers:

Function	Use
memccpy	Copies from source to destination
memchr	Searches the buffer for the first ch
memcmp	In buf1 and buf2 - compares n characters
memcpy	Copies n characters from source to destination
memicmp	As for memcmp - but remains case-insensitive
memset	Copies ch into n character positions in buf
strcat	Appends one string to another
strchr	Finds first occurrence of a character in a string
strcmp	Compares two strings
strcpy	Copies one string to another
strcspn	Finds the first occurrence of a character in a string from a given character set
strdup	Replicates a string
strerror	Saving of system error message
stricmp	Behaves the same as **strcmpi**
strlen	Length of a string
strlwr	Converts string to lowercase
strncat	Character of string appended
strncmp	Character of separate strings compared
strncpy	Character of one string copied to another
strnicmp	Character s of two strings compared - case insensitive
strnset	Sets string characters to given character
strpbrk	First occurrence of character from one string in another string
strrchr	The last occurrence of a character in a string
strrev	Reverses the character in a string
strset	Sets the character in a string to a given character
strspn	Locates the first sub-string from another given character set in a string
strstr	Loates one string in another string
strtok	Locates tokens within a string
strupr	Converts string to uppercase

393

Memory Operator - Syntax Statements

```
void *memccpy(void *dest,void *source,int ch,unsigned count)
void * memchr(void *buf,int ch, unsigned count)
int memcmp (void *buf1,void *buf2,unsigned count)
void *memcpy (void *dest,void *source,unsigned count)
int memicmp (void *buf1,void *buf2,unsigned count)
void *memmove (void *dest,void *source,unsigned count)
void *memset (void *dest,int ch,insigned count)
```

String .h String Functions

Some of the useful syntax statements for this function are listed below:

Syntax	Use
char*sterror(int errnum)	ANSI supplied number
char*_strerror (char*s)	A user originated message
size_t strlen(const char*s)	A Null terminated string
char *strlwr(char*s)	St string to lowercase
char *strncat(char*s1,	
const char *s2,size_tn)	Append **n char s2 to s1**
int strncmp(const char*s1,	
const char *s2,size_tn)	Compares the first n characters of two strings
int strnicmp(const char *s1,	
const char *s2,size_tn)	Compares the first two character of two strings (case insensitive)
char*strncpy(char *s1,	
const char *s2,size_tn)	Copies n character of s2 in s1
char *strnset(char *s,	
int ch,size_tn)	Sets the first n character of a string to a **char** setting
char *strpbrk(const char *s1,	
const char *s2)	Locate a character from s2 that's in s1
char *strrchr(const char *s,int ch)	Locate the last occurrence of ch in a string
char *strrev(char*s)	Set string to reverse
char *strset(char *s,int ch)	String to be set by ch

Syntax	Use
size_t strspn(const char *s1, const char*s2)	Search through s1, with **char** set in s2
char *strstr(const char *s1, const char *s2)	Set a search through s1 using s2
char *strtok(char *s1, const char *s2)	Finds a token in s1 (s1 has tokens/s2 has the delimiters)
char *strupr(char *s)	Set string to uppercase

Note: ***s** is a pointer to a string
*s1 and ***s2**, are pointers to two strings
char is a character value

The other string functions are similar to the above.

Math Functions

math.h has prototyped functions which permit mathematical, trigonometric and algebraeic actions (for complex functions use **complex.h**). Remember that **math.h** contains many of the oft used mathematical constants. See below:

Function	Use
M_E	2.71828182845904523536
M_LOG2E	1.44269504088896340736
M_LOG10E	0.434294481903251827651
M_LN2	0.693147180559945309417
M_LN10	2.30258509299404568402
M_PI	3.14159265358979323846
M_PI_2	1.57079632679489661923
M_PI_4	0.785398163397448309616
M_1_PI	0.318309886183790671538
M_2_PI	0.636619772367581343076
M_1_SQRTPI	0.564189583547756286948
M_2_SQRTP1	1.12837916709551257390
M_SQRT2	1.41421356237309504880
M_SQRT_2	0.707106781186547524401

Math Operators in C/C++

Operator	Use
double acos (double x)	Arc cosine
double asin (double x)	Arc sine
double atan (double x)	Arc tangent
double atan2 (double y, double x)	Arc tan
double cell (double x)	Greatest integer
double cos (double x)	Cosine
double cosh (double x)	Hyperbolic cosine
double exp (double x)	Exponential
double fabs (double x)	Absolute
double floor (double x)	Smallest integer
double fmod (double x, double y 0	Modula
double frexp(double x,int *exponent)	Separate to a mantissa and an exponent
double hypot (double x, double y)	Hypotenuse
double ldexp (double x, int exponent)	x times 2 to the power of the exponent
double log (double x)	Log (natural)
double log10 (double x)	Log (common)
double modf (double x, double *ipart)	Mantissa and exponent
double poly (double x, int degree,	
double co-efficients[ ])	Polynomial
double pow (double x, double y)	x to the power of y
double sin (double x)	Sine
double sinh (double x)	Hyperbolic sine
double sqrt (double x)	Square root
double tan (double x)	Tangent
double tanh (double x)	Hyperbolic tangent

Complex Math

You may use the C++ class **comlex.h** for complex arithmetic. As well as the previous functions, the following operations are additional in **comple.h**:

Function	Use
friend double real (complex&)	A complex number's real part
friend double image (complex&)	A complex number's imaginary part
friend complex conj (complex&)	Complex conjugate
friend double norm (complex&)	The square of the magnitude
friend double arg (complex&)	Angle in the plane
friend complex polar (double mag, double angle = 0)	Complex object with polar coordinates as arguments

Time Function

Time.h conveniently contains many of the time and date formats regularly used in your programs:

Function	Use
asctime	Translates date/time to ASCII string - uses the *tm* structure
clock	Processor clock time in current session
ctime	Translates date/time to a string
difftime	Difference between two times
gmtime	Translates date/time to Greenwich Mean Time - uses *tm* structure
localtime	Translates date/time to *tm* structure
mktime	Translates time to calender format - uses *tm* structure
stime	Date/time set on the system
strftime	Formats date/time for output
time	Current system time
tzset	Set the time variables for the environment variable *TZ*

Many of the date and time functions use the *tm* structure defined in **time.h**.

```
struct     tm
{
int   tm_sec;
int   tm_min;
int   tm_hour;
int   tm_mday;
int   tm_mon;
int   tm_year;
int   tm_wday;
int   tm_yday;
int   tm_isdst;
};
```

Appendix

Operator Overloading

To understand how to design and create overloaded operator functions you need to know a bit about how these statements are translated into function calls. The translation depends on whether the operator is binary or unary and whether the overloaded operator function is a member of a class.

Unary/Binary	Member of Class	Syntax	Call
Binary	Yes	A Opr B	A.operatorOpr (B)
Binary	No	A Opr B	operatorOpr (A,B)
Unary	Yes	Opr A	A.operatorOpr()
Unary	Yes	A Opr	A.operatorOpr()
Unary	No	Opr A	operatorOpr (A)
Unary	No	A Opr	operatorOpr (A)

Instant

Index

WIN FREE BOOKS

TELL US WHAT YOU THINK!

Complete and return the bounce back card and you will:

- Help us create the books you want.
- Receive an update on all Wrox titles.
- Enter the draw for 5 Wrox titles of your choice.

FILL THIS OUT to enter the draw for free Wrox titles

Name _____

Address _____

_____

_____

_____ Postcode/Zip _____

Occupation _____

How did you hear about this book?

☐ Book review (name) _____

☐ Advertisement (name) _____

☐ Recommendation

☐ Catalogue

☐ Other _____

Where did you buy this book?

☐ Bookstore (name) _____

☐ Computer Store (name) _____

☐ Mail Order

☐ Other _____

I would be interested in receiving information about Wrox Press titles by email in future. My email/Internet address is:

_____

What influenced you in the purchase of this book?

☐ Cover Design

☐ Contents

☐ Other (please specify) _____

How did you rate the overall contents of this book?

☐ Excellent   ☐ Good

☐ Average   ☐ Poor

What did you find most useful about this book? _____

What did you find least useful about this book? _____

Please add any additional comments. _____

What other subjects will you buy a computer book on soon? _____

What is the best computer book you have used this year?

_____

WROX PRESS INC.

Wrox writes books for you. Any suggestions, or
ideas about how you want information given in
your ideal book will be studied by our team.
Your comments are always valued at WROX.

Free phone in USA 800 814 4527
Fax (312) 465 4063

Compuserve 100063,2152
UK Tel. (44121) 706 6826   Fax (44121) 706 2967

Computer Book Publishers

NB. If you post the bounce back card below in the UK, please send it to:
Wrox Press Ltd. Freepost BM6303, Unit 16, 20 James Road, Birmingham, B11 2BR

NO POSTAGE
NECESSARY
IF MAILED
IN THE
UNITED STATES

BUSINESS REPLY MAIL

FIRST CLASS MAIL   PERMIT#64   CHICAGO,IL

POSTAGE WILL BE PAID BY ADDRESSEE

WROX PRESS
2710 WEST TOUHY AVE
CHICAGO IL 60645-3008
USA